KU-044-551

Shaw's Theater

THE FLORIDA BERNARD SHAW SERIES

THE FLORIDA BERNARD SHAW SERIES
Edited by R. F. Dietrich

This series is devoted to works of and about Shaw, Shaw's literary production, and Shavian topics of interest. While supportive of traditional approaches, the series also aims to encourage scholars with new critical paradigms to engage Shaw's works.

Pygmalion's Wordplay: The Postmodern Shaw, by Jean Reynolds (1999)
Shaw's Theater, by Bernard F. Dukore (2000)

Shaw's Theater

Bernard F. Dukore

University Press of Florida

Gainesville · Tallahassee · Tampa · Boca Raton
Pensacola · Orlando · Miami · Jacksonville

KING ALFRED'S COLLEGE
WINCHESTER

792.0233 KAO 259231
/SUA

Copyright 2000 by the Board of Regents of the State of Florida
"Bernard Shaw, Director," copyright by Bernard F. Dukore, 1971
"The Director as Interpreter: Shaw's *Pygmalion*," copyright by the
Pennsylvania State University Press, 1983
Printed in the United States of America on acid-free paper
All rights reserved

The drawings in Figures 1–7 are reproduced in this volume by permission of
the Hanley Collection of the Harry Ransom Humanities Research Center,
University of Texas at Austin. The drawings in Figures 8–10 are reproduced
courtesy of the Bernard F. Burgunder Collection of George Bernard Shaw,
Division of Rare and Manuscript Collections, Cornell University Library.

05 04 03 02 01 00 6 5 4 3 2 1

Library of Congress Cataloging-in-Publication Data
Dukore, Bernard Frank, 1931–
Shaw's theater / Bernard F. Dukore.
p.cm. — (The Florida Bernard Shaw series)
Includes bibliographical references and index.
ISBN 0-8130-1757-2 (alk. paper)
1. Shaw, Bernard, 1856–1950—Stage history. 2. Shaw, Bernard, 1856–1950—
Dramatic production. I. Title. II. Series.
PR5368.S75 D85 2000
792.9'5—dc21   99-050695

The University Press of Florida is the scholarly publishing agency for the
State University System of Florida, comprising Florida A&M University,
Florida Atlantic University, Florida International University, Florida State
University, University of Central Florida, University of Florida, University of
North Florida, University of South Florida, and University of West Florida.

University Press of Florida
15 Northwest 15th Street
Gainesville, FL 32611-2079
http://www.upf.com

Contents

Illustrations

Foreword

Although the great majority of works in the Shaw Series will be original works, from time to time we will resurrect a classic of Shaw criticism or scholarship, particularly when it does not seem to have been superseded. Bernard F. Dukore's *Shaw's Theater* is not entirely a reprint, but it begins with an updated version of Dukore's 1971 work, *Bernard Shaw: Director,* a work that is still the standard in its field. It then follows with a revised version of his 1983 article, "The Director as Interpreter: Shaw's *Pygmalion*," and concludes with an original, unpublished study, "The Theater in Bernard Shaw's Drama." This progression of studies, reflecting as well the development of Dukore's thinking about Shaw's use of the theater, completes, as Dukore himself puts it, a "tripartite study of Shaw's theater: his theatrical direction of his plays, his view of the interpretation of the drama, and his dramatic use of the theater." It is likely that with this volume we have as complete and expert an account of Shaw's directorial, interpretative, and creative uses of the theater as we are likely to get for some time.

R. F. Dietrich
Series Editor

Preface

The basis of *Shaw's Theater,* connecting its three sections, is the fruitful interrelationship between the drama and the theater. Its subjects are, on the one hand, Shaw's presentation of his drama on stage and, on the other, his incorporation of the theater itself in the dramatic text: in brief, Shaw's putting his plays in the theater and putting the theater in his plays.

The book divides into three parts of unequal length. The emphasis of the first part, "Bernard Shaw, Director," is not on Shaw's role as a dramatist or critic, although these enter the picture, but on his role as a play director, both in theory and in practice, and on how his mastery of the pragmatic aspects of theater, chiefly in staging his own plays, informs his art. The second part, a supplement to the first, is "The Director as Interpreter: Shaw's *Pygmalion,*" which focuses on his views of how directors interpret the drama they are staging, examines these views in general, and then applies them to his productions of *Pygmalion,* one of his best-known and most popular plays. The third, final part of *Shaw's Theater,* "The Theater in Bernard Shaw's Drama," takes the subject of his plays and his stage from a different viewpoint, that of his incorporating the theater itself in the text of his plays. To my knowledge, no one else has examined this aspect of his dramaturgy in depth. Together, I hope these complementary analyses of Shaw and the theater—the function and practice of the director in staging his plays in the theater, the director interpreting them there, and the playwright using the theater and its components as dramatic devices in writing his plays—offer fresh insights into Shaw's dramatic practice.

This antithesis—Shaw's plays in the theater and the theater in his plays—is more than the type of verbal balance that is one of Shaw's stratagems as a writer of comedy. As both director and writer, he wanted to convince audiences that what they saw on the stage were real things happening to real people. Yet neither his sole nor main interest was in depicting a slice of life: no cup-and-saucer or kitchen-sink dramatist, he. For that matter, his realism was hardly the "slice of life" drama that has been associated with that of the Théâtre Libre. He bragged that his dramaturgy consisted of old-fashioned methods, but his ideas were fresh and he used new methods as well, intermingling with and at times overlaying or supplanting the old. Shaw was eclectic, and his tribute to Lillah McCarthy—that she had the executive ability of the old-school actress combined with a desire to murder the Victorian womanly woman—applies, *mutatis mutandis,* to Shaw himself. His realism was never simple; he called himself a realist, but he also bragged that his plays were akin to Italian operas—the two claims containing more than a hint that these characteristics are not mutually exclusive. As a theatrical as well as a dramatic realist, he probed the facade of orthodox values and ideals to the reality they unsuccessfully tried to hide. Employing both conventional and newfangled methods, he exposed the tensions between appearance and reality in the theater and in real life. Indeed, his plays use different aspects of the theater as means of dramatizing these tensions. He staged the outlandish with degrees of realism and he used theatrical devices to offset or break through the semblance of reality, not to assault, but to help awaken audiences to the reality in which they lived.

The three parts of *Shaw's Theater* were written at different times. *Bernard Shaw, Director* was first published in 1971. It is basically unchanged. Were I to rewrite it today, I might resemble, to choose a somewhat older person as analogy, the Clint Eastwood of *In the Line of Fire* remaking the Clint Eastwood of *Dirty Harry.* The author of *Bernard Shaw, Director* was a younger man than I am, with virtues and liabilities different from those of the older writer of *Shaw's Theater.* I believe that the integrity of the 1971 book should remain intact, both for better or for worse, and for better and for worse. However, I have taken the opportunity to correct errors of which I am aware and to insert, as footnotes, new information on the subject that has become available since the time that book was written. To enable the reader to consult printed sources, I have also updated those of its citations which were unpublished when that book came out but which have been published subsequently.

In its original form, "The Director as Interpreter: Shaw's *Pygmalion*" was an essay published in 1983, independently of *Bernard Shaw, Director* but indebted to that book, of which it repeated portions. Since "Bernard Shaw, Director" now precedes "The Director as Interpreter" in this volume, I have abridged, deleted, or otherwise revised, mostly in its introductory section, passages that repeat those in the book.

By contrast with these works, the third part of *Shaw's Theater,* "The Theater in Bernard Shaw's Drama," is new. I hope that the progression from "Bernard Shaw, Director" through "The Director as Interpreter" to the fresh long essay that concludes this book provides a comprehensive treatment of the relation between Shaw's views of dramatic production and his use of the theater in his role as playwright.

Throughout this book I reproduce Shaw's idiosyncratic punctuation and spelling. He eliminates the apostrophe from such words as *don't, doesn't,* and *they'll,* although *I'll* remains the same. *Show* becomes *shew,* and *Shakespeare* may be *Shakespear* or *Shakspere.*

Acknowledgments

For permission to quote from Shaw's published and unpublished work, I am grateful to the Society of Authors on behalf of the Bernard Shaw Estate.

For their assistance in locating Shavian material for "Bernard Shaw, Director" (first published in 1971) and for their permission to quote from works or reproduce drawings by Shaw in their collections, my sincere thanks go to the British Library; the Bernard F. Burgunder Collection of George Bernard Shaw, Division of Rare and Manuscript Collections, Cornell University Library; Harvard Theatre Collection, Houghton Library, Frederic Woodbridge Wilson, Curator; the Berg Collection of English and American Literature, New York Public Library, Astor, Lenox and Tilden Foundations; the Academic Center Library (now the Harry Ransom Humanities Research Center), University of Texas at Austin; the Theatre Museum, London (for material I examined in the Enthoven Collection of the Victoria and Albert Library); and the Beinecke Rare Book and Manuscript, Yale University. I should also like to thank Norman Philbrick for making available to me unpublished Shavian letters in his private library.

It is a pleasure, too, to acknowledge my obligations to colleagues and friends in the theater and academe, and at home, for their generous help on "Bernard Shaw, Director." I owe thanks to Dame Sybil Thorndike, Wendy Hiller, and Ronald Gow. I am beholden to Sidney P. Albert for our hours of dialogue on Shaw's plays in general and on my production of *Major Barbara* in particular. For Ruby Cohn's constructive advice upon reading an early draft I am most grateful. For detailed comments on the final draft of the 1971 edition and for valuable suggestions, I am greatly indebted to my late wife Joyce. I hope I have profited from their criticisms.

"The Director as Interpreter: Shaw's *Pygmalion*" first appeared as an article in *SHAW: The Annual of Bernard Shaw Studies*, vol. 3, *Shaw's Plays in Performance,* ed. Daniel Leary (1983), pp. 129–47. For permission to reprint it, I thank the Pennsylvania State University Press. For permission to quote from unpublished Shavian writings in their collections, I thank the British Library and the Bernard F. Burgunder Collection of George Bernard Shaw, Division of Rare and Manuscript Collections, Cornell University Library.

I am grateful to Fred D. Crawford and Stuart Baker, who read an early draft of "The Theater in Bernard Shaw's Drama" and who made valuable suggestions. In November 1997, a small portion of this work, in a different form, was presented orally as the Hoffman Lecture at the School of Theater, Florida State University, Tallahassee. In July 1998, another small portion, in a still different form, was given orally as the keynote address of the Shaw Seminar of the Shaw Festival, Niagara-on-the-Lake, Canada. I thank both institutions for giving me the opportunity to test my ideas in a public forum.

I Bernard Shaw, Director

To Joyce (1943–71)

BERNARD SHAW devoted many years of his life to the art of play directing. Not only was he a director of considerable experience, he was extremely good, and his practices, moreover, anticipated those of modern directors. As early as the 1890s, when he was relatively inexperienced, his writings vividly demonstrated a knowledge of theater practice. Blaming Ellen Terry for making it appear that another actor had fluffed his lines, he explained why she was probably at fault: "I suppose you didnt give him his cue, and he waited long enough to be detected before he made up his mind that he was not going to get it."[1] In his weekly theater criticisms for the *Saturday Review,* backstage terminology spiced his comments on stagecraft. He reprimanded one director, for instance, for having "so far neglected the ancient counsel to 'jine his flats' as to leave a large gap in the roof [. . .]."[2] These examples could easily be multiplied. As Shaw remarked in an uncharacteristic understatement, "I am not a dreamer who doesnt understand the practical exigencies of the stage [. . .]."[3]

Understanding, however, is different from experience. Shaw had both. His knowledge of "the practical exigencies of the stage" derived from several sources. By 1895, he had written four plays, started a fifth, and participated in the London productions of two—as supervising author of *Widowers' Houses* and as director of *Arms and the Man.*[4] In the years that followed his 1894 production of *Arms and the Man,* he directed many plays. At the Court Theatre, under the management of J. E. Vedrenne and Granville Barker, Shaw was as actively and successfully engaged in directing his plays as he was in writing them. By the end of World War I, he was a seasoned director as well as an experienced playwright.

When a major dramatist expends so much of his creative energies on the art and craft of play production, it becomes mandatory to examine just what he did. Surprisingly, there has been little attempt to do so. Eight pages of Raymond Mander and Joe Mitchenson's *Theatrical Companion to Shaw* are devoted to accounts by Dame Sybil Thorndike and Sir Lewis Casson of Shaw as director; Archibald Henderson's major biography *George Bernard Shaw: Man of the Century* gives only twenty of its almost one thousand pages to this topic; Eric Bentley comments on "Shaw and the Actors" in a thirteen-page appendix to the 1957 edition of his *Bernard Shaw;* and William A. Armstrong has written a fifteen-page article on Shaw as director.[5] Heretofore, there has been no full-length treatment of the subject.[6]

This book studies Shaw as artist of the theater, mainly from the point of view of director (or producer, as the director was until recently called in England). My primary concern is not Shaw's playwriting practices or his theories of playwriting, but rather his ideas and methods of putting the play on the stage. The subject of the initial chapter is Shaw's background and experiences in the theater before he began to direct plays. Following this chapter, the book divides into different aspects of play directing and various areas with which the director is concerned. My procedure is to analyze first Shaw's theoretical and critical pronouncements, and then his practices. For the theory-criticism, my sources are Shaw's theater and op-era reviews, essays, letters, prefaces, and the like. In these, he frequently refers to the plays of Shakespeare and Ibsen. The practical problems center almost exclusively on his own plays. Sources of this information are chiefly notes that Shaw made during rehearsals. In addition, I use Shaw's letters to various actors. Where possible, and in most cases it is possible, I choose examples from Shaw's comments on productions of his better-known plays rather than of his less well-known plays: *Cæsar and Cleopatra* and *Pygmalion,* for instance, rather than *Augustus Does His Bit* and *The Inca of Perusalem.* Although Shaw did not direct plays by other au-thors, he did on a few occasions advise on their production, and I have used certain of these comments in order to demonstrate his consistent approach.

Shaw's basic concern is the actor, who is the major element of produc-tion. In working with actors, he employed virtually all of the techniques that a modern director might use—ranging from animal imagery to me-chanical, technical instruction. But Shaw was a director, not merely an acting coach. He supervised every element of production: scenery (con-struction and painting, as well as design), lighting, costuming, make-up— even business and house management.

Is this so unusual? What may surprise the reader is not that Shaw's practice was different from that of the modern director but that it was similar. His practice was completely harmonious with the twentieth-century tradition of the director as guiding artist in the production of a play. However, in 1894, when he began to direct plays, this tradition had not yet been established. In late-nineteenth-century London, the tradition was that of the actor-manager: a star actor supervising his satellite company. Unity of production under the guidance of a director, a commonplace idea today, was not at all commonplace in England in the late nineteenth century. A supervising, powerful figure who was not a star actor was rare; the authoritarian play directing of an author—W. S. Gilbert, for example—was unusual. For that matter, play production under the leadership of a strong director was exceptional on the Continent as well as in England. The Meiningen Company (1874–90) was outside then-current theatrical traditions. The Moscow Art Theatre, which at its start had a strong director guiding the actors, was organized in 1898, four years after Shaw's directorial debut. Gordon Craig's influential pronouncements advocating unity of production under the supervision of a single directing mind did not appear until 1905, when *The Art of the Theatre* was published—eleven years after Shaw directed *Arms and the Man*. Shaw's work as a director is therefore important for three reasons: first, because he is a major playwright who directed his own works; second, because he was a good director; and third, because he is an early example of the modern idea of the director as guiding artist in the production of a play.

Theater Background and Experience

By the time he was ten years old, says Shaw, he was "saturated" with both Shakespeare and the Bible. As a child, he adored the theater. On his first visit he saw Tom Taylor's *Plot and Passion,* which was followed by a full-length Christmas pantomime, *Puss in Boots,* whose attractions included a fairy queen, a policeman shooting a gun, and a disappearance through a grave-trap.[1] His theater reviews contain numerous references to plays and performances that he saw in Dublin, as well as an explicit statement that he had ten years of play-going experience before moving to London.[2]

Growing up in Dublin, Shaw attended the Theatre Royal, the Gaiety, and the Queen's, where he saw tragedies and melodramas, high comedies and farces, musical extravaganzas and Christmas pantomimes—virtually every type of play. His reminiscences include comments on the scenery and performances, for he was attentive not only to the plays themselves but also to the manner in which they were produced. In these theaters, stock scenery served for each play; staging techniques included closing flats, the descent of sky borders and front-scenes, wings-and-grooves, and illumination by coal-gas; and resident stock companies supported such visiting stars as Charles Mathews, John Hare, Dion Boucicault, Kate Bateman, Edward Sothern, and Barry Sullivan.[3] Sullivan—whose repertoire featured *Richard III, Hamlet, Macbeth, Othello,* and *Richelieu*—made so deep an impression on young Shaw that as late as 1947 he vividly described details of Sullivan's athletic performance of Richard III.[4]

Not only did Shaw attend the professional theater in Dublin, he also participated in amateur theatricals. At the Dublin English Scientific and Commercial Day School, which he entered at the age of thirteen, he and Matthew Edward McNulty organized a drama club that aimed to produce the major works of Shakespeare. The results were disastrous. For their first production, *Macbeth,* none of the actors memorized his lines, and the performance collapsed after twenty minutes when the prompter gave up. In the club's second and final effort, *Hamlet*, Shaw tiptoed on stage as Ophelia and used a falsetto voice that turned the tragedy into a comedy.[5]

His early experience with amateur theatricals included the operatic stage, for his mother became involved with George John Vandeleur Lee, voice teacher and conductor, whose enthusiasms included opera. In the two years between April 1871 and March 1873, Lee produced and conducted a series of amateur operas in which Shaw's mother performed. She played Azucena in Verdi's *Il Trovatore*, Donna Anna in Mozart's *Don Giovanni*, Margaret in Gounod's *Faust*, and the title role in Donizetti's *Lucrezia Borgia*. Since all of these operas were rehearsed at home, Shaw "whistled and sang them from the first bar to the last [. . .]." During this period Lee extended his range from opera to theater. Merging his Amateur Musical Society with another Dublin amateur group, the Operatic and Dramatic Society, he produced Racine's *Athalie* in 1872.[6] The closeness of the relationship between Lee and the Shaw household, as well as the evidence of Shaw's letter, make it appear likely that at the very least Shaw attended rehearsals of Lee's Dublin productions.

In 1873 Lee and Mrs. Shaw moved to London, and three years later, young Shaw followed. In London, Lee organized a musical society called the Troubadours, which performed operas. After Mrs. Shaw ended her association with Lee, her son occasionally assumed her role of piano accompanist during rehearsals and once (in 1881) during the actual performance. Prior to 1883, he assisted Lee in productions of *Faust, Il Trovatore, Don Giovanni,* and Gilbert and Sullivan's *Patience* and *Pinafore*. Apart from piano accompaniment, we do not know the specific nature of Shaw's contribution to Lee's operatic ventures, though on at least one occasion Lee asked him to prepare press releases.[7] As far as we know, none of the contributions was on the actor's side of the footlights.

On a few occasions Shaw acted in the nonmusical theater. He played Stratton Strawless in a benefit performance of *Alone*, by Palgrave Simpson and Herman Merivale, which the Socialist League presented on 30 January 1885. The cast included Edward Aveling (the model for the unscrupulous artist Dubedat in *The Doctor's Dilemma*), Eleanor Marx Aveling (Karl Marx's daughter and Aveling's mistress), and May Morris (William Morris's daughter).[8] On 15 January 1886, Shaw also played Krogstad in a drawing room performance, at the Aveling house near the British Museum, of Ibsen's *A Doll's House*, with Eleanor Marx Aveling as Nora Helmer; on 6 November 1886, at the Novelty Theatre, he acted Chubb Dumbelton in a copyright performance of Edward Rose's *Odd: To Say the*

Least of It; and early in 1888, under the pseudonym "I. Roscius Garrick," Shaw, himself an amateur photographer, appeared as a photographer in a sketch, *The Appointment,* by his friend Dolly Radford, a poet, in an amateur performance at William Morris's house during one of the Socialist League's soirées.[9] These amateur performances may have given him a nodding acquaintance with the problems of the actor and of play production, but Shaw certainly did not gain a great deal of directing experience as an actor.

Some of the knowledge and background that Shaw brought to his directing, he gained as a critic. Although he was not a regular play reviewer until after his directorial debut in 1894—writing weekly theater criticisms in the *Saturday Review* during the years 1895–98—he was, during the 1880s and 1890s, a regular critic of music and a frequent reviewer of art and theater.[10] In his capacities of art and music critic, as well as in his irregular theater reviews, his directorial eyes and ears were being developed. As an art critic, he dealt with composition, color, emphasis, and balance. This background not only helped Shaw the director to supervise the scenery for his productions, it also helped him to visualize the composition and movement of the actors within that scenery. As a music critic evaluating the staging of operas, he analyzed directing, acting, scenery, lighting, costuming, and make-up—all of the aspects of play production with which he would soon be concerned as a director.

Until his own plays were staged, however, Shaw did not become seriously involved with the actual business of play production.[11] On 9 December 1892, J. T. Grein's Independent Theatre performed *Widowers' Houses,* Shaw's first play. Five days later he confided to Charles Charrington: "I have spent so much time at rehearsal that I am stark ruined, and am ruefuly asking myself whether a continental trip for my health would not have been far more economical than all this theatrical glory."[12] Herman de Lange received directing credit for the production that occasioned this lament, but Shaw, as supervising author, assumed some, perhaps many directorial chores.[13]

The next London production of a Shaw play (his first in the West End) was *Arms and the Man,* which he directed in 1894. Between 1894 and 1924, according to Raymond Mander and Joe Mitchenson, Shaw directed nineteen productions of his plays and codirected four others (two productions of *Cæsar and Cleopatra* with Forbes Robertson, *Heartbreak House* with J. B. Fagan, and *Saint Joan* with Lewis Casson). Even when someone else is given credit for having directed the early plays, Mander and Mitchenson assert, "one may be certain that G.B.S. was behind him at rehearsals."[14] This statement is verified by the thousands of notes Shaw made during rehearsals of plays for which others are listed as directors: for example, Arnold Daly's 1911 production of *Arms and the Man* and Robert Loraine's 1919 production of the same play.[15] During the famous "Vedrenne-Barker seasons" at the Court Theatre, from 1894 to 1907, Shaw was one of the Court's directors as well as its "house playwright." He claims, and Granville Barker admits, that even though Barker is credited with having staged most of Shaw's plays, Shaw himself was responsible for their direction.[16]

At the Court, Shaw and Barker eliminated artificial acting in favor of what Desmond MacCarthy calls "actuality in gesture, diction, and sentiment." Audiences saw realistic, believable performances, dedicated to the requirements of the role rather than to the exhibition of an actor's bag of tricks. And they saw ensemble acting, which was very different from the practice at other theaters. At the Court, a performer with a major part in one play might appear in a walk-on in another. Edmund Gwenn, for instance, played the important role of Enry Straker, Tanner's chauffeur in *Man and Superman,* and the minor role of Bilton, custodian of the guncotton shed in the last act of *Major Barbara.* Devotion to the ensemble and to the requirements of the play, rather than to self-display, led to far better acting than otherwise would have been the case. "At the Court," MacCarthy declared, "the acting pleased from the first. People began to say that the English could act after all, and that London must be full of intelligent actors, of whom nobody had ever heard. Yet, strange to say, these actors, when they appeared in other plays on other boards, seemed to sink again to normal insignificance."[17] Under the guidance of Shaw and Barker, productions at the Court were, according to McCarthy, "remarkable enough to challenge the highest standards [. . .]. I should not have felt so keenly when anything was lacking in their performances had they not shown me at the same time to what pitch of excellence it is possible to attain."[18]

In "The Art of Rehearsal" (1922), Shaw described directing as "hard work" because of the "incessant strain on one's attention (the actors have their exits and rests; but the producer is hard at it all the time), the social effort of keeping up everyone's spirits in view of a great event, [and] the dryness of the previous study of the mechanical details [. . .]." He called it a "grind [. . .] which I face with greater reluctance as I grow older [. . .]."[19] But he did face it, for he consistently maintained that "the art of producing plays [. . .] is as much in my profession as writing them [. . .]."[20] He also invariably contended, "*The most desirable director of a play is the au-*

thor." The most undesirable director, on the other hand, is the actor, when that actor is also performing in the production. One or both, he insisted, is bound to suffer. "Producing kills acting: an actor's part dies if he is watching the others critically. You cannot conduct an orchestra and play the drum at the same concert."[21]

What did Shaw do when he "conducted his orchestra"? To answer this, we must first answer two related questions: What is the purpose of "conducting"? Does the process of "conducting" begin when the "conductor" meets the "orchestra" at rehearsal? The subjects of the next chapter are Shaw's ideas of the purposes of play directing and the nature of the director's prerehearsal work.

2 The Director: Goals and Groundwork

The Director's Aims

In Shaw's opinion, "The director, having considered the play, and decided to undertake the job of directing it, has no further concern with its literary merits or its doctrine (if any)." If a director's notes contain such statements as "'Shew influence of Kierkegaard on Ibsen in this scene,' or 'The Edipus complex must be very apparent here. Discuss with the Queen,' the sooner he is packed out of the theatre and replaced the better." If, on the other hand, he has noted "'Ears too red,'" "'further up to make room for X,'" "'Mariar Ann,'" "'Contrast,'" "'Unladylike: keep knees together,'" "'More dialogue to give them time to get off,'" "'Tibbeeyrnottibeethat iz'" (meaning that Hamlet should clearly enunciate, "'To be? Or NOT to be? THAT is the question'"), "'chaste tars'" (meaning that Othello should not slur "chaste stars"), and the like, then the director knows his business.[1] But these notes represent means, not ends. In "The Art of Rehearsal," Shaw announced one of the director's aims: "The beginning and end of the business [of play production] from the author's point of view is the art of making the audience believe that real things are happening to real people."[2]

This was a Shavian critical criterion of long standing. As a music critic, using the pen name Corno di Bassetto, he implored the opera impresario Augustus Harris to remove the "barnstorming absurdities" of the operatic stage:

[Harris] should go to his singers and say gently "Do not saw the air thus. You think yourselves fine fellows when you do it; but the public thinks you idiots. The English nation, among whom I am a councillor, no longer supposes that attitudinizing is acting. Neither would I have you suppose that all native young men wear dove-colored

tights, and have pink cheeks with little moustaches. Nor is it the case
that all men with grown-up daughters have long white beards reach-
ing to the waist, or that they walk totteringly with staves, raising
hands and eyes to heaven whenever they offer an observation. The
daughters of Albion do not, when in distress, leave off wearing bon-
nets in the open air, assume mourning, keep their hands continually
on their hearts, and stagger and flop about like decapitated geese."
And so on. Harris's advice to the opera singers would become more
celebrated than Hamlet's to the players.[3]

As theater critic for the *Saturday Review,* Shaw similarly satirized unrealistic staging and stereotyped acting. In 1897 he called a production of
John Gabriel Borkman "old fashioned" because it conceived the play as a
conventional tragedy and ignored realistic behavior. This production concept, he complained, "lends itself to people talking at each other rhetori-
cally from opposite sides of the stage, taking long sweeping walks up to
their 'points,' striking attitudes [. . .] with an artificiality which, instead of
being concealed, is not only disclosed but insisted on, and being affected in
all their joints by emotions which a fine comedian conveys by the faintest
possible inflexion of tone or eyebrow."[4] The basis of such complaints was
that the directors ignored what Shaw believed to be the fundamental aim
of play production: "making the audience believe that real things are happening to real people."

An important aspect of this goal of credibility—indeed, its basis, according to Shaw—is the desire of the author. Not only must the director
arrange the stage to produce an illusion of reality, he must also produce
the particular illusion intended by the author.[5] The "real people" are the
people the author created, and the real things happen in the world he
created. Contributing to the illusion are the duration of the play, the relationship between stage and auditorium, and the nature of the scenic effects. Shaw insisted that a play should be neither shorter nor longer than
its author intended, nor should its scenes be rearranged. The distance
between the stage and the spectators should not place the actors in a less
intimate relationship to the audience than the author planned—which is
what happens, for example, when a Shakespearean play is transferred
from the platform stage to behind the proscenium arch. He further insisted
that the attention of the spectators not be "divided and distracted by
quantities of furniture and appointments greatly in excess of the author's
demands," and that neither director nor actors "take advantage of

modern contrivances to make effects that the author never contemplated [. . .]."[6]

Another major goal of the director concerns the actors. Shaw recalls having asked William Reed "whether he agreed with Wagner that the first duty of a conductor is to give the right time to the band. 'No,' said he. 'The first duty of a conductor is to let the band play." Agreeing with this precept, Shaw applied it to the theater: "the perfect producer lets his actors act, and is their helper at need and not their dictator. The hint is meant specially for producers who have begun as actors. They are the first instead of the last to forget it."[7] He condemned Henry Irving for "not allowing his company to act. He worked hard to make them do what he wanted for his own effects; but if they tried to make independent effects of their own, he did not hesitate to spoil them by tricks of stage management." On the other hand, he praised Herbert Beerbohm Tree for giving members of his company "as big a chance as himself in the production." Tree "surrounds himself with counter-attractions and lets them play him off the stage to their heart's content as long as he takes the money at the door. Good policy [. . .]."[8]

The Director's Training

Shaw made few statements on how a director should be trained. He advised R. E. Golding Bright: "When a Shakspere play is coming out—or a Sheridan one, or any old published one—buy a copy & *stage manage* [block] it yourself, marking all the business. *Then* go and see it, and you will be astonished at the grip you will have of it & how much you will learn about the stage from your mistakes & *theirs.*"[9] Customary at the first rehearsal was a reading of the play by the author (at which Shaw excelled). He advised his German translator, Siegfried Trebitsch, to practice reading the play to all of his friends until he learned how to read effectively. Later, when he read the play to the actors, he would be able to make a good initial impression.[10]

A knowledge of theater history could be useful to the director, said Shaw, for he "may be called on to direct a play by, say, Euripides or Aristophanes as it was produced in Athens 2356 years ago. Or one of the pious Mysteries as the Church produced them in the Middle Ages. Or an Elizabethan drama on an Elizabethan stage. Or a Restoration or early Victorian play on a stage with proscenium, wings, and flats."[11] His music and theater criticism demonstrates that Shaw himself knew theater history. In

a music review, for instance, he refers to Jeremy Collier.[12] One of his theater reviews contains a reference that could only be understood in the
context of Coleridge's description of Edmund Kean playing Shakespeare:
"I have no objection whatever to Satan, after elaborately disguising himself as a modern *chevalier d'industrie,* giving himself away by occasional
flashes of lightning. Without them the audience would not know that he
was the devil: besides, it reminds one of Edmund Kean."[13]

By resorting to analogy, we might glean a final Shavian prescription on
the subject. If we substitute the words "directing a play" for "writing a
book," we can apply to directing the precept Shaw gave to a young writer:
"If I advised you to learn to skate, you would not reply that your balance
was scarcely good enough yet. A man learns to skate by staggering about
and making a fool of himself. You will never write a good book until you
have written some bad ones."[14] Although analogies should never be
pushed too far, it must be remembered that Shaw himself had no formal
training in directing. Indeed, there was no institution where he could have
acquired such training. As a director (and as a writer as well), Shaw followed his own precepts, and, having observed productions and acquainted himself with dramatic literature and theater history, he "learned
by doing."

The Director's Prerehearsal Planning

In his Induction to *Fanny's First Play,* Count O'Dowda tells Cecil Savoyard that his daughter Fanny "had some difficulties at the first rehearsals with the gentleman you call the producer, because he hadnt read the
play" (4, 355).[15] This would not have been the case with Shaw, who constantly urged careful prerehearsal planning. The elaborate stage directions
in the printed texts of his plays were designed in part to make the plays
more readable, but they also aimed to serve as blueprints for production.[16]
"A director cannot ignore many of [Shaw's] stage directions with impu-
nity," Lee Simonson realized.[17] Sir Cedric Hardwicke agreed: "Any director who attempts to stage a Shaw play without following his stage directions finds himself in trouble. They cannot be improved upon. I know,
because I have tried the experiment myself."[18]

Shaw's stage directions are intended for both director and actor. "Take
the ordinary actor at a rehearsal," he wrote to Henry Arthur Jones. "How
often does he divine without a hint from you which way your lines are to
be spoken in scenes which are neither conventional nor otherwise obvious?"[19] Shaw provided such "hints" in his stage directions, which also aim

at helping the actor to understand the character's motivation, such as "the political or religious conditions under which" he "is supposed to be acting. Definite conceptions of these are always implicit in the best plays, and are often the key to their appropriate rendering" (1, 31). Since what is implicit is not always understood, Shaw makes these matter explicit in his stage directions.

But these stage directions are also designed for the reader. How many people, Shaw wondered, would have read Charles Dickens's novels if they had been written in the style of acting editions? He offers an example of a Dickensian novel adapted to that style: "Sykes *lights pipe—calls dog—loads pistol with newspaper—takes bludgeon from R. above fireplace and strikes* Nancy. Nancy: Oh, Lord, Bill! *(Dies. Sykes wipes brow—shudders—takes hat from chair O.P.—sees ghost, not visible to audience—and exit L.U.E.).*" If this practice is permissible for stage directions, why might it not be permissible for dialogue? Answering the question with an example, Shaw takes the first four lines of *Richard III* —

Now is the winter of our discontent
Made glorious summer by this sun of York;
And all the clouds that lour'd upon our house,
In the deep bosom of the ocean buried.

—and abbreviates them in the conventional shorthand of prose stage directions:

Now is the winter of our discon't
Made glorious summer by sun of York;
And all clouds th. lowered, &c.
In deep bosom of ocean buried.[20]

Employing readable prose as a blueprint for action, his own stage directions block the movement, describe characters, provide motivations, and tell the actor what impression he should produce, though they leave the method of producing it up to him. In *Getting Married*, for instance, we find: "*Mrs Bridgenorth, her placidity quite upset, comes in with a letter; hurries past Collins; and comes between Lesbia and the General.*" Shortly thereafter, Leo "*runs in fussily, full of her own importance, and swoops on Lesbia, who is much less disposed to spoil her than Mrs Bridgenorth is. But Leo affects a special intimacy with Lesbia, as of two thinkers among the Philistines*" (3, 563, 567). These instructions provide the same specific blocking instructions as stage directions written in traditional abbreviations but serve other functions as well. The movement is more clearly visualized because it is given in terms not of abstract stage area (such as *XRC*) but in terms of characters ("*comes between Lesbia and the General*"). We also receive information on characterization (Leo is "*full of her own importance*"), emotional state (Mrs. Bridgenorth's placidity is upset), manner of movement (Leo "*runs in fussily [. . .] and swoops on Lesbia*"), and character relationships (Leo and Lesbia).

In the second act of *Major Barbara*, we are not merely told that "*Jenny Hill enters L, XLC—Peter Shirley on arm.*" Instead, we receive a vivid and much more complete description: "*Jenny Hill, a pale, overwrought, pretty Salvation lass of 18, comes in through the yard gate, leading Peter Shirley, a half hardened, half worn-out elderly man, weak with hunger.*" This stage direction includes not only the blocking but also an account of Jenny's emotional state ("*overwrought*") and a brief character sketch of Peter Shirley that indicates the effect he should produce. Snobby Price does not simply "*XLC*"; Shaw states the manner of his movement and its motivation: "*hurrying officiously to take the old man off Jenny's hands*" (3, 98–99). The scenery for the second act of *Major Barbara* is not described in such shorthand terms as: "*Yard. Salvation Army Shelter. January. Morning. Building U., with door C. and another door in loft above. Gateway to street L. Penthouse R., with table and benches.*" Rather, the description reads:

> The yard of the West Ham shelter of the Salvation Army is a cold place on a January morning. The building itself, an old warehouse, is newly whitewashed. Its gabled end projects into the yard in the middle, with a door on the ground floor, and another in the loft above it without any balcony or ladder, but with a pulley rigged over it for hoisting sacks. Those who come from this central gable end into the yard have the gateway leading to the street on their left, with a stone horse-trough just beyond it, and, on the right, a penthouse shielding a table from the weather. There are forms at the table" (3, 95).

This stage direction gives the same information as the shorthand, but at the same time describes the appearance of the building, the weather, and the reason for scenic appurtenances. Useful to the scene designer, this information is also helpful to the actors who, in this "*cold place on a January morning,*" must walk from the center of the yard to the area shielding them from the weather, and then from the penthouse to the more open yard—their sensory responses changing as they cross.

The value of this method of writing stage directions is perhaps more apparent when one compares it with Shaw's practice *before* the first edition (1898) of *Plays: Pleasant and Unpleasant*. Prior to that edition, Shaw used precisely the type of stage direction he later deplored. The first act of the 1894 typescript of *Arms and the Man* has "*Door R.2.E. with lock and key*,"[21] while the corresponding stage direction now reads, as it did in 1898, "*The door is on the side nearest the bed*"—which is easier to visualize, for the placement of the door is described in relation to another scenic unit. In 1894, "*Balcony and mountain snow backing*"; now, "*Through an open window with a little balcony a peak of the Balkans, wonderfuly white and beautiful in the starlit snow, seems quite close at hand, though it is really miles away*"—which is more helpful to the scene designer, for it conveys more clearly the effect to be produced. In 1894, "*Exit*"; now, "*She goes out, swaggering*"—which is more helpful to the actress, for it specifically indicates the manner in which she leaves (1, 389, 394). In each case, the later version is more informative and far easier to read.

From a director's viewpoint, however, the later treatment is still incomplete. Shaw the author planned the blocking and stage business when he prepared the play for the printer. Shaw the director refined the author's blocking and stage business when he prepared the play for production.

Shaw believed that the director must plan meticulously, never leaving anything to chance that he could arrange beforehand.[22] He should prepare a prompt book in order to save time and come to the first rehearsals "with the stage business thoroughly studied, and every entry, movement, rising and sitting, disposal of hat and umbrella, &c. [. . .] ready for instant dictation; so that each player will be in the most effective position to deliver his lines and not have to address an intimate speech to a player at the other side of the stage, nor to follow such a player without a line or movement to transfer the attention of the audience accordingly. The exits must be carefully arranged so that the players leave the stage immediately on their last word, and not hold up the play until they have walked to the door." Unless the director blocks the play in advance, he will waste a great deal of time during rehearsals, and unless he sets down this blocking in his prompt book, he might, no matter how extensive his experience, forget some movements, such as exits.[23]

Before blocking the action, however, the director needs a floor plan. Shaw often sketched a plan in the margin of his prompt book. In preparing *The Philanderer* for production, he drew such a plan above the scenic description of the second act—

A long room, with glass doors half-way down on both sides, leading respectively to the dining room corridor and the main staircase. At the end, in the middle, is the fireplace, surmounted by a handsome mantelpiece, with a bust of Ibsen, and decorative inscriptions of the titles of his plays. There are circular recesses at each side of the fireplace, with divan seats running round them, and windows at the top, the space between the divans and the window sills being lined with books. A long settee faces the fire. Along the back of the settee, and touching it, is a green table, littered with journals. Ibsen, looking down the room, has the dining room door on his left, and beyond it, nearly in the middle, a revolving bookcase, with an easy chair close to it. On his right, between the door and the recess, is a light library step-ladder. [. . .]

Cuthberton is seated in the easy chair at the revolving bookstand, reading the Daily Graphic. Dr Paramore is on the divan in the recess on Ibsen's right, reading the British Medical Journal.

—thus:[24]

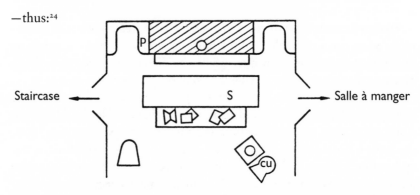

Staircase ← — — — — — — — — S — — — — — — → Salle à manger

With this plan, he could more easily visualize the stage picture and the movements while blocking the action. The possibilities for varying the positions of the actors are made clearer in the floor plan, which shows graphically the different stage areas created by the furniture "breaking" the stage space.

In the margins of the prompt script, Shaw the director blocked the action—transforming explicit movements in the text into pictorial patterns or reduced cues, elaborating and refining implicit movements, and inventing new movements that Shaw the author did not indicate. For the introduction scene at the end of the first act of *Mrs. Warren's Profession,* for example, the author provided few stage directions. In preparing the play for production,[25] Shaw had to devise blocking that would accomplish several goals: as Reverend Samuel Gardner is introduced to the other characters, he must see and be seen by each person to whom he is introduced; Mrs. Warren should have an unobstructed view of him; she should have time to observe him before crying out her recognition; and her movement should build to that recognition. As the dialogue begins, Mrs. Warren and Crofts are upstage, Vivie and Frank stage center, Praed downstage right, and Gardner downstage left. Vivie and Frank are designated by the initials of their first names, the others by the initials of their last names. Shaw blocked the scene in six movements:

	FRANK. [. . .] Let me introduce—my
(1) G to LC	father: Miss Warren. (1)
	VIVIE. (*going to the clergyman and*
(2) V to C	*shaking his hand*) (2) Very glad to see
(3) F to L	you here, Mr Gardner. (3) Let me
(4) W down to RC	introduce everybody. (4) Mr Gardner—Mr
	Frank Gardner—Mr Praed—Sir George
(5) V a step up	Crofts, and—(5) (*As the men are raising*
	their hats to one another, Vivie is
	interrupted by an exclamation from her
	mother, who swoops down on the Reverend
	Samuel).
(6) W to G	MRS WARREN. (6) Why, it's Sam Gardner,
	gone into the church!

These movements comprise a shifting picture that begins with Mrs. Warren, in a crowded center area, almost hidden by Frank and Vivie. The center area becomes less congested when Frank moves to stage left. Mrs. Warren gradually gains more prominence: she moves toward Gardner, Vivie then clears the way for her, and finally she goes directly to center stage to greet him. The gradual shifts can be seen in a series of plans (only the first of which Shaw drew in the margin of his script). At the beginning of the dialogue, when Vivie asks Frank to introduce her to his father, the focus is on her and Frank; Mrs. Warren is almost hidden.

When Gardner and Vivie meet each other—(1) and (2)—the focus is on them, but Vivie's movement provides Mrs. Warren with space: she becomes more prominent and we can observe her.

W

C

F

VG

P

After Vivie introduces herself to Gardner, Frank moves to the left (3), in sufficient time to clear the space so that his father and Crofts can see each other when they are introduced. The central area is now less crowded; Mrs. Warren is set off by more space.

W

C

F

VG

P

During these introductions, as Gardner turns from downstage right to upstage left, Mrs. Warren begins to move toward him (4): she can now do so without being observed by him. Gardner first looks downstage right, at Praed.

C

W   F

VG

P

Vivie then moves upstage a step (5), giving the focus to her mother and Gardner, who is at this point looking upstage left, at Crofts.

C

WV   F

G

P

Mrs. Warren steps forward to Gardner, calling his name and making him turn in a sweeping movement from upstage left to stage right.

C

V   F

WG

P

Mrs. Warren has moved from upstage to stage center as Vivie and Frank relinquish the center area and Gardner turns more than 180 degrees to focus on her. Shaw the director has fulfilled the requirements of the scene, and the entire process occurs so quickly and smoothly that the stages are unobtrusive.

The movements in this scene derive from a basic situation in the text (one character is introduced to other characters) as well as from two explicit stage directions (Vivie going to Gardner and Mrs. Warren swooping down upon him). Early in the first act, when Vivie and Praed discuss Mrs. Warren, Shaw the director—in order to delineate character and help generate atmosphere—suggests movement where the stage directions indicate only that Praed rises.

PRAED. [. . .] Of course you and your mother will get on capitally. (*He rises, and looks abroad at the view*).

PRAED rises—down to float [footlights]—back to audience.

What a charming little place you have here!

VIVIE. (*unmoved*) If you think you are doing anything but confirming my worst suspicions by changing the subject like that, you must take me for a much greater fool than I hope I am.

P up to VIVIE—intimately.

PRAED. Your worst suspicions! Oh, pray dont say that. Now dont.

VIVIE. Why wont my mother's life bear being talked about?

PRAED. Pray think, Miss Vivie. It is natural that I should have a certain delicacy in talking to my old friend's daughter about her behind her

(1) Away a little R from V.

back. (1) You will have plenty of opportunity of talking to her about it when

(2) Up, fidgeting.

she comes. (*Anxiously*) (2) I wonder what is keeping her.

VIVIE. No: she wont talk about it either. (*Rising*)

(3) P down again to her, protesting.

However, I wont press you. (3) Only, mind this, Mr Praed. I strongly suspect there will be a battle royal when my mother hears of my Chancery Lane project.

(4) P stock still.

PRAED. (4) (*ruefully*) I'm afraid there will.

All of the movements in this scene are stimulated by Praed's attitude to Vivie, which is based on who she is and what she does not know. Although the text indicates urbane replies to Vivie's questions and charges, the subtext implies nervousness, for Praed fears she will learn the truth. Shaw creates movement from this subtext. As Vivie dominates the situation by remaining strongly anchored in the same stage area, Praed nervously moves about—going downstage, moving to and then away from Vivie, walking upstage as he fidgets, returning to her. The tension between text and subtext is enhanced by the movement devised by the director.

Shaw also utilized movement to underscore themes and character attitudes implicit in his dialogue. When he and Forbes Robertson jointly directed the first professional English-language production of *Cæsar and Cleopatra* in 1906, Shaw carefully planned the stage business, refining to a considerable degree the directions in the printed text.[26] Here, as a final example, is a small portion of Shaw's blocking for Act I, Scene ii (the throne room of Cleopatra's palace):

CLEOPATRA. I will make all the men I love kings. / I will make you a king. / I will have many young kings, with round strong arms; and when I am tired of them I will whip them to death; / but you shall always be my king: my nice, kind, wise, good old king.

Kiss.
They laugh, he with a wry face.

She takes his arm & makes him walk about with her.
L then back to C.
    C   CL

CÆSAR. Oh, my wrinkles, my wrinkles! And my child's heart! / You will be the most dangerous of all Cæsar's conquests.

Puts his hands on her shoulders & looks at her.
Cl recoils.

CLEOPATRA (*appalled*) Cæsar! I

Returns—pets his
arm—whispers in his
ear

forgot Cæsar. (*Anxiously*) You
will tell him that I am a Queen,
will you not?—a real Queen. /
Listen! (*stealthily coaxing him*):
let us run away and hide until
Cæsar is gone.

Shaw's inventive movement and business, typical of his blocking, enrich the play by creating a visual obligato to the dialogue. It has become commonplace to say that Shaw's stage directions are so detailed that they do the director's work for him and stifle his creativity. Although they are certainly more elaborate than those of most authors, they still provide leeway enough for the imaginative director, and Shaw himself was such a director.

Among the production problems upon which Shaw exercised his imagination was the staging of crowd scenes. As a music critic he had condemned Sir Augustus Harris's production of *Les Huguenots*, comparing the staging of the crowd scenes to "blindman's buff from beginning to end, the crowd caring for nothing but to get out of the way of the principals"; he demanded a "stage full of people who are punctual, alert, in earnest [. . .]." He had praised a production of *The Basoche*: "the movements of the crowds engaged in the action are free alike from the silly stage-drill of *opéra bouffe* and the hopeless idiocy and instinctive ugliness of our Italian choristers."[27]

As a director, Shaw gave crowd scenes the attention he demanded from others, blocking the action carefully. In preparing the 1906 production of *Cæsar and Cleopatra*, he wrote dialogue for the extras,[28] since it was "the only way of getting a natural effect."[29] In the first act, for instance, Belzanor tells the Persian that Cleopatra "is descended from the River Nile and a black kitten of the sacred White Cat," and immediately asks, "What then?" In the dialogue for extras, Shaw added a response. On the cue "the sacred White Cat," there should be a "*reverential murmur.*" In composing lines that give the impression of this murmur he differentiated among the extras, one of whom becomes an irreverent guardsman whose blasphemy starts a small argument. This conflict helps convey the impression that "real people" rather than mere "extras" are on stage.

Yes: the White Cat.
Yes: it is magic.
We must be careful.
I have felt that myself.

Magic.
Meaow!
Blaspheme not.
Hush-sh-sh-sh!
Silence.

When the text indicates or implies reactions from the crowds, the director specifies particular reactions. Shortly after the "White Cat" speech, a mob tries to leave the palace. While Shaw the playwright described only the fact that there is "*An affrighted uproar in the palace,*" Shaw the director worked out the "*affrighted uproar*" in detail. As the women-servants and nurses rush out of the palace in panic, their panic is individualized. Some want only to get away. Others are concerned with their material possessions: one checks packages, another asks help in carrying a bundle, another realizes she has left something behind. Each responds to the others in a different way: one looks out for a friend's safety as they descend the steps, another angrily replies to someone who has apparently bumped into her.

Be quick, be quick.
Come on: Do come on.
Have you the other bundle?
Take care of the steps.
Ayisha, Ayisha!
I am here. Come on.
Take care where youre coming, will you?
Its too heavy! help me.
I'll take the other end.
Oh, Ive forgotten the panther skin.

When in the fifth act Cæsar suggests to Rufio that he become governor of Egypt, the text indicates no response from anyone but Rufio. Shaw the director, however, was concerned with the responses of all within hearing distance of Cæsar's suggestion and specified that there should be "whispering & chattering—both soldiers & ladies." Upon hearing Cæsar's words, the Egyptian women exclaim:

What! Rufio governor.
That vulgar common man!
What will Cleopatra say?
Its a shame, so it is.
Oh, scandalous!
Who did he say?

Is he actually making that great brute our governor?

The soldiers exclaim:

Did you hear that?
Rufio is to be a governor.
One of us! A freedman.
Well, why not? He is a Roman.
Catch Cato making Rufio governor of a province.
We are the real Republicans after all.

The women's reactions range from indignation to incredulity, the men's from delighted surprise to pride. Shaw used extras not merely to populate the stage and give the impression of a crowd, but to enrich the action by varied responses and to help build the climaxes. Nor is *Cæsar and Cleopatra* an isolated instance of detailed work on crowd scenes. For the 1912 production of *Captain Brassbound's Conversion,* for example, Shaw wrote exclamations and dialogue for the five extras representing Brassbound's crew.[30]

Much of the director's preproduction planning involves such drudgery as the compilation of a property list. For the second act of *The Devil's Disciple,* Shaw went through the tedious labor of making up a detailed prop list that included a "big loaf" of bread (large because it is homemade), a table cover that must be cloth and also recognizably American, and a powder horn and bullet bag attached to the leather belt holding a pair of pistols.[31]

Whereas the properties for *The Devil's Disciple* were necessary, they were not at all unusual. When unconventional properties were required, as in *The Admirable Bashville,* Shaw gave specifications: "A knockout sceptre for Cetewayo, not too unwieldy for a broadsword combat with Lucian's umbrella," "Four enormous boxing gloves stuffed with feathers (eider down preferred)," "A mossgrown tree trunk for Lydia to sit on, not too low, and really round, so that she can get her heels well under herself when Cashel lifts her with one finger under her chin."[32]

Movements and motivations, business and exclamations (of the extras as well as the principals), even properties were thoughtfully planned prior to rehearsals. In order to produce the effect he wanted, to save time, and to leave as little as possible to chance, Shaw meticulously prepared every detail of production in advance of his rehearsals with the actors. Before examining Shaw's rehearsal practices, however, we must first discuss his methods of casting. The next chapter analyzes both, as well as a third directorial problem, cutting the script, which may occur before or during rehearsals.

3 General Directing Practices

Casting

On 6 January 1905, Shaw suggested to Gilbert Murray that Gertrude Kingston play Helen of Troy in Murray's translation of *The Trojan Women* by Euripides. "Of course," he added, "I make the suggestion as a practical stage manager, comparing her, not with the ideal Helen of your imagination, but with the next best Helen you are likely to get."[1] When Shaw cast a play, a major consideration was practicality. If Ben Webster were in the company of *John Bull's Other Island,* he considered, pondering several casting possibilities, there would be three combinations for the roles of Larry and Keegan: "1 Webster-[William] Poel, 2 [Granville] Barker-Webster, 3 Webster-Barker." The first, he wrote to Barker, "would set you free altogether. No. 3 would save you the trouble of learning a new part. No. 2 would save the situation if Poel proved impossible as Keegan, and Webster as Larry." (As it turned out, Number 1 was used.) Shaw usually considered numerous possibilities and combinations. In a letter to J. E. Vedrenne, he proposed Alfred Bishop, Henry Ainley, H. B. Irving, and William Haviland as possibilities for the Bishop in *Getting Married.* "Unless the Bishop has a touch of charm & distinction the play will fail: a stage bishop wont do. For Cecil Sykes [Clarence] Blakiston, [Lewis] Casson, Basil Gill, [Julian] Lestrange, [Leon] Quartermaine, Vernon Steele, [George F.] Tully, Harcourt Williams, [Dawson] Milward are none of them right exactly; but they are not grossly impossible."[2]

Despite his practicality, however, Shaw did not lose sight of the necessity of placing the right actor in the right role. After advising James Welsh, an actor-director who planned to produce *You Never Can Tell,* that he would be better as the Waiter than as Phil, Shaw warned him that although the play as a whole is "absolutely actor proof," it has a ten-minute episode "during which it is the most difficult comedy in the Irish language": the scene between Valentine and Gloria at the end of Act II. "If that scene fails, the play fails. And nobody but a comedian of the very first forty-pound-a-week order can touch that scene. It is not that a lesser man can only do it badly: it is that *he can't do it at all* [. . .]. Can you get [Charles] Hawtrey, or [Charles] Wyndham, or John Drew, or [Charles] Bourchier?"[3] To Lawrence Langner, of the Theatre Guild, Shaw suggested several doubling combinations for *Back to Methuselah.* The same actor could play Adam, Conrad, the Accountant General, and the Envoy; the same actress, Eve, Mrs. Lutestring, the Oracle, and the She-Ancient. Caine, Burge, Burge-Lubin, Napoleon, and Ozymandias could be played by the same actor, and Savvy, Zoo, and the Newly Born by the same actress.[4]

In attempting to persuade actors to undertake certain roles, Shaw used charm, wit, and blarney. On 30 March 1894, he tried to interest Alma Murray in playing Raina in *Arms and the Man:* "I want Miss [Florence] Farr to play, *not* the heroine, but the servant. If I can persuade her to do this, and to crown her magnanimity by allowing you to play the heroine, will you consent to be approached on the subject, or have you any decisive objection or prior engagement that puts you out of the question? The lady does not swear, nor does she throttle the servant like the heroine in my other play [*Widowers' Houses*]. She has to make herself a little ridiculous (unconsciously) once or twice; but for the most part she has to be romantically beautiful or else amusing in a bearably dignified way. She is a Bulgarian, and can, I suppose, wear extraordinary things if she wishes."[5] In an effort to convince Louis Calvert that he should play Undershaft in *Major Barbara,* he described the role as "Broadbent and Keegan rolled into one, with Mephistopheles thrown in," and prophesied that Calvert's performance as Undershaft would immediately thrust Henry Irving and Beerbohm Tree into the third rank of their profession. "There are the makings of ten Hamlets and six Othellos in his mere leavings," wrote Shaw. "Learning it will half kill you; but you can retire next day as preeminent and unapproachable." Since the character must play the trombone, the playwright added, Calvert would receive a fringe benefit: "trombone players never get cholera nor consumption—never die, in fact, until extreme old age makes them incapable of working the slide."[6]

In selecting a cast, Shaw believed, the director should not be concerned with whether the actors understand the play, but whether their ages, physical appearances, and personalities are suitable.[7] Refusing to offer Lillah McCarthy the role of Ellie Dunn in *Hearbreak House,* he explained

to her in one letter that Ellie must be "born to immaculate virginity" and
asked in another, "How can you, at your age and with your reputation as
a Siddonian 'heavy,' play an ingenue of eighteen against two women of
forty playing off their sexual fascinations for all they are worth? You could
do it perfectly well [as Margaret Knox in *Fanny's First Play*] against Mrs
Gilbey and Mrs Knox, but not against Hesione and Ariadne."[8]

The peculiar "quality" of an actor was another important consideration. Shaw complained that Elizabeth Robins projected youthful indi-
vidualism in revolt too strongly to play successfully the role of Ella
Rentheim in *John Gabriel Borkman*.[9] Charles Charrington, he said, completely failed as Helmer in *A Doll's House*, not through any fault of his
own but because the role was uncongenial to his natural quality: "What is
wanted for Helmer is complacency *without* conviction. Charrington has
conviction without complacency; and the result is disastrous to the play. It
is a case of congenital incapacity [. . .]." To Granville Barker, he explained
the difficulty of casting Snobby Price in *Major Barbara*: "Unless I can get
[Fred] Cremlin and [Oswald] Yorke [as Peter Shirley and Bill Walker]
fitted with the right sort of Snobby we shall get the usual stock-company
ensemble with no character at all in it. Of course [Edmund] Gwenn can
play a thief. He can also play the emperor of China. An actor is an actor
and a part is only a part when all's said. [. . .] I want a slim, *louche*, servant-
girl-bigamist, half-handsome sort of rascal, *not* a costermonger, *not*
an Artful Dodger, not anything like Gwenn."[10] The *Lumpenproletariat*
Snobby Price is an unlikable scoundrel, not an ingenious, colorful cut-
purse. Shaw may have feared that Gwenn, unable to eradicate his own
charm and warmth, would turn Snobby into a likable scoundrel, appealing to the audience in a way that Snobby should not appeal, and, in effect,
justifying the character. As Shaw said in another context, "making
[wicked characters] lovable is the most complete defence of their conduct
that could possibly be made."[11]

Shaw frequently referred to the roles in his plays in terms of stock
company types: Judith Anderson (*The Devil's Disciple*) should be played
as a melodramatic heroine, Lady Britomart (*Major Barbara*) as a *grand
dame*.[12] He also referred to these roles in operatic terms. In casting plays,
he said, the director should pay attention to vocal contrast. "The four
principals should be soprano, alto, tenor, and bass."[13] In *Arms and the
Man*, Raina and Louka should be soprano and contralto, respectively.
Bluntschli's voice should be dry, and Sergius's ringing.[14]

Shaw was aware, too, of the importance of securing believable family
relationships. For example, it is easy to cast the roles in *You Never Can Tell*

separately, but difficult when the family is taken into account, for the actors must be convincing not only as the characters but also as parents, children, sisters, and brother of each other. Mrs. Clandon and Dolly should be believable as mother and daughter, Gloria and Dolly as sisters.[15]

Conducting Rehearsals

At the start of rehearsals, Shaw believed, the author should read the play to the company. If the author was not a competent reader, a substitute should do the job. If a good substitute were unavailable, however, it would be better to have no reading at all, rather than a bad one.[16] Shaw himself usually read the play to the cast. From this first reading, Sir Cedric Hardwicke recalls, the actors learned "how the author wished the various parts to be acted. [. . .] The inflexions of voice peculiar to each character were steadily maintained until the end. [. . .] Shaw's soft Irish tones never became monotonous, nor even in the most dramatic moments did he resort to gesture; he merely relied on the modulations of his voice to make his meaning clear." Once this "monumental reading was over, it was difficult for any of us to go seriously astray, knowing now precisely what the author had in mind."[17]

Ideally, Shaw would like to have "half a dozen rehearsals seated round a table, books in hand, to get the *music* right before going on to the stage." Since these conditions did not exist in the British theater, he did his best "to get, not what I want, but what is possible under the circumstances."[18] Because of this, blocking began immediately. "If the scenery is not ready," he told Siegfried Trebitsch, remarking that in England it is never ready, "I seize chairs, forms &c. with my own hands, and arrange them to mark doors and objects of furniture. (The stage manager waits until he can order a carpenter to do it, as such manual work would compromise his dignity). I open the prompt book; seize the actor or actress who begins; lead them to their entrance in my pleasantest and busiest and friendliest manner, and say, 'Here you are: this is your entrance — now down here and across to here' letting them read the words just as they please, and simply piloting them through the movements." After blocking the first act, he asked the actors to run through the act again in order to settle the movements and business in their memories. The two run-throughs took up one rehearsal. The following day he would run through the second act twice in the same manner, and the next day the third.[19] At this point, according to Shaw, the director should be on the stage with the actors, prompting them as they go through the business. They should be asked not to learn their roles until after the first week of rehearsals (the blocking rehearsals), for "nothing is a greater nuisance than an actor who is trying to remember his lines when he should be settling his position and getting the hang of the play with his book in his hand." Once the blocking has been completed and the movements mastered, the director should ask the actors whether they were comfortable in these movements, and if not, which movements were uncomfortable. He should then adjust the movements so that the actors can perform them comfortably.[20]

At the end of this first stage of rehearsals, Shaw would have the director call "'[line] perfect'" rehearsals. As the actors go through the scenes without scripts in hand, the director should leave the stage and sit in the auditorium. During this phase of rehearsals, he must not stop the scene and demand that the actors repeat a passage again and again until they get it right. This, Shaw believed, is schoolmastering rather than directing. Such repetitions cause the performance of that passage to deteriorate rather than to improve. If anything goes wrong, or if the director thinks of an improvement, let him make a note and give this note to the actor at the end of the act. But he should not mention or attempt to correct a fault unless its repetition reveals that the actor will not correct it in his own way as he is learning the play. When "'[line] perfect'" rehearsals begin, Shaw reminds the director, there will be at least a week of disappointing and agonizing backsliding, for as the actors try to memorize their lines, everything else will be lost. At this stage, the director should be especially considerate of the actors, for they are under a heavy strain. Only the inexperienced director will betray dismay at this stage of rehearsal and permit himself outbursts of reproach or frenzied attempts to make sure that everything is perfect at rehearsals. Once the memorizing stage has been passed, says Shaw, the director must watch the act run-throughs and take careful notes, appending "'Rehearse this'" after some of them. At the end of the act, he should have the actors go through those bits to get them right. Still, he must refrain from schoolmastering, that is, ordering them to repeat a scene even if it means staying there all night. During this phase, he may return to the stage, interrupting as often as he finds necessary. Shaw implies that this should not occur often, and ideally not at all.[21]

"Remember that no strangers should be present at a rehearsal," Shaw advised. Since he recognized that it was sometimes expedient for strangers — such as newspapermen — to attend, he suggested a prearranged interruption to remind the visitors that they were witnessing a rehearsal rather than a performance. This interruption should consist of an instruction to a member of the technical staff about a technical detail. The director should never direct an actor in the presence of strangers, and he should always get the consent of every actor before admitting a stranger to rehearsal.[22] According to Sir Cedric Hardwicke, Shaw practiced what he preached: "Rehearsals to Shaw were as confidential as the confessional." If a stranger were present, "Shaw punctiliously abstained from giving a single word of instruction to any actor until the auditorium was clear again." Hardwicke called this an "infallible instinct for good theatrical etiquette."[23]

Consideration for the actor is also evidenced in Shaw's advice on scheduling rehearsals. First, the director should not waste the actor's time. Actors with only a few lines should not wait all day while the principals rehearse. Second, he should avoid late-night rehearsals. If he cannot, then he should see that the actors receive taxi fare home if they are kept until the last trains and buses have stopped.[24]

"Never find fault until you know the remedy," Shaw urged the director. If something is wrong and the director does not know how to correct it, he should say nothing, for it is discouraging for an actor merely to be told that something is wrong. The director should be silent until a solution comes to him—or to the actor, as it probably will. Since the actor cannot assimilate more than two or three suggestions at a time, the director should remember not to give him too many notes at any one rehearsal. If the director thus controls his zeal and saves the other notes for future rehearsals, the actor may correct some of the errors by himself. Further, the director should not discuss such trifles as mistakes in lines or business as if the fate of the world hinged on them. Nor should he discuss anything that is not essential. And he should be prepared for the actor to make the same mistake several times in succession, and to forget the director's notes until they have been given, also in succession, for several days.[25]

If an actor "repeatedly omits some physical feat or movement, the director must conclude that it is made impossible by some infirmity which the player would rather die than disclose. In such cases the business must be altered." The director should not discuss a passage with the actor, nor should he tell him that a scene is essentially either pathetic or comic. If he does, "the player will come to the next rehearsal bathed in tears from the first word to the last, or clowning for all he is worth all the time." Instead, he should demonstrate to the actor—not as an order, but as a suggestion— how the passage or scene should be performed. These demonstrations should be so exaggerated that there is no chance of the actor merely imitating them. "A performance in which the players are all mimicking the director, instead of following his suggestions in their own different ways, is a bad performance."[26]

Imitative performances, Shaw knew, followed the law of doing what was done the last time, whereas living, organic performances obeyed the innermost impulse of the text. "And as that impulse is never, in a fertile artistic nature, the impulse to do what was done last time, the two laws are incompatible, being virtually laws respectively of death and life in art." Shaw recalls having laughed at a provincial Iago who, at the words "Trifles light as air," twitched his handkerchief into space. A theatrical acquaintance rebuked him, claiming that the actor was right because he had copied every gesture, movement, and inflection of his performance from Charles Kean. "Unfortunately," Shaw points out, "he was not Charles Kean: consequently Charles Kean's [by-]play no more fitted him than Charles Kean's clothes. [. . .] In the old provincial stock companies, most of which have by this time died the death they richly deserved, there was often to be found an old lady who played Lady Macbeth when the star Shakespearean actor came his usual round. She played it exactly as Mrs Siddons played it, with the important difference that, as she was not Mrs Siddons, the way which was the right way for Mrs Siddons was the wrong way for her."[27] While this was written in 1889, before Shaw had any directing experience, the principles of "death and life in art" apply to Shaw's directing. He wanted the actor to use his own methods, to follow his own impulses, rather than to imitate Shaw's or anyone else's techniques. "There is only one effect to be produced," he pointed out; "but there may be fifty different ways of producing it." Furthermore, "a good part can be played a dozen different ways by a dozen different actors and be none the worse: no author worth his salt attaches a definite and invariable physiognomy to each variety of human character. Every actor must be allowed to apply his own methods to his own playing."[28]

Shaw followed these precepts. "Dont hamper your inspiration," he urged Annie Russell, who was rehearsing the title role of *Major Barbara*. "If I make suggestions or offer criticisms freely it is only on the understanding that you need not give them a second thought if they do not chime in with your own feeling." Reluctant to suggest a method of playing the final scene with Cusins because he did not know exactly how she got her effects ("except that it is not in my rather rhetorical, public-speaker kind of way"), he implored her to play the role in her way rather than in his: "You have much greater resources in the direction of gentleness than

I have; and I assure you that you will go wrong every time you try to do what *I* like instead of letting yourself do what *you* like."[29]

One must remember that in this instance Shaw was dealing with an accomplished actress, not a novice. To a novice, his advice was different. He told Molly Tompkins not to take the bit between her teeth all at once, but to take a night for herself, or an act, or—as a beginning—a speech or two, and test whether her method proved to be as good as the coached method. The only way to win a conflict with the director, he assured her, was to make her method convincing. Possibly, her method was right but she did not yet have the skill to put it across. If this were the case, then for the moment she must accept the coaching. Nevertheless, "in the end you must make yourself something more than a marionette worked mostly by somebody who is not a successful actor or author or critic or connoisseur or anything else that commands an unquestioning deference."[30]

The director should not get angry and complain in the pedantic manner of a schoolmaster that he has repeatedly called attention to such and such a point, for he "will destroy the whole atmosphere in which art breathes, and make a scene which is not in the play, and a very disagreeable scene at that."[31] Nor should he shame the actor by calling out his deficiencies before the entire company. Shaw's practice was to give quiet, individual advice to the actors after each run-through.[32]

Numerous actors praised Shaw's good manners, his tact, and his ability to communicate his ideas.[33] According to the Frank Harris biography (in a passage that may have been written by Shaw himself, who corrected the galleys after Harris died),[34] "Shaw's manners were always ingratiating, his directions always helpful, and altogether he carried an air of angelic sweetness while he sometimes undid the work of weeks of another man quite as competent as himself in the matter at issue. His manners alone saved him from being hit with an axe." The only instance I have found of Shaw's having lost his temper was when Mrs. Patrick Campbell's violent refusal to execute a mechanical movement provoked him into calling her an amateur.[35]

Shaw understood that there are different types of actors, each of whom must be treated differently. The director "must distinguish between born actors who should be let alone to find their own way, and spook actors who have to be coached sentence by sentence and are helpless without such coaching. There are so many degrees between these extremes that the tact and judgment of directors in their very delicate relations with players are sometimes strained to the utmost [. . .]."[36]

He often tried to ease the strain by clowning. "What Raina wants," he insisted to Lillah McCarthy, whose performance in the 1907 revival of *Arms and the Man* had deteriorated over a month into its run, "is extremity of style—style—Comédie Française, Queen of Spain style. Do you hear, worthless wretch that you are?—s t y l e." He demanded that Mrs. Patrick Campbell, as Eliza in *Pygmalion*, not run to Higgins like her pet dog and then "forget everything in an affectionate tête à tête with him. Imagine that he is the author, and be scornful."[37] The day after the first performance of *Major Barbara*, he wrote to Louis Calvert, who had failed to learn his lines,

> I see with disgust that the papers all say that your Undershaft was a magnificent piece of acting, and Major Barbara a rottenly undramatic play, instead of pointing out that Major B. is a masterpiece and you the most infamous amateur that ever disgraced the boards.
>
> Do let me put Cremlin into it. A man who could let the seven deadly sins go for nothing could sit on a hat without making an audience laugh. I have taken a box for Friday and had a hundredweight of cabbages, dead cats, eggs, and gingerbeer bottles stacked in it. Every word you fluff, every speech you unact, I will shy something at you. Before you go on the stage I will insult you until your temper gets the better of your liver. You are an imposter, a sluggard, a blockhead, a shirk, a malingerer, and the worst actor that ever lived or ever will live. I will apologize to the public for engaging you: I will tell your mother of you. Barker played you off the stage; Cremlin dwarfed you; Bill annihilated you. Clare Greet took all eyes from you. If you do not recover yourself next time, a thunderbolt will end you. If you are too lazy to study the lines, *I'll* coach you in them. That last act MUST be saved, or I'll withdraw the play and cut you off with a shilling.[38]

Shaw's extravagant manner may have softened his criticism, but it did not conceal that criticism, nor did it hide the unmistakable urgency of his effort to make Calvert learn his lines.

Shaw's clowning sometimes took the form of parody. Writing to Alma Murray that her performance in *Arms and the Man* lacked "the sincerity of the noble attitude and the thrilling voice," he exaggerated that attitude in his complaint: "What—oh what has become of my Raina? How could you have the heart to play that way for me—to lacerate every fibre in my being? [. . .] Oh, that first act! that horrible first act! could anything expiate it? I swear I will never go to that theatre again. Here is my heart, stuck full of swords by your cruel hands." Beneath a drawing of a heart with nine swords in it, the letter is signed, "yours, agonized." A few weeks later, his tone was considerably different as he apologized to his leading lady:

> I have now to entirely withdraw all my former observations, which you will please attribute to temporary aberration. It is quite impossible that you could ever have played Raina otherwise than beautifully. [. . .] I shall not now accept your invitation to call and talk the part over, because whenever any woman gives me the pleasure your playing tonight did, I cannot help falling violently in love with her; and I can no longer support the spectacle of [A. W.] Forman's [her husband's] domestic happiness. He is a most intolerable usurper and monopolist; and the advantage he has taken of the mere accident of his knowing you before I did appears to me to be altogether unjustifiable.

In case she might think he was in such good humor that his appreciation was worthless, he added some adverse criticism before signing the letter, "yours contritely."[39] In this instance, the actress herself resolved the errors that prompted Shaw's tirade. When Wendy Hiller was rehearsing *Saint Joan* at Malvern in 1936, Shaw wrote her a letter containing devastating criticisms of her acting. She called at his hotel to discuss the points raised in his letter. "He was charming & courteous," she reports, "but not inclined to take me or his notes too seriously—I was overcome with earnestness which I think he found amusing."[40]

Shaw did not on all occasions use a charming manner to soothe ruffled feelings. When the circumstance called for it, he was frank. To Lillah McCarthy, for example, he wrote, "Raina has gone to bits [. . .] and the effect is disastrous." He then gave reasons. But at other times, he would offer praise, telling the same actress that her Ann Whitefield (*Man and Superman*) "was one of the best performances I have seen you do."[41] His praise was valid partly because he did not give it indiscriminately. In his discussions with and letters to actors, he did not withhold praise. He used it sincerely but also as a way to reassure the actor that his performance was not "all wrong." This obvious device—honored as often in the breach as in the observance—was nonetheless effective. Shaw made special use of it in the "pep-talks" (or "pep-letters") he gave to actors shortly before opening night. After offering several pieces of adverse criticism on Lillah McCarthy's Raina, he called them "only counsels of perfection," reassuring her that "even if you miss a few points, you have enough in hand for a handsome success." He used the same tactic with John L. Shine, who played Larry Doyle to Louis Calvert's Broadbent in *John Bull's Other Island*. This time he called the adverse criticisms "danger signals" and went on to say, "Even if we make a slip or two, there is enough in hand now for success. [. . .] On the whole, whatever happens to the play, you will score." But his pre-opening night letters did not always contain such praise. His letter to Mrs. Patrick Campbell, headed "FINAL ORDERS," written just before the opening of *Pygmalion*, contains no praise, but a series of instructions and an admonition to leave as little as possible to chance.[42]

Prior to opening night, however, is the final stage of preparation, dress rehearsal. During this stage—when the actor must accustom himself to performing in costume, under lights, using full properties and scenery— the director should be prepared for everything to go wrong. This should not deter him: after the run-throughs he should return to the stage—with his notes—to rehearse the sections that need polishing. Shaw believed the theatrical superstition that a bad final rehearsal means a good performance, since the actors would otherwise be too confident to achieve success on opening night.[43]

The time needed to direct a play, Shaw estimated, was four weeks: one week for blocking the action; two weeks for memorizing, with the director seated in the house, taking notes; and a week for dress rehearsal.[44] He apparently adapted these methods to traditional rehearsal practices in England, for he also stated that ideally he would like a rehearsal period of from six weeks to two months.[45]

Cutting and Changing the Script

Shaw issued numerous critical strictures against cutting and changing Shakespeare's plays. "In a true republic of art," he declared in a review of the Lyceum *Cymbeline*, "Sir Henry Irving would ere this have expiated his acting versions on the scaffold. He does not merely cut plays: he disembowels them. In Cymbeline he has quite surpassed himself by extirpating the antiphonal third verse of the famous dirge. A man who would do that would do anything: cut the coda out of the first movement of Beethoven's Ninth Symphony, or shorten one of Velasquez's Philips into a kitcat to make it fit over his drawing room mantelpiece."[46] Irving, he predicted, "will have an extremely unpleasant quarter of an hour if he is unlucky enough to come across the bard in the heavenly Pantheon."[47] But Irving was not the only villain. Shaw chastised John Barrymore for having cut an hour and a half of the text of *Hamlet*, including the recorder scene, the scene with the King after Polonius's death, and the speech beginning "How all occasions do inform against me." And Augustin Daly's rearrangement of the scenes in *Two Gentlemen of Verona,* he claimed, made the plot and the character relationships unintelligible.[48]

In 1887, in a review of Richard Wagner's *On Conducting,* he approvingly quoted Wagner's charge that cutting is the conductor's "'means of accommodating to [his] own incompetence the artistic tasks which [he finds] impossible.'" In 1919 he made the same charge against producers who cut Shakespeare:

> The moment you admit that the producer's business is to improve Shakespear by cutting out everything that he himself would not have written, and everything that does not make prosaic sense, you are launched on a slope on which there is no stopping until you reach the abyss where Irving's Lear lies forgotten. The reason stares us in the face. The producer's disapprovals, and consequently his cuts, are the symptoms of the differences between Shakespear and himself; and his assumption that all these differences are differences of superiority on his part and inferiority on Shakespear's, must end in the cutting down or raising up of Shakespear to his level.

According to Shaw, the only workable plan is to perform Shakespeare's plays in their entirety. This plan makes Shakespeare, not the director, the ultimate authority. If the latter thinks Shakespeare's language is half-dead and often unintelligible, these are excellent reasons for not producing the plays, but poor reasons for "breaking them up and trying to jerrybuild modern plays with them, as the Romans broke up the Coliseum to build hovels." Those people who really want to see Shakespeare want all of him, and not merely a director's "favorite bits; and this is not in the least because they enjoy every word of it, but because they want to be sure of hearing the words they do enjoy, and because the effect of judiciously selected passages, not to mention injudiciously selected passages, is not the same as that of the whole play [. . .]." Cutting, Shaw concludes, "must be dogmatically ruled out [. . .]." Either perform a Shakespearean play in its entirety or else leave it alone. "If Shakespear made a mess of it, it is not likely that Smith or Robinson will succeed where he failed."[49]

Shaw praised William Poel's productions of Shakespeare *in toto* and applauded Forbes Robertson for breaking with stage tradition by including Reynaldo and Fortinbras in his production of *Hamlet*. In Shaw's short story "The Theatre of the Future" (1905), a Utopian theater performs the three parts of *Henry VI* plus *Richard III* on four different evenings, without altering or revising the texts, since the management "has, unfortunately, not succeeded in obtaining the services of a stage manager whose judgment in these matters can be accepted as unquestionably superior to Shakespear's."[50]

But what of Shaw's own judgment in this regard? At times, he himself was willing to cut Shakespeare. In 1896 he offered Ellen Terry advice on cutting and rearranging the dialogue of *Cymbeline,* and in 1937 he rewrote the last act, calling his version *Cymbeline Refinished.* Parts of the character of Imogen were "idiotic," he told Ellen Terry on the former occasion, and it would be brainless to retain such "tawdry trash" from Act III, Scene iv, as "'No, 'tis slander, / Whose edge is sharper than the sword, whose tongue / Outvenoms all the worms of Nile,'" and so forth. He suggested that Imogen not read aloud Posthumous's letter to her in this scene, but instead have Pisanio read it aloud in Act III, Scene ii, so that the first sentence of the letter would motivate his "'How! of adultery!'" and the remainder provoke his "'How! That I should murder her. . . . I! her!'" Then, in the fourth scene, Imogen would read the letter in silence and exclaim, "'I false!'"—thus moving the words sixteen lines earlier. Pisanio would reply, "'What shall I need to draw my sword? The paper / Hath cut her throat already. What cheer, madam?'"—cutting Shakespeare's eight lines to two. Imogen's entire speech beginning "'Thou didst accuse him of incontinency'" should be deleted, Shaw urged, together with the "rubbish" about "'false Aeneas.'"[51]

This advice seems to contradict Shaw's condemnation of those who cut Shakespeare's texts. However, because he knew that Irving would cut the play, his letter might also be regarded as an effort to secure an intelligent cutting. Supporting this suggestion is a statement in Shaw's Foreword to *Cymbeline Refinished:* "I shall not press my version on managers producing Cymbeline if they have the courage and good sense to present the original word-for-word as Shakespear left it, and the means to do justice to the masque. But if they are halfhearted about it, and inclined to compromise by leaving out the masque and the comic jailor and mutilating the rest, as their manner is, I unhesitatingly recommend my version" (7, 185–86).

About his own plays he unhesitatingly insisted upon his version.[52] He ordered Siegfried Trebitsch to tell the people at the Volkstheater of his absolute refusal to have a line deleted or a comma changed. "If they know how plays should be written let them write plays for themselves. If they dont, they had better leave the business to those who do." And if they are too backward to be capable of performing his plays as he wrote them, "they can let them alone [. . .]." "If you find at rehearsal that any of the lines [in *Candida*] cannot be made to go," he wrote to Richard Mansfield, "sack the whole company at once and get in others. I have tested every line of it in my readings of the play; and there is a way of making every bit of it worth doing." By cutting *Misalliance*, according to Shaw, William Faversham caused the play's failure and made himself useful only as an example of an actor-manager who succeeded when he followed Shaw's instructions and failed when he did not.[53]

Actually, it was not cutting that Shaw objected to, but bad cutting. "I don't mind cuts," he said, "but I'll make them myself so that the point of my sermons is not destroyed."[54] In his "Rules for Directors," he admitted, "A play may need to be cut, added to, or otherwise altered, sometimes to improve it as a play, sometimes to overcome some mechanical difficulty on the stage, sometimes by a passage proving too much for an otherwise indispensable player."[55] But cutting to save time is never satisfactory, for it usually saves time at the expense of the play.[56] Intelligent cutting, however, is a skilled job which "should be done by the author, if available, or if not, by a qualified playwright, not by a player, nor by the callboy."[57]

When Max Reinhardt agreed to direct *Cæsar and Cleopatra* for Berlin's Deutsches Theater, Shaw suggested that in order to bring the performances into the traditional time limits, Reinhardt cut Act III (the lighthouse act). Reinhardt did not follow this advice but instead cut the burning of the library at the end of Act II and also the first scene of Act IV. Shaw was furious: "May the soul of Reinhardt scream through all eternity in boiling brimstone!" he wrote to Granville Barker and wondered how the second act could possibly be intelligible without the burning of the library.[58] It is always a mistake, he explained, to trust people like Reinhardt to alter a play: "They see the effects, but they dont see the preparation of the effects—the gradual leading of the audience up to them. They cut the preparation out, and then are surprised because the effects miss fire." Reinhardt, he concluded, "has done everything that a thoroughpaced blockhead could do to achieve a failure; and he has achieved it accordingly. [. . .] May his soul perish for it!"[59]

Although Shaw refused to sanction other people cutting and changing his plays, he often did so himself.[60] On some occasions, he made cuts only for specific productions, later restoring the passages—sometimes with minor modifications—to the printed texts. Shaw removed part of the following passage from a speech by Barbara, for example, in Act III, Scene ii of the 1905 production of *Major Barbara* (double brackets indicate deletions):

But you came and shewed me that I was in the power of Bodger and Undershaft. [[Today I feel—oh, how can I put it into words? Sarah: do you remember the earthquake at Cannes, when we were little children?—how little the surprise of the first shock mattered compared to the dread and horror of the second? That is how I feel in this place today.]] I stood on the rock I thought eternal; and without a word of warning it reeled and crumbled under me. I was safe with an infinite wisdom watching me—an army marching to Salvation with me; and in a moment, at a wave of your cheque book, I stood alone; and the heavens were empty. [[That was the first shock of the earthquake: I am waiting for the second.]][61]

While he provided no explanation for the deletions, the cut passage is essentially digressive. Without Barbara's reminiscence her speech is more straightforward, compact, and vigorous. In the Standard Edition of his plays (beginning 1931), and more recent printings, Shaw restored these deletions but changed "at a wave of your cheque book" to the more accurate "at a stroke of your pen in a cheque book" (3, 170). Shortly after this speech he cut part of an exchange between Undershaft and Barbara:

UNDERSHAFT. [. . .] Only fools fear crime: we all fear poverty. Pah! (*He turns on* BARBARA) [[You talk of your half saved ruffian in West Ham: you accuse me of dragging his soul back to perdition. Well, bring him to me here; and I will drag his soul back again to salvation for you. Not by words and dreams; but by thirty eight shillings a week, a sound house in a handsome street, and a permanent job. In three weeks he will have a fancy waistcoat; in three months a tall hat and a chapel sitting; before the end of the year he will shake hands with a duchess at a Primrose League meeting, and join the Conservative Party.

BARBARA. And will he be the better for that?

UNDERSHAFT. You know he will. Dont be a hypocrite, Barbara. He will be better fed, better housed, better clothed, better behaved; and his children will be pounds heavier and bigger. That will be better than an American cloth mattress in a shelter, chopping firewood, eating bread and treacle, and being forced to kneel down from time to time to thank heaven for it—knee drill, I think you call it.]] It is cheap work converting starving men with a Bible in one hand and a slice of bread in the other.

Here, too, Shaw restored the passage to the printed edition, and the dialogue remains unchanged (3, 172–73). Again, he gave no reason for the cut. A reasonable speculation, however, is prompted by Shaw's letter to Calvert after the play's opening night (above, p. 34): since Calvert had difficulty memorizing the lines, Shaw may have cut some long speeches to enable him to devote his time to other, more important passages.

For the 1921 production of *Heartbreak House,* Shaw cut sixty-five lines from the third act (1919 edition), all of which he retained in subsequent editions of the play. For these cuts, however, he provided a reason: the actors were unable to deliver the lines convincingly. "There are always lines which are dud lines with a given cast. Change the cast and you get other lines dud. The line which strikes on A's box will only bother B."[62]

The different versions of Shaw's plays demonstrate that he made numerous changes in the dialogue and stage business. In the second act of *Arms and the Man,* the 1894 typescript copy contains this exchange between Petkoff and Catherine:

PET-   The war's over. The treaty was signed three days ago at Bucharest; and the decree for our army to demobilize was issued yesterday. It's an honorable treaty: it declares peace but not friendly relations; the two words have been expressly struck out. If the Austrians hadnt interfered we'd have annexed Servia and made Prince Alexander Emperor of the Balkans. Confound them!

CATH-   (*Sitting R. of table*) Well, never mind, dear. So glad to have you back again with me.

PET-   Thank you, my love. I missed you greatly!

CATH-   (*Affectionately*) Ah! (*Stretches her hand across the table to squeeze his.*)

In the Standard Edition and subsequent printings of his plays, this was changed to:

PETKOFF. [. . .] The war's over. The treaty was signed three days ago at Bucharest; and the decree for our army to demobilize was issued yesterday.

CATHERINE (*springing erect, with flashing eyes*) Paul: have you let the Austrians force you to make peace?

PETKOFF (*submissively*) My dear: they didnt consult me. What could I do? (*She sits down and turns away from him*). But of course we saw to it that the treaty was an honorable one. It declares peace—

CATHERINE (*outraged*) Peace!

PETKOFF (*appeasing her*)—but not friendly relations: remember that. They wanted to put that in; but I insisted on its being struck out. What more could I do?

CATHERINE. You could have annexed Serbia and made Prince Alexander Emperor of the Balkans. Thats what I would have done.

PETKOFF. I dont doubt it in the least, my dear. But I should have had to subdue the whole Austrian Empire first; and that would have kept me too long away from you. I missed you greatly.

CATHERINE (*relenting*) Ah! (*She stretches her hand affectionately across the table to squeeze his*). [1, 416]

The later version, partially the result of several productions of the play, is richer. When Petkoff informs Catherine of the demobilization order, the later version has her responding violently, forcing him to explain that he was unable to prevent the action. In the earlier version, his declaration that the treaty was honorable and declares peace merely follows the information about the demobilization. In the later version, it is an attempt to pacify Catherine, who has first accused him and then turned away from him. Far from pacified, Catherine is outraged, interrupts him again (as she does not do in the earlier version), and motivates him to deliver the remainder of his speech as a further effort to appease her. In the earlier version, Petkoff pompously announces the desirability of annexing Serbia and making Prince Alexander a Balkan Emperor. In the later version, Shaw transfers this speech from the romantic husband to the ferocious wife, deleting her uncharacteristically conciliatory dismissal of the proposed annexation. Petkoff then—in the later version—gives a romantic explanation of his inaction, which functions as a transition to wooing his wife. Her acquiescence is a gradual development in the newer version. In 1894 Catherine's jingoism, firmly established in the first act, disappears from this second-act scene. She is not angry at the peace; she ignores it, telling Petkoff that she is glad he has returned. When he confesses that he missed her, she cries, "(*Affectionately*) Ah!" and reaches across the table to squeeze his hand. In the new version, she is angry and he is conciliatory. Only after his flattering explanation that a prolongation of hostilities would have kept him from her for too long, does she change. When he confesses that he missed her, she is still not immediately affectionate but cries, "(*relenting*) Ah!" and *then* reaches "*affectionately*" across the table to squeeze his hand. The new version is more polished; uncharacteristic lines are cut or changed and new lines added to reveal more clearly each character's attitudes and relationship to the other character.

Shaw frequently incorporated into his printed texts changes made during rehearsals. When he was preparing the first collected edition of his plays,[63] he wrote to Edith Craig, who had played Prossy in *Candida:*

> Will you send me a line to remind me of the business in the scene with Eugene at the place where you say "Pray are you flattering me or flattering yourself[?]" Do you go back to the typewriter at the end of that speech or at "I'll leave the room, Mr Mb [Marchbanks]: I really will. It's not proper." I want to get it right for the printer.
>
> Also, if you have accumulated any effective gags, you might let me have them for inclusion in the volume.[64]

Although there is no record that he did include any gags that she had accumulated, the edition shows that she starts to return to the typewriter at the first speech, that Marchbanks stops her, and that she resumes her seat at the typewriter after the second speech.

Another example of Shaw's practice of revising the printed text to include business that was added during rehearsals is a series of changes he made in a key dramatic moment of the first act of *Arms and the Man*. In the 1894 typescript, Raina gives Bluntschli the box of chocolates. He eats the contents and says, "Creams! Delicious!" Shaw expanded this for the first edition of *Plays Pleasant*. After the exclamation, Bluntschli "*looks anxiously to see whether there are any more. There are none. He accepts the inevitable with pathetic goodhumor* [. . .]." During rehearsals for the 1919 revival, Shaw suggested to Bluntschli that after he has gobbled the contents of the box, "Search for another & lick your fingers."[65] This note was incorporated into the Standard Edition and later printings, where the earlier stage direction was enlarged to read: "*He looks anxiously to see whether there are any more. There are none: he can only scrape the box with his fingers and suck them. When that nourishment is exhausted he accepts the inevitable with pathetic goodhumor*" (1, 402).

Pygmalion offers a further example of the printed text incorporating rehearsal changes. In the 1913 rehearsal edition, the action of the third act begins:

> *The door is opened violently; and Higgins enters.*
> MRS HIGGINS (*dismayed*) Henry! What are you doing here today? It is my at-home day: you promised not to come.

During rehearsals of the 1914 London production, Shaw wrote a note for Higgins and Mrs Higgins: "Hat biz."[66] In the Standard Edition and subsequent editions, the "Hat biz" is spelled out for future directors: "*Higgins enters with his hat on.*" Following Mrs. Higgins's line is the business: "*As he bends to kiss her, she takes his hat off, and presents it to him.*" Exclaiming, "Oh bother!" Higgins then "*throws the hat down on the table*" (4, 721).[67]

Shaw frequently cut and changed his plays—to shorten the running time, to assist an actor who could not adequately deliver the lines, to improve the play. On some occasions, Shaw restored cut passages to the printed editions of his plays. We may conclude that in such cases the deletions were made because of the requirements of a particular production. At other times, changes (often extensive) were incorporated in printed editions of the play. All changes and cuts, Shaw insisted, were the prerogatives of the author, who understood the relationship of each line to the total fabric of the play. Rather than entrust the cutting of his plays to an unskilled vivisector—however capable a director or actor he might be—Shaw preferred that his plays be produced in their entirety.

4 The Actor

According to Shaw, the actor's function, like the director's, is "to make the audience imagine for the moment that real things are happening to real people."[1] Shakespeare, according to Shaw, had a similar idea when he made Hamlet declare that "it is the business of the players to make their highly artificial declamation seem to be natural human speech. One can almost hear him say to Burbage at rehearsal 'Speak as if you were a human being, Dick, and mean something by what you are saying. Dont rant.'"[2] The actor's job "is not to supply an idea with a sounding board, but with a credible, simple, and natural human being to utter it when its time comes and not before."[3] Nor is it his task to make a play pleasing or interesting, for that is the author's business. He advised the young actress Molly Tompkins not to confuse "the appreciation and understanding of parts with the ability to act them. If the two were the same faculty then Shakespear would have been a greater actor than Burbage, and I should be able to play Cleopatra better than you. An actor stands in much the same relation to an author as a carpenter or mason to an architect: he need not understand the entire design in the least; and he would not do his part of the job any better for such understanding."[4] In creating a credible human being, moreover, the actor should display no sign of effort. The title character of Shaw's novel *Cashel Byron's Profession* probably speaks for the author when he says, "If a thing cant be done light and easy, steady and certain, let it not be done at all. [. . .] The more effort you make, the less effect you produce. [. . .] But in all professions any work that shews sign of labor, straining, yearning [. . .] or effort of any kind, is work beyond the man's strength that does it, and therefore not well done." As Cashel Byron observes, "the same is true in other arts."[5] The actor who displays physical strain not only fails to produce the effects for which he strives, he also makes his audience acutely uncomfortable. To play his role without physical strain, he must have training.

The Actor's Training

On 12 June 1927, the *New York Times* printed a letter from Shaw to Alexander Bakshy, who had analyzed Shaw's plays in *The Theatre Unbound*. Shaw admitted that Bakshy was right "in saying that my plays require a special technique of acting, and in particular, great virtuosity in sudden transitions of mood that seem to the ordinary actor to be transitions from one 'line' of character to another. But, after all, this is only fully accomplished acting; for there is no other sort of acting except bad acting, acting that is the indulgence of imagination instead of the exercise of skill."[6] "The exercise of skill" is a frequent theme in Shaw's writings on the actor. Deriding unskilled actors who spend their time "idly nursing their ambitions, and dreaming of 'conceptions' which they could not execute if they were put to the proof," he maintained that the "'conceptions'" of the unskilled "are mere impertinences."[7] The art of acting is "impossible without tremendous practice and constant aiming at beauty of execution, not through a mechanical study of poses and pronunciations (though every actor should be a plastic and phonetic expert), but through a cultivation of delicate feeling, and absolute renunciation of all the coarser elements of popularity."[8] Training is essential.

> The defect of the old fashioned systems of training for the stage was that they attempted to prescribe the conclusions of this constantly evolving artistic sense instead of cultivating it and leaving the artist to its guidance. Thus they taught you an old fashioned stage walk, an old fashioned stage voice, an old fashioned stage way of kneeling, of sitting down, of shaking hands, of picking up a handkerchief, and so on, each of them supposed to be the final and perfect way of doing it. The end of that was, of course, to discredit training altogether. But neglect of training very quickly discredits itself [. . .].[9]

Cannot an actor acquire the necessary training in the process of performing first smaller and then larger roles? Although a public speaker might learn his profession at the expense of his audience, Shaw did not believe that an actor could do so, for "a public speaker practises his whole art every time he speaks, whereas an inexperienced actor applies only a small portion of his art to such minor parts as he is likely to obtain at first. Repeating that minor part every night for six months will not advance him as a skilled actor [. . .]." Suppose a young man is cast as Paris in *Romeo and Juliet*. Since, in all likelihood, he is unable to dance a minuet or to fence, he will have to be coached in both a minuet and a stage duel. Just as the repetition of this minuet for 150 performances will not make him a fully qualified dancer, nor that of the stage duel a fully qualified fencer, neither will his repetition of the role of Paris make him a fully qualified actor.[10] "A fully qualified actor," according to Shaw, is one who "can perform and sustain physical feats of deportment, and build up vocal climaxes with his voice through a long crescendo of rhetoric." He also has a "feeling for the splendor of language and rhythm of verse."[11] He "knows the visible symptoms of every human condition, and has such perfect command of his motor powers that he can reproduce with his own person all the movements which constitute such symptoms." Conceding that this "ideal standard has not yet been realized," Shaw nevertheless maintains that "it is necessary to determine the standard in order to keep [. . .] actors [. . .] from going astray."[12]

Since this ideal standard, admittedly unattained, may also be unattainable, cannot the actor rely on inspiration to prevent him from going astray? Although Shaw valued the role of inspiration in art ("I depend entirely on inspiration," he once said,[13] using an exaggerative adverb), he also valued hard work (he researched the American Revolution, for example, in preparation for *The Devil's Disciple*).[14] More important, perhaps, he understood their relationship: groundwork should be so thorough that if inspiration does not arrive, the job will still be done adequately. When Ellen Terry worried that her performance as Imogen in *Cymbeline* would misfire, Shaw reminded her that she had prepared the role thoroughly and pointed out that if she played for all she were worth, she could not "fall below a good weekday performance, even if [she were] not in the vein for a regular Sunday one."[15] In order "to make effective & visible *all* [his] artistic potentialities," the actor must study and master all of the technical devices of his profession. "In my own art I am ready," he affirmed, "if only time be given me, to answer for the workmanship to the last comma; and now, if 'inspiration' comes, it does not half escape me: I know how to seize it and knead it so as to exhaust all the nutriment in it." He would have the actor do the same, developing his physical, intellectual, and emotional resources to the point that he is capable of seizing, kneading, and exhausting the nutriment of any inspiration that may come to him.[16] If the inspiration does not arrive, these resources should be sufficiently developed to enable him to give the "good weekday performance" he mentioned to Ellen Terry.

Physical training is essential, for the actor must have full command of his motor powers. As a music critic, Shaw called attention to operatic performers who failed to train their bodies. He mocked some of the singers at early Bayreuth performances of Wagner as "animated beer casks, too lazy and conceited to practise the self-control and physical training that is expected as a matter of course from an acrobat, a jockey or a pugilist." As a drama critic, he advised gymnastic training to enable the actor to control all parts of his body.[17] As a director, he gave the same advice. Lillah McCarthy relates that when Shaw noticed that she acted with her muscles contracted, he had her learn muscular control. After a month of such lessons, "I could move any muscle and relax it as I wished, and from this time my acting developed a greater naturalness. I learned to move more easily and, when standing still, to remain if need be quite immobile."[18]

The actor's voice, as well as his body, should be trained so that he can communicate intelligibly without shouting. Shaw, who strongly emphasized voice and articulation, had considerable knowledge of these skills. The voice teacher George John Vandeleur Lee had moved into the Shaw household when Bernard was eleven, and singing became part of his upbringing. Beyond learning the Lee method of voice production, he worked on a revision of Lee's 1869 book *The Voice: Its Artistic Production, Development, and Preservation*.[19] And, of course, Shaw also reviewed concerts and operas for many years and wrote a book on Wagner, *The Perfect Wagnerite*.

Shaw advised diaphragmatic breathing, together with a steady, economical, unforced expulsion of air, rather than a voice-cracking "walnut system, scientifically known as 'tension of [vocal] cords and force of blast,'"[20] for the latter produced "a muscular strain [. . .] that [. . .] destroyed the voice, and sometimes killed the vocalist."[21] Because tension and force could destroy the speaking as well as the singing voice, Shaw cautioned Molly Tompkins, "Do not imagine [. . .] that the vigorous speech that is needed for public purposes is shouting because at first it seems more violent than ordinary conversation. Real shouting is no use: it does not travel; and it worries the audience. As far as mere loudness goes, never go to the utmost of your power: always keep well inside it. It is articulation that tells." He also condemned the exaggerated force achieved by what is called the glottal shock, which is defined as the "'sudden and energetic drawing together of the lips of the glottis an instant before expiration commences.'" In less technical terms, he explained: "I myself, in the very rare instances when I pronounce the word 'I' in a self-assertive mood, may sometimes attack it with a *coup de glotte;* but I always regret it the moment the sound strikes my conscience, which, in my case, as in that of all musical critics, is situated in my ear."[22] Not only does the glottal shock offend the ear of the sensitive hearer, its habitual use would offend the voice of the speaker or singer.

Deprecating as "all nonsense" the "artificial woolly boom" that results from using the throat to obtain resonance, Shaw urged the speaker and singer to develop all resonating chambers. In a review of J. P. Sandlands's *How to Develop General Vocal Power*, he repudiated the author's advice that all students should learn to speak at the pitch of "F in the bass," which Sandlands identified as "'the foundation tone.'" The reverse is true, said Shaw, for the "so-called 'foundation tones' vary with each individual [. . .]." The consequence of attempting to use "F in the bass" as a foundation tone, when one's voice is too high, is apt to be "'clergyman's sore throat,'" which is "brought on by persisting in what Artemus Ward called 'a sollum vois' [. . .]."[23] Unless the voice employs its widest range, strain develops. Censuring both Verdi and Sir Arthur Sullivan for allowing the singer to use only a part of his vocal range, Shaw praised Handel and Wagner for employing "the entire range of the human voice," which helped to relieve any particular vocal register from fatigue and also exercised all registers.[24] With a full knowledge of the necessity for vocal variety, he disparagingly defined both William Butler Yeats's "cantilation" and Sarah Bernhardt's *voix d'or* as "intoning." He compared the latter to "holding down one key of an accordion [. . .]. Some critics speak of 'the melody' of it, as to which I can only say that the man who finds melody in one sustained note would find exquisite curves in a packing case."[25]

Shaw demanded good diction. Ellen Terry, whose articulation he particularly admired, "had had her professional technique hammered into her in her childhood by Mrs Charles Kean, who would sit in the gallery and see to it that every word of Ellen's reached her there."[26] To develop what Shaw called an "athletic articulation," the actor must be drilled in a "staccato alphabet so staccatisimo that every consonant will put out a candle at the back of the gallery. Not until her tongue and lips are like a pianist's fingers should she begin to dare think of speaking to an audience." "Alphabet" meant chiefly "consonants," for Shaw agreed with "the old rule": "take care of the consonants and the vowels will take care of themselves."[27] For purposes of public speaking, he himself "practised the alphabet as a singer practises scales until I was in no danger of saying 'Loheerylentheethisharpointed sword' instead of 'Lo here *I* lend *th*ee *th*iss *sh*arp *p*ointed sword.'"[28] To Janet Achurch he suggested alphabet exercises:

To practise R (trilled), repeat L. M. N. R: this will, if you leave your tongue loose, bring it into the right position. Then try, first eer, ér, èr &c, and ree[,] ré, rè &c; and then such combinations as BRee, bré, brè &c, and eebr, ébr, èbr &c, proceeding with CR, DR, FR, GR, PR, SR, TR. The terminal RD is very important; and there is RF (serf) RP (harp) RT (art) &c. Also of course, such combinitions as SP, TH, BL, CL, DL, FL, GL, PL, SL, TL, & so on, compiling them out of the alphabet in order.²⁹

Shaw was familiar with exercises for vowels as well as for consonants. In his revision of Lee's technical manual on the voice, for instance, he set down exercises designed to prevent vowels from becoming diphthongs: "if the a in ray ends as ee, it is a diphthong, and the student must persevere until the sound of the French é can be sustained as long as the breath lasts, the tip of the tongue never once rising to the front teeth after the articulation of the initial r [. . .]."³⁰ In a scene written for the film version of *Pygmalion,* he composed a diction scene on the same subject:

HIGGINS. [. . .] Say A, B, C, D.
LIZA (*almost in tears*) But I'm sayin it. Ahyee, Bəee, Cəyee—
HIGGINS. Stop. Say a cup of tea.
LIZA. A cappətə-ee.
HIGGINS. Put your tongue forward until it squeezes against the top of your lower teeth. Now say cup.
LIZA. C-c-c—I cant. C-Cup.
PICKERING. Good. Splendid, Miss Doolittle.
HIGGINS. By Jupiter, she's done it at the first shot. (4, 718)

Since the language of poetry is not colloquial, poetry involves special problems of articulation. To Molly Tompkins, he urged, "you must take great care of the words that are not used in ordinary conversation, because the audience cannot guess them and will not take the meaning in so quickly as when you are giving them common idiomatic phrases. If you say Woff terangelsthrough thisguise, Fa rabove yonazh erplane you might as well say it in Chinese. You must say Waftt hher, no matter how pedantic it sounds. But it wont sound pedantic to the audience unless you articulate sounds that are spelt but never spoken." Vowels, though, should not be distorted. *Angels* should not rhyme with *bluebells* or *organ* with *dustpan.* The second vowel of each, "the Obscure Vowel," must rhyme with the second vowel in *butter.*³¹

Still, vocal technique was to Shaw not an end but a means and should therefore be unnoticed by the audience. Tompkins, he demanded, "should practice all this until it becomes completely automatic; for there is nothing more annoying than an actress or a singer who is thinking about her technique when she ought to be thinking only of the sense and feeling of her part."[32] All of the technical skills which the actor so painstakingly acquires should be concealed, and the actor's behavior on stage appear so spontaneous and inevitable that it would be impossible to persuade the audience that any art or study is involved. Finally, there is the old saw—nonetheless true—that to be a complete actor one must be a complete human being. In an interview, the pianist Madame Backer-Gröndahl told Shaw (as Corno di Bassetto) "that it is as wife and mother that she gets the experience that makes her an artist." He responded, "I collapse. Bassetto is silenced. He can only bow to the eternal truth, and think how different his column would be if all artists were like this one."[33]

Although the acting skills that have been discussed can be taught in a classroom or rehearsal room, an academy aiming to train actors should not confine its instructional program to the classroom or rehearsal room, for part of the actor's necessary training includes appearing before audiences. As analogy Shaw uses the medical profession. Just as the apprentice doctor must "walk the hospitals as well as [. . .] pass examinations" in order to receive his degree, so should the apprentice actor "walk the stage for a couple of years before receiving a diploma as master of what can be taught in his art." Unless an acting academy includes this period of internship for the trainee, the graduates of this institution will earn their livelihoods "by teaching others to win the same degree for the same purpose," and thereby leave the art of acting "to be practised by people without degrees, who, when they are conspicuously successful, can be made honorary graduates, and thus throw a radiance on the institution which can never proceed from within itself."[34]

Shaw knew that the conditions he postulated as desirable did not exist. In his novel *Love among the Artists,* which describes some of the conditions that did exist, he gives the case history of the development of an actress, who studies elocution and learns her craft by performing in provincial stock companies before coming to London.[35] Far from upholding the provincial stock company as a training ground for actors, Shaw deplored it, calling the notion that stock companies taught versatility "the wildest of delusions. Versatility was the much-needed quality of which [stock company actors] became quite incapable." With weekly or nightly program changes, actors "have to 'swallow' their speeches as best they can, and deliver them, not in the author's characterization, but in their specialities such as juvenile lead, ingénue, walking gentleman, light comedian, low comedian, singing chambermaid (soubrette), heavy old man (*père noble*), old woman, utility, and so forth." The most that he could say for the stock company was that it taught the actor "the routine of his business." The routine items included "conscientiously articulated elocution which reached the back row of the pit effectively (it is really more satisfactory to hear an actor say meechee-yah-eeld and know that he means my child than to hear him say msha and wonder what on earth the fellow thinks he is mumbling)," a "pompous entrance which invited and seized the attention of the audience," and a "momentous exit on the last word of his last speech (your modern novice as often as not finishes in the middle of the stage and stops the play until the audience has enjoyed the spectacle of his walking to the door)." This "routine of his business," however, was satisfactory only for routine acting. With such abilities an actor could "completely [. . .] kill the dramatic illusion of a modern play."[36]

In 1886 Shaw invited the theatergoer nostalgic for the "palmy days of the drama" to study "palminess" at the opera, which still operated on the basis of the theatrical stock company. There, such abuses of the stock company system as the substitution of mannerisms for acting, the use of the same stage caricature for each role, and the insufficiency of rehearsal would make it obvious that "the palmy theory lacks experimental verification." Shaw preferred the long run system, for the actor who knows one role thoroughly "is superior to the actor who can scramble with assistance through a dozen. The one gets into the skin of one character: the other only puts on the clothes of twelve."[37]

But the long run system, too, has its curses, for it engenders mechanical repetition and saps vitality. Reviewing the 789th performance of *Dorothy,* Shaw asserted that the tenor, "evidently counting the days until death should release him from the part of Wilder," sang "as if with the last rally of an energy decayed and a willing spirit crushed." Similarly, a lackluster languor characterized the ninety-fifth of the one hundred performances of Forbes Robertson's production of *Hamlet,* whose actors "were for the most part sleepwalking in a sort of dazed blank verse dream. Mr Barnes raved of some New England maiden named Affection Poo," Mrs. Patrick Campbell's "subtle distinctions [. . .] between madness and sanity had blurred off into a placid idiocy turned to favor and to prettiness," and Forbes Robertson's "lightness of heart [was] all gone [. . .]." This deterioration was the result of "the torturing fatigue and monotony of nightly repetition," which drove the actor to limit himself to such effects as he can repeat to infinity without committing suicide."[38]

Admitting that "the playing-every-night system is only possible for *routine* acting,"[39] Shaw still found it superior to the stock company system, for "the modern actor may at all events exhaust the possibilities of his part before it exhausts him, whereas the stock actor, having barely time to apply his bag of tricks to his daily task, never varies his treatment by a hair's breadth from one half century to another." To avoid the debilitating effects of the long run system without returning to the old stock company system, some actors and actresses had a repertory of plays that provided resting places: Charles Surface, for instance, relieved Richard III, Mirandolina relieved Magda. While an improvement on both the stock company and the long run systems, this method was more of a mitigation than a solution, for "no actor can possibly play leading parts of the first order six nights a week all the year round unless he underplays them, or routines them mechanically in the old stock manner, or faces a terrible risk of disablement by paralysis, or, finally, resorts to alcohol or morphia, with the usual penalties." Shaw's answer to the problem was a repertory company with alternate casts: Sir Henry Irving and Ellen Terry, for example, playing *Hamlet* on Thursdays and Saturdays, Forbes Robertson and Mrs. Patrick Campbell playing it on Wednesdays and Fridays. On the other two nights, all four would appear in a comedy.[40] To put it in more general terms: Shaw would have a repertory company with a sufficient number of major performers that the burden on any one of them would not be too heavy.

Degrees of Realism

As a director wanting his actors to convince the audience that real things were happening to real people, Shaw demanded illusionistic acting. He noted that on the French stage, a kiss was "as obvious a convention as the thrust under the arm by which Macduff runs Macbeth through." It was "purposely unconvincing," designed to make it impossible for anyone to believe that it was real. On the English stage, by contrast, realism was carried to the point at which only the actors were aware that the kiss was not real. Shaw favored the English method, for whatever question may arise as to the propriety of representing an incident on the stage, he found it offensive, once it was decided to represent that incident, to do it other than convincingly (4, 839).

Shaw's directorial practices followed the English tradition. During rehearsals of *You Never Can Tell,* he demanded that the members of the company behave "as if they were coming into a real room instead of [. . .] rushing to the float to pick up the band at the beginning of a comic song."[41] Charles Charrington's activities in the Fabian Society, Shaw suggested, might be spoiling his acting: "You are getting rhetorical; and you expound and illustrate your parts like the Ghost in Hamlet."[42] Shaw's rehearsal notes contain many similar injunctions, as the following examples illustrate. When Louka tells Sergius that Bluntschli is worth ten of him, she should merely refer to Bluntschli rather than make an obvious stage cross. Liza's interruption of Higgins's departure, "Before you go, sir," should not be rendered melodramatically, as "Before you go, Serrrrr," but instead should be spoken naturally. When Higgins equates Liza's offer of a shilling for English lessons with a millionaire's sixty to seventy guineas, he should avoid declaiming.[43]

Rhetorical dialogue, on the other hand, requires rhetorical speech, which is realistic delivery when a character is making a speech. Thus, in the passage between Tarleton and The Man (Gunner) in *Misalliance*—

> TARLETON. [. . .] youll get no justice here: we dont keep it. Human nature is what we stock.
> THE MAN. Human nature! Debauchery! gluttony! selfishness! robbery of the poor! Is that what you call human nature?
> TARLETON. No: thats what you call it. Come, my lad! Whats the matter with you? You dont look starved; and youve a decent suit of clothes.
> THE MAN. Forty-two shillings.
> TARLETON. They can do you a very decent suit for forty-two shillings. [4, 212–13]

—he advised Gunner, "'Debauchery, selfishness, gluttony, robbery of the poor'—rhetoric, not realism—prepare for 42/-." Despite Shaw's distinction between realism and rhetoric, and despite the obvious desire for a build so that Tarleton can get a laugh on his last speech in this exchange, his request for a rhetorical delivery of Gunner's first speech is not inconsistent with realism. Because Gunner is pontificating, consciously making a speech for Tarleton's benefit, Shaw wanted him to be rhetorical. Again, when Sergius declares to Louka, "Oh, *(fervently)* give me the man who will defy to the death any power on earth or in heaven that sets itself up against his own will and conscience: he alone is the brave man" (1, 454), Shaw urged the actor to "Give it to the gallery—forget her." These lines are, after all, the climax of an oratorical passage spoken by a man given to speechifying. Earlier in the speech, however, Shaw had Sergius cross downstage in order to "avoid taking the stage at the end" of the speech.[44] The distinction is vital: to take the stage would be unrealistic, for Sergius is not an actor; but to deliver the speech as if he were giving it to the gallery would be realistic, for he is a man who breaks into declamation.

Although Shaw wanted realism, he also wanted his plays to be performed broadly. Calling his methods "a throwback to the art of Barry Sullivan and Italian opera," he requested "the drunken, stagey, brass-bowelled barnstormers my plays were written for," and exclaimed, "Bumptiousness for me!"[45] Once, an actor who was cast as Burgess in *Candida* rehearsed the first act "in subdued tones like a funeral mute [. . .]." As the author was about to protest, the actor "solemnly put up his hand," saying, "'Mr Shaw: I know what you are going to say. But you may depend on me. In the intellectual drama I never clown.'" Intellectual drama, the equation apparently went, meant serious drama, which called for a solemn attitude toward the role and an *ex cathedra* delivery of all speeches. "And it was some time before I could persuade him that I was in earnest when I exhorted him to clown for all he was worth. I was continually struggling with the conscientious efforts of our players to underdo their parts lest they should be considered stagey."[46] The word "underdone" occurs frequently in Shaw's rehearsal notes. Morrison's consternation at Undershaft's arrival was "Underdone." When Sergius touched the bruise on Louka's arm, causing her to flinch, both the stroke and the flinching were "underdone." At rehearsals of Lewis Casson's production of *Macbeth,* Shaw counseled Sybil Thorndike (Lady Macbeth) about the line, "screw your courage to the sticking-place" (I,vii), "Dont soften — scold like a fury — underdone."[47] Granville Barker, Shaw confessed, "rebukes me feelingly for wanting my parts to be 'caricatured.'" Shaw, on the other hand, chided Barker for underplaying, comparing him to Robert Loraine, who performs "quite in my old fashioned way, with a relish and not under protest, like you."[48]

Shaw demanded that expansiveness and technical proficiency be part of a convincing performance.[49] But conviction, carried to its extreme, is total identification of the actor with the character. Did Shaw intend this? On the one hand, he wrote to Ellen Terry that the only thing "not forgivable in an actor is *being* the part instead of playing it[.]" As example, he pointed to Eleonora Duse's performance in Dumas *fils's La femme de Claude,* in which she acts "with an impossible perfection, and yet never touches the creature with the tips of her fingers."[50] On the other hand, he said, "On the highest plane one does not act, one i s." As examples, he pointed to Mrs. Patrick Campbell's performances in John Davidson's *For the Crown* and in Sheridan's *School for Scandal* (in which she played Lady Teazle). Yet he reviewed unfavorably a performance by Dorothea Baird which lacked this quality. Admitting that Miss Baird did precisely what the role demanded that she do, that she was "letter perfect, gesture perfect, paint perfect, dress perfect, beauty perfect, and imitation pathos perfect," he nevertheless concluded that "if a play depends on the part being lived from the inside instead of put on as a shepherd putteth on his garment, then it will fail, though Miss Baird may seem to succeed."[51] Although the familiar paradox of the actor being the character yet at the same time being detached from the character might reconcile these apparently contradictory statements, Shaw did not explicitly reconcile them. He did so implicitly, however, by his demand that the actor have thorough control over everything he did.

The Actor and the Character

As critic and as director, Shaw despised the actor's use of stage tricks, clichés, artificial indications of emotions the character is supposed to be feeling, posturing, posing—in general, anything destructive of the illusion of real things happening to real people. He defined "'character actor'" as "a clever stage performer who cannot act, and therefore makes an elaborate study of the disguises and stage tricks by which acting can be grotesquely simulated."[52] As Mrs. Alving in *Ghosts*, he maintained, Mrs. Theodore Wright used such stage tricks: her "application of the conventional stage method to the final situation, with advances and recoils and screams and general violent oscillations between No—yes—I cannot—I must &c&c&c, only proved, interestingly enough, that it cannot be done that way."[53] Olga Nethersole's performance in the title role of Arthur Wing Pinero's *The Notorious Mrs. Ebbsmith*, he wrote, was marked by posturing: "When she pretends to darn a stocking she brings it down to the footlights, and poses in profile with the stockinged hand raised above the level of her head. She touches nothing without first poising her hand above it like a bird about to alight, or a pianist's fingers descending on a chord. She cannot even take up the box containing the rich dress to bundle it off into the next room, without disposing her hands round it with an unmistakable reference to the conventional laws of grace." Shaw objected to actors who played comedy by delivering all their actions in high spirits, obstreperously, archly, with squawking voices and grinning faces intended ostentatiously to indicate their funniness. Once the audience becomes aware that an actor is trying to make an effect, the attempt fails. The actor whose performance does not portray the character but merely describes him or suggests how the audience should react to him will be applauded only by spectators like Partridge, in Henry Fielding's *Tom Jones,* who preferred the actor playing Claudius—since "anyone can see that he is an actor"—to David Garrick's realistic portrayal of Hamlet.[54] Because of this, Shaw frequently said that he wished actors would not act, by which he meant grotesque indicating rather than convincing representation. He implored Trebitsch to prevent Carl Wiene from "acting" when Richard Dudgeon is arrested in the second act of *The Devil's Disciple:* "Good God! imagine the idiot whispering & crying out and 'springing about,' with the sergeant & the soldiers & the woman standing round admiring him like a Donizettian opera chorus!" When the sergeant arrests him, there must be complete silence. Richard should speak "with frightful *quiet* distinctness," so that each of his words terrifies Judith. Then, after he turns and confronts a suspicious-looking sergeant, comes "the great effect" when he gets the idea of having Judith kiss him in order to remove the sergeant's suspicion. "All that will be utterly ruined if the damned scoundrel *acts.* He will want to act—to agonize, to make convulsive movements & play tricks with his voice. Dont let him. Tell him I say that he shall not act. He may pray and fast and weep and go to confession; but *act,* by God, he shall not. I will have no monkey tricks with my play."[55]

Shaw especially disapproved of the actor or actress who tried to secure personal admiration rather than to play the character. A prominent example was Sarah Bernhardt, whose dazzling appearance, he noted, seemed virtually to say to the audience, "'Now who would ever suppose that I am a grandmother?'" This effect, part of what he called "the childishly egotistical character of her acting," was "not the art of making you think more highly or feel more deeply, but the art of making you admire her, pity her, champion her, weep with her, laugh at her jokes, follow her fortunes breathlessly, and applaud her wildly when the curtain falls." He regretted "the shameless prostitution of the art of acting into the art of pleasing. The actor wants 'sympathy': the actress wants affection. They make the theatre a place where the public comes to look at its pets and distribute lumps of sugar to them." When the average actress was asked to play an "'unsympathetic'" role, she refused to do so "on exactly the same grounds as she might refuse to let her lover see her in curl papers. And the actors are worse than the actresses." As a critic, he objected to an actress who played an elderly lady but refused to conceal the fact that she was young and pretty.[56] As a director, he worried that the actress portraying

Mrs. Higgins wanted to avoid appearing middle-aged.[57] As a critic, he objected to Mrs. Patrick Campbell's removal of the unpleasant aspects of *Little Eyolf* in an attempt to secure admiration of her charm, beauty, and self-possession. As a director, he insisted that she refrain from making "a sympathetic point" in *Pygmalion* when Higgins remarks that at times he would call her attractive.[58]

Shaw admired the actor who played the character, instead of substituting himself or his stage self for that character. He accused Henry Irving of having had "only one part; and that part was the part of Irving. His Hamlet was not Shakespear's Hamlet, nor his Lear Shakespear's Lear: they were both avatars of the imaginary Irving, in whom he was so absorbingly interested." Sometimes this was an improvement, at other times a disgrace. "His Iachimo, a very fine performance, was better than Shakespear's Iachimo, and not a bit like him. On the other hand, his Lear was an impertinent intrusion of a quite silly conceit of his own into a great play." Irving did not adapt himself to the role he played: "his creations were all his own; and they were all Irvings." By comparison, Ellen Terry played "Beatrice, Juliet, Portia, Imogen, &c., intelligently and charmingly just as Shakespear planned them [. . .]." Similarly, he contrasted Sarah Bernhardt and Eleonora Duse. Like Irving, Bernhardt "does not enter into the leading character: she substitutes herself for it." With Duse, as with Ellen Terry, "every part is a separate creation."[59]

Shaw distinguished between "the actor's tendency to adapt the play to his own personality and the author's desire to adapt the actor's personality to the play."[60] Acting, he advised Laurence Irving, "must always depend on the success of the pretence that the character is you, not on the pretence that you are the character—the amateur's notion [. . .]."[61] The distinction is subtle but important. The actor who pretends that he is the character imagines himself in the situation the author has imagined, and so behaves as he himself might behave, thus adapting the play to his own personality. The character then becomes an embodiment of him, rather than he of the character. On the other hand, the actor who pretends that the character is himself tries to find the aspects of himself which will elucidate and embody the character, thereby adapting his personality to the play. In 1889 Shaw declared that while there had been only one genuine clown, Grimaldi, "we all have a clown in us somewhere; and Garrick's Petruchio, Lemaître's Macaire, and Mr Irving's Jingle and Jeremy Didler may be regarded as the outcome of the impulse felt by these actors to realize for a moment the clown in themselves."[62] Shaw preferred that the actor try to find the role in himself, rather than merely try to play himself in the role.

The printed texts of his plays contain character descriptions designed to help the actor play the character the author drew. The "*stout and fatherly*" Father Dempsey, for example, in *John Bull's Other Island,* is described as falling

> *far short of that finest type of countryside pastor which represents the genius of priesthood; but he is equally far above the base type in which a strongminded unscrupulous peasant uses the Church to extort money, power, and privilege. He is a priest neither by vocation nor ambition, but because the life suits him. He has boundless authority over his flock, and taxes them stiffly enough to be a rich man. The old Protestant ascendency is now too broken to gall him. On the whole, an easygoing, amiable, even modest man as long as his dues are paid and his authority and dignity fully admitted.* (2, 931)

Characterization is not simply a matter of a few stock attitudes. Shaw criticized Evelyn Millard's performance as Pinero's *The Second Mrs. Tanqueray* for merely dividing the role into sympathetic passages and outbursts of temper and then shifting quickly from the one to the other. Nor is characterization a matter of a few "points." The beginner, says Shaw, will find several points in a role, play them, and, in between, allow the role to play itself. When these points are smoothly executed, he will invent more points, executing them more smoothly and forcefully. After a time, he will continually make points. With some, this is the final stage. "But with the greatest artists there soon commences an integration of the points into a continuous whole, at which stage the actress appears to make no points at all, and to proceed in the most unstudied and 'natural' way."[63]

But characterization, Shaw maintained, involves more than this. It means understanding the sort of person the playwright has created and using this understanding as a guide to his actions and behavior. As a director, Shaw tried to help the actor achieve this understanding. Coaching Ellen Terry for the role of Imogen in *Cymbeline,* he first described the character in general terms: "Imogen is an impulsive person, with quick transitions, absolutely frank self expression, and no half affections or half forgivenesses." Following this, he explained general behavioral characteristics: "The moment you abuse anyone she loves, she is in a rage: the moment you praise them she is delighted." With these observations in mind, he interpreted specific scenes in Act II:

> It is quite easy for Iachimo to put her out of countenance by telling her that Posthumus has forgotten her; but the instant he makes the

mistake of trying to gratify her by abusing him—"that runagate"—
he brings down the avalanche. It is just the same with Cloten: she is
forbearing with him until he makes the same mistake. And Iachimo
has nothing to do but praise Posthumus, and lay the butter on thick,
and she is instantly as pleased as Punch, and void of all resentment.
It is this that makes her pay him the extra-special compliment of
offering to take the chest into her own bedroom, *a thing she would
never have done if she had not forgiven him* quite thoughtlessly—
honest Injun.[64]

In commenting to actors about his own characters, he frequently
wanted to convey an impression about the sort of person that was being
represented. He told Sybil Thorndike that Joan of Arc was nineteen years
old, not a child or an angelically sweet little girl, but a sturdy woman.[65]
Trying to create a similar image for Wendy Hiller, he advised her not to rub
her ankle pathetically when the chain was removed but rather to "bend
your legs at the knee and stretch them as if you were going to take on the
whole court at all-in wrestling. And call the man a noodle heartily, not
peevishly. Get a big laugh with it.[66] He explained certain aspects of Major
Barbara to Annie Russell:

> "Nonsense! of course its funny" might be a little more peremp-
> tory. There are one or two points, like the "Nonsense! she must do as
> she's told" (about Rummy) in which Barbara, with all her sweetness,
> shews that she is her mother's daughter, and that it comes very natu-
> ral to her to order people about. There is a curious touch of aristo-
> cratic pride at the very end, where she says she does not want to die
> in God's debt, and will forgive him "as becomes a woman of her
> rank" for all the starvation & mischief he is responsible for. Barbara
> has great courage, great pride & a high temper at the back of her
> religious genius; and you need not hesitate to let them flash through
> at moments if any of the passages catch you that way.[67]

To Irene Vanbrugh, he described the Polish aviatrix Lina as "the St Joan of
Misalliance": she is not a thrill-hunter but "a religious force." Trained as
an acrobat, she devotes herself to dangerous exercises but "has a nun's
grave disapproval of stunts that are not really either difficult or dangerous
[. . .]." Her dedication, however, is coupled with independence: "she is
very like a modern nun except that her sexual morality is not that of the
Church: marriage is to her a sale of herself: she must be free. Her stage
foundation is a grave and almost mystical beauty; and Tarleton has the

surprise of his life when, touched by it, he finds that he cant buy it, even for love [. . .]. When she takes Bentley she is devoting him to death, as she devotes herself every day. Something like that should be felt by the audience; for it is to that that Bentley responds. It is a hieratic act on her part."[68] Comments such as these can be extremely helpful to the actresses playing Joan, Barbara, and Lina, for they contain precise images that can be translated into behavior.

For Shaw, characterization was incomplete unless the actor understood the class characteristics of the person he played. After attending a performance of *Captain Brassbound's Conversion,* for instance, he informed Janet Achurch that she would be unable to play Lady Cicely convincingly until she had completed "a careful study of the English lady. Mind: I dont mean the English bourgeoise, nor the English artist-Bohemian: I mean the great lady." Shaw claimed that he, like Molière, consulted his cook about his plays. According to the cook, according to Shaw, when Janet Achurch "'sat down she got her dress tucked in between her knees: no high lady would do that.'" Heartily agreeing with his cook's criticism, he told the actress that she played the entire role with her dress tucked between her knees. A great lady, he observed,

> would hardly ever shew real excitement, or lose her distinction and immense self conceit & habit of patronage. She [. . .] might be childish, and make little jokes & puns that only courtiers laugh at; she might even go on with men in a way which in a shopgirl would lead to overtures & be understood to have that intention; she might do forty thousand things that no woman who was not either above or below suspicion would do (the coincidences between the tramp & the aristocrat are very interesting); but in everything external she would be distinguished from the middle-class woman, who lives her whole life under suspicion & shortness of cash.

Until Miss Achurch had mastered all of these marks of caste and could imitate them as easily as she could distinguish between one shade of greasepaint and another, she would be unable to act Lady Cicely. "It is not that ladylikeness is difficult, but it is antipathetic to the free Bohemian middle-class *revoltée:* the essence of it is flunkeyism, upper servantism," which she must study dispassionately until she is able to perform it mechanically.[69]

Shaw's intent was to relate social to psychological realism. The social themes of modern plays, especially those of Ibsen, create difficulties for the actor accustomed to the English theater's stock characters, which are often based on moral judgments. Puzzled by Ibsen's high-minded characters whose high-mindedness causes mischief, the conventional actor assumes that if a stage character is selfish, he must be a villain; if self-sacrificing, a hero; and if unconsciously ridiculous, a comedian. Not only do these assumptions reduce Ibsen's characters to stage stereotypes, but they are impossible to execute in a satisfactory manner. It is difficult for an actor or actress to be laughed at while playing a serious part, such as Gregers Werle in *The Wild Duck,* but this is exactly what Ibsen demands: his plays expose the very conventions upon which the actor bases his conceptions of stock types. Ibsen does not distribute sympathy according to traditional moralistic assumptions. He makes "'lost'" women lovable, portraying them as compassionate *because* they are "'lost'" and giving them the sympathy that usually goes to the righteous character. Moreover, by having women describe men as "'lost'" and "'ruined,'" he ridicules such moralistic terms. His characters must be portrayed from their own points of view. This, in fact, is a consistent Shavian principle: dramas that deal realistically with modern men and women cannot be presented according to conventional stage conceptions; rather, they must be played from the viewpoint of the characters' own conceptions of themselves.[70]

Shaw was not satisfied with mere descriptive acting. He praised James Pursail for noticing that, "as [Don Giovanni] was not a professional singer, however masterfully he may sing all the dramatic music, he should sing the serenade like an amateur. I do not mean that he sang it badly: on the contrary, he sang it very nicely [. . .]. I mean that Mr Pursail sang it, not in the traditionally ardent and accomplished manner, but in the manner of a modest amateur."[71] Shaw's advice to Janet Achurch on playing Candida had a similar basis: although dignity must underlie all of Candida's behavior, "the least attempt on your part to be dignified will be utterly fatal."[72] The actress, in other words, should behave as the character would behave. Candida does not try to *be* dignified: she *is* dignified. The quality should not be described for the benefit of the audience, or paraded as if it were an elaborate accomplishment, but taken for granted and allowed to underlie her behavior.

As a director, Shaw tried to prevent the actor from inserting business which was inconsistent with the character—warning Straker, for example, "not to touch his hat" to Violet in the fourth act of *Man and Superman* (had he not told Tanner in the second act that his grandfather, but not he, would have touched his hat to members of the upper class?). Alert to the danger of the actor substituting his own reaction for the character's reaction, Shaw told Stephen not to laugh at Lady Britomart's laugh lines, even though the audience may do so; instead, he should maintain "a strain of seriousness [. . .] all through." When Raina reacts to Bluntschli's description of Sergius leading the cavalry charge "like an operatic tenor" (1, 404), the actress must realize that Raina "likes an operatic tenor."[73]

In comedy, too, the actor should maintain the character's viewpoint and not play for laughs (unless, of course, the character himself is trying to be amusing). Shaw assured Arnold Daly, who directed the American première of *John Bull's Other Island* in 1905, that Broadbent "will get endless laughs until he begins to play for them," but he warned that "With the exception of the stage Irishman in the first act [Tim Haffigan], the performers must not behave as if it were funny to be Irish and to speak with an Irish accent."[74] Broadbent and the Irishmen in Acts II, III, and IV are unconsciously funny, whereas Tim Haffigan, deliberately playing the stereotyped comic Irishman, is trying to amuse and to ingratiate himself. Most of the company of the 1919 revival of *Arms and the Man,* noted Shaw, played for laughs and thus produced "that detestable effect as of all the characters being so many Shaws spouting Shavianisms, and provoking first a lot of shallow but willing laughter, and then producing disappointment and irritation." The antidote, he told Robert Loraine, was to ignore the audience and play the characters in the situation.[75] When Liza tells of her father ladling gin down her mother's throat, Higgins must not laugh but must behave as though drops of sweat were pouring down his brow[76] (for he is anxious during his pupil's first encounter with cultivated people). Shaw also warned that unless "Not bloody likely" (4, 730) is said in perfect seriousness, unconscious of the fact that it may produce a laugh, it will ruin the play.[77]

Thus, the actor should be believable as the character. Avoiding clichés, posturing, and artificial indications of emotion, he should play not himself but a fully individualized character responding to a particular situation, behaving as that character would behave, and playing the role from the character's point of view.

Motivation

In an obvious sense, stage motivation means that the actor should have a reason for what he does. It implies that the audience should perceive that he has one. The absence of motivation is often the basis of Shaw's rehearsal notes, which record, for instance, that the General (*Getting Married*) should motivate his sitting down, and that Liza's "Slow walk" is "not motivated." Shaw warns the actor against anticipating the business or the line to which he reacts: the cue must come before the result. Since the church clock reminds Higgins that he should be charitable to the flower girl, he must not get out his money before the clock strikes. Leo (*Getting Married*) should not anticipate Reginald's line "You damned scoundrel, how dare you throw my wife over like that before my face" (3, 651), which is her cue for preventing him from assaulting Hotchkiss: earlier, she had no inkling of his intentions.[78]

In order for the actor to show his reasons for speaking and acting, he should first understand them. Some of Shaw's rehearsal notes explain the motivation: he told Hotchkiss, for example, that when the Bishop says, "'soldiers & servants'—this is where he recognizes the baptism service. Up to that he is at a loss."[79] In his letters to actors, Shaw combined statements on motivation with prescriptions on externals. He advised Louis Calvert, "In the scene with Cusins (the drum scene) you must be on the lookout for 'Not Paganism either, eh?' 'I admit that,' because the next speech, 'You have noticed that she is original in her religion' comes with sudden force and pride. Indeed, the change comes from the line 'And now to business.' Up to that, Undershaft has been studying Cusins and letting him talk. But the shake-hands means that he has made up his mind that Cusins is the man to understand him; and he therefore takes the lead in the conversation and dominates Cusins at once."[80] Not only did Shaw explain why Undershaft has been allowing Cusins to expound on the activities of the Salvation Army and to declaim passages from *The Bacchae,* he also prescribed the way the speech should be given and described the effect of Undershaft's change of manner. The motivational and non-motivational advice are linked. In his advice to Matthew Boulton, who played Boanerges in *The Apple Cart,* he more clearly differentiated them:

B. comes to court with a powerful conception of himself as a man of the people leading them in the struggle against the governing classes. All the Boanerges do. The notion that there is no governing *class*— that government is carried on by the strong men, no matter what class they belong to, and that his lot is with the strong men and not with the people (whether he is on their side or not) is quite new to him, though everything he has been saying to the king about democracy proves it. Consequently the princess's "anyone can see that you belong to the governing class" is a flash of revelation to him. I have given him no dialogue to express this: it has to come out between the lines; but every time I see it I feel that he *must* play to it. I cannot make him exclaim "Yes, by God! it's true" because it would run the scene right off the rails; but [it] can be done quite easily by suddenly unfolding the arms, opening the mouth, and lifting the eyes at the cue "governing class." Just try it. You will find yourself doing it involuntarily when you get the idea.[81]

Here, Shaw first explained Boanerges's motivation: his conception of himself and his internal reaction to what is told him. Then, he suggested physical, external business to convey the character's thoughts.

As his advice to Matthew Boulton suggests, Shaw was concerned with motivation not only in its obvious sense but also in its sense of revealing a character's thoughts and desires—what actors call the inner life. In one of his theater reviews, he wrote, "I suspect that Miss [Violet] Vanbrugh has hitherto lamed herself by trying to arrive at Miss Ellen Terry's secret from without inward, instead of working out her own secret from within outward."[82] As a director, he worked on both approaches.

To help the actor understand the character, Shaw sometimes used models and images. On one occasion, he told Sybil Thorndike that Joan of Arc was like a suffragette. At times, he would name a specific person as a model, suggesting that the actor imitate him.[83] The actor playing Cusins in *Major Barbara*, he told Theresa Helburn, should use Gilbert Murray as a model; if he had never seen Murray, the next best model was Harold Lloyd. Shaw asked Granville Barker, who acted the role in London, to play Puck to Louis Calvert's Mephistopheles. Apollodorus's dive into the sea in *Cæsar and Cleopatra*, Shaw wrote to Gabriel Pascal, might make Caesar "so excited [. . .] that he snatches off his helmet and hurls it at Britannus like a ball at cricket; and Britannus fields it like a first class wicket keeper."[84] He told Beerbohm Tree that "Tosh, Eliza" should be "Miltonic," and he suggested that Mrs. Patrick Campbell use the image "Blind terror of a hunted animal" when Higgins reproduces her words and accent.[85]

Shaw also tried to make visual both character relationships and motivations that come from other characters. In the third act of *John Bull's Other Island*, for example, Matt Haffigan tells Father Dempsey, "If I might make so bould, Fadher, I wuldnt say but an English Prodestn mightnt have a more indepindent mind about the lan, an be less afeerd to spake out about it dhan an Irish Catholic" (2, 960). Shaw told the actor to wait after "'If I might make so bould, father'" [until you get] leave to speak." Later in the act, Larry Doyle responds to Matt Haffigan's calling him a turncoat:

LARRY. St Peter, the rock on which our Church was built, was crucified head downwards for being a turncoat.

FATHER DEMPSEY (*with a quiet authoritative dignity which checks*

Doran, who is on the point of breaking out) Thats true. You hold
your tongue as befits your ignorance, Matthew Haffigan [. . .].
(2, 964)

After "Thats true," Matt was asked to open his mouth in order to motivate the priest's next line. In *Cæsar and Cleopatra*, Cleopatra is provoked
to jealousy when Cæsar asks her brother,

> CÆSAR. [. . .] Come here, my boy, and stand by me.
> *Ptolemy goes over to Cæsar, who, resuming his seat on the tripod,
> takes the boy's hand to encourage him. Cleopatra, furiously jealous,
> rises and glares at them.*
> CLEOPATRA *(with flaming cheeks)* Take your throne. I dont want it.
> (*She flings away the chair, and approaches Ptolemy, who shrinks
> from her*). (2, 202)

In order to explain the fury of Cleopatra's jealousy, Shaw noted during
rehearsal that more was needed than Caesar's line: "there must be some
petting by Caesar. REHEARSE." In *Arms and the Man*, Bluntschli draws up
orders and then passes them to Sergius, who signs them with difficulty. In
the 1894 typescript (and also in the first edition of *Plays Pleasant*), he signs
"*with the air of a man resolutely performing a difficult and dangerous
feat.*" In the Standard Edition (1931), prepared after the play had been
produced several times, and in subsequent editions, Shaw made this "air"
visual: Sergius "*signs with his cheek on his elbow and his protruded
tongue following the movements of his pen.*" Following the signature (in
all versions), Sergius tells Bluntschli, "This hand is more accustomed to
the sword than to the pen" (1, 440). During rehearsals of the 1911
production, Shaw had Bluntschli provoke the explanation by reacting to
Sergius's manner of signing his name: "When Serg lays his head on his arm
to sign, look at him in alarm."[86]

The stage directions in the printed editions of Shaw's plays help give the
actor motivation for what he says and does. In the third act of *Widowers'
Houses*, for instance, Blanche tells Trench, "*I* dont want you to stay."
Then: "*For a moment they stand face to face, quite close to one another,
she provocative, taunting, half defying, half inviting him to advance, in a
flush of undisguised animal excitement. It suddenly flashes on him that all
this ferocity is erotic: that she is making love to him. His eye lights up: a
cunning expression comes into the corners of his mouth: with a heavy
assumption of indifference he walks straight back to his chair, and plants
himself in it with his arms folded*" (1, 119). A clear description of the

motivation of the two characters, this stage direction prompts the remainder of Blanche's speech. In *Man and Superman,* when Straker accuses Mendoza of funk, the latter springs to his feet, telling Enry that he comes from "a famous family of fighters" and that Enry "would have as much chance against me as a perambulator against your motor car." Although Straker says, "I aint afraid of you," a stage direction reveals that he is "*secretly daunted, but [rises] from his knees with an air of reckless pugnacity*" (2, 628). The subtext, implicit in the text, is often explicit in the stage directions.

As a director too, Shaw attended to subtext. Advising Ellen Terry how to play Imogen, he persuaded her that her speech after Posthumus puts a bracelet on her arm—"O the gods! / When shall we see again?" (1,i)—"is really two separate speeches. When Posthumus puts the bracelet on your arm, look for a moment with delight at the present if you like; but that doesnt matter: the great thing is that you shiver with love at his touch on your arm, and say 'Oh the gods!' as a sigh of rapture. It is when that subsides that you ask the question a woman always does ask—it being the nature of her sex never to be satisfied—'When will you come again?'" He also suggested that in the same scene, her speech to Cymbeline—"I beseech you, sir, / Harm not yourself with our vexation"—should be "thoroughly petulant and full of temper, Cymbeline having not only sent Posthumus away, but called him 'thou basest thing.' What she really means is 'You may save your breath to cool your porridge, you old wretch.'"[87] Shaw continually tried to enrich the text by helping the actor understand and express the subtext, or "What she really means." When he assisted Lewis Casson in the direction of *Macbeth,* he noted that when Macbeth said "'If I stand here, I saw him [Banquo's ghost]'" (III,iv), there should be more "relief [. . .] at the vanishing." In *Pygmalion,* when Mrs. Pearce tells Higgins that they must be "very particular with this girl as to personal cleanliness. [. . .] I mean not to be slovenly about her dress or untidy in leaving things about," Higgins agrees and turns to Pickering, saying, "It is these little things that matter, Pickering. Take care of the pence and the pounds will take care of themselves is as true of personal habits as of money" (4, 704). Shaw suggested to Higgins, "Imply that Pick is careless of his person."[88]

In his concern for motivation, and for internal reality, Shaw wanted the actor to achieve a moment-to-moment reality, to think on his feet, as it were, and to give the illusion that events were happening to him for the first time. "An actor's cue," he maintained, "is not a signal to take up the running thoughtlessly, but a provocation to retort or respond in some clearly differentiated way. He must, even on the thousandth night, make the audience believe that he has never heard his cue before."[89] As a critic, he berated Lewis Waller for having "delivered his lines with the automatic gravity of a Brompton Cemetery clergyman repeating the burial service for the thousandth time," and he reprimanded Mrs. Patrick Campbell for having delivered a long speech "as a schoolgirl repeats her catechism: its happy indifference of manner and glib utterance almost unhinged my reason."[90] As a director, he warned Candida that certain responses were "too glib" and asked Malcolm not to rattle off the string of epithets he heaps on Macbeth:

> I grant him bloody,
> Luxurious, avaricious, false, deceitful,
> Sudden, malicious, smacking of every sin
> That has a name. (IV,iii)[91]

Often, his advice contained specific suggestions to help the actor convey the impression that he was speaking his lines for the first time. Macbeth's response to the Witches addressing him as Thane of Cawdor and King was "too prompt—not puzzled enough." When Raina asks Bluntschli to tell her about the cavalry charge, Shaw noted that he is at first "Rather puzzled at how to describe it." Actors who must describe something, Shaw pointed out, should not have the adjectives ready to hand, but should let the audience see them trying to find the right words. When Percival (*Misalliance*) mentions the possibility of asking a woman to share his "degrading poverty" (4, 241), he should "pick out 'degrading.'"[92] And if Baudricourt (*Saint Joan*) "goes for PACE and picks up his cues smartly, evidently knowing all about them beforehand, he will ruin the first scene. Everything that Joan says to him takes him aback. [. . .] He is trying to bully her; but she counters all his leads in an utterly unexpected way. She always *surprises* him."[93] This moment-to-moment reality, acting and reacting as if events were occurring and words spoken for the first time, helps to achieve the illusion of real things happening to real people.

Shaw insisted that the actor dissect the individual speech as well as the scene, breaking it down into small, precise, and clearly differentiated units, each with a separate meaning and purpose. As a critic, he objected to a singer in *Das Rheingold*: "Every line he uttered was exactly like every other line."[94] As a director, he tried to guard against this. In *You Never Can Tell*, Crampton's "'She told you what I am—a father—a father robbed of his children' is all right as a frantic retort to Valentine, but [. . .] he must then collapse, and begin 'What are the hearts of this generation' brooding brokenheartedly to himself."⁹⁵ When Dubedat admits that he pawned Walpole's cigarette case—"It's quite safe: he cant sell it for a year, you know. I say, my dear Walpole, I a m sorry" (3, 386)—he should "get the change" between the sentences. Macbeth's line about Banquo's heirs—"To make them kings, the seed of Banquo kings!" (III,i)—should be delivered: "'to make them kings.' Change—'the seed of B. kings!!!'"⁹⁶

In a letter to John L. Shine, he gave detailed instructions on breaking down Larry Doyle's long speech in the first act of *John Bull's Other Island:*

> BROADBENT The usual thing in the country, Larry. Just the same here.
>
> LARRY (not too quick, and shaking his head) No, no: the climate is different. Here, (in this sanguinary England,) if the life is dull, you can be dull too, and no great harm done. (Laughter at the expense of English dulness. So far, shew no sign that there is a long speech coming; and keep your eye on Louis [Calvert as Broadbent], or he'll immediately bung in a corruscation of some kind, probably out of the fourth act).
>
> (Now go right into sheer poetry with) "But your wits cant thicken &c" down to "dreaming dreaming." Get back to prose in the "No debauchery" sentence by a shiver of disgust and a nervous fidget; and then turn to Broadbent and *tell* him about "An Irishman's imagination"—rub it into him, the climax being your quoting his own words "agreeable to strangers." Then add bitterly and with a sort of half tender reproach to him "like a good-for-nothing woman on the streets," meaning "A nice compliment to pay me, Tom: to tell me that I have the accomplishments of a whore—*agreeable to strangers.*"
>
> Then comes "Its all dreaming—all imagination," which you have got all right. It brings you quite back to cool description, which you need not trouble about, as the audience will be satisfied with the political interest of what you are saying, and will perhaps laugh at Yeats's expense when you mention Kathleen ni Hoolihan [the title of a play by Yeats].
>
> Then you get back to work again on "It saves thinking." Go ahead angrily, contemptuously, disgustedly, but not poetically; and finish on "useless devils like yourself."
>
> Now comes the final section. At "And all the while" you drop your voice in a sort of horrible shame, because you are no longer describing what the other people do, but remembering what you did

yourself. Get the change right; and your talent will pull you through the rest without any further suggestion, the last part of the speech being purely poetic and emotional.

I think this will help you to get command of the speech, and sufficient variety to save you from the feeling of holding on to it for dear life and not being able to stop yourself. But dont worry yourself by trying to carry out my suggestions exactly or hampering yourself in any way with them. Very likely when you study them over you will be able to improve on them.[97]

Employing explanatory paraphrase ("Here" means "in this [bloody] England"), mechanical business ("a shiver of disgust and a nervous fidget"), subtext ("a sort of half tender reproach"), literary analysis (poetry, prose, and description), and inner feeling (shame when he remembers what he himself did), Shaw's analysis separates the speech into distinct units—not *always* in motivational terms, to be sure, but nevertheless designed to create variety and assist the illusion that a character is formulating and enunciating his thoughts step by step, moment by moment, to another character, instead of repeating a set speech.

When the actor was in a scene with several characters, Shaw asked him to dissect his speeches so that he demonstrated different attitudes toward each of them. On Macbeth's "How does your patient, doctor?" (V,iii), spoken immediately after ordering Seyton to scour the country and kill defeatists, Shaw urged, "contrast to order to Seyton." Similarly, he suggested that Higgins provide a "Contrast between speech to Pick[ering] & speech to Liza."[98]

Another factor in establishing a feeling of reality is the actor's awareness of and reaction to physical conditions. Shaw apparently missed this quality in the James Hackett–Mrs. Patrick Campbell *Macbeth,* for he wrote to Mrs. Campbell, "You should not have forgotten that there was blood on your hands and on his, and that you dared not touch one another for fear of messing your clothes with gore."[99] He advised Higgins not to throw Liza's hat on the piano, for that action "would shake the creepy crawlies out of it," and reminded Louka that since her arm had been bruised by Sergius's grasp, "Dont forget the sore arm in crossing arms."[100] An awareness of mood and milieu also helps make the action credible. The beginning of *Misalliance,* for instance, should not be too rapid, for it is a "Lazy afternoon."[101] The actor must be alert not only to the time of day, but also to other characters who might influence his behavior. "Only dont *slam* the window when youre running away," he advised Ellen Terry, who was playing the title role in *Olivia:* "the Vicar might hear you."[102]

Shaw also wanted the actor to be constantly aware of—and reacting to—the other actors on stage. Throughout his rehearsal notes, he told actors to "play to"—meaning "react to"—a line or action. Sometimes, he simply indicated that there should be a response. When Shotover (*Heartbreak House*), in reply to Ellie Dunn's statement that her father is not a pirate but a good man, maintains, "He must be greatly changed" (5, 63), Ellie should "Play to this." And when Undershaft testifies that he has conscientious scruples against attending prayer services, Lady Britomart should "play to 'conscientious scruples.'" Sometimes, Shaw indicated *how* the characters should react. After Candida calls Morell "a thorough clergyman!" he replies, "So Eugene says" (1, 564); Shaw asked her to react to his line with "surprise & delight." Nicola's "We shall have our evenings to ourselves" (1, 451) should cause Louka to "shudder at the prospect." The uncomprehending Liza should greet Higgins's explanation of the uses of a handkerchief with a "vacant stare."[103] Shaw sometimes noted the motivation for a response. Tanner's comment on "the New Man" (2, 590) is "new to Straker." When Catherine tells Petkoff that the blue closet contains his raincoat, her overcoat, and two old dressing gowns belonging to their daughter, Raina "Doesnt like her two old dressing gowns being mentioned."[104]

As the note about Raina's dressing gown indicates, Shaw the director attended to the responses of characters not engaged in the dialogue. During Ramsden's statement to Ann (*Man and Superman*), "Suppose you were to discover that I had been guilty of some disgraceful action—that I was not the man your poor dear father took me for!" (2, 552), Tavy should "play to the 'disgraceful action.'" Ross's announcement (*Macbeth,* I,ii) that the Norwegian King has disbursed "Ten thousand dollars to our general use" should prompt a general reaction: "'10,000 dollars'—all play to it."[105]

This was part of Shaw's desire to help establish a feeling of ensemble among the actors. He suggested the interpolation of business in order to help them create the sense of give and take so crucial to realistic acting. In *Misalliance*, Tarleton confesses that he has a yen for Lina, which prompts Lord Summerhays to remind him that she is his guest; Tarleton responds, "Well, is she? A woman I bring into my house is my guest. A woman y o u bring into my house is my guest. But a woman who drops bang down out of the sky into my greenhouse and smashes every blessed plane of glass in it must take her chance" (4, 198). Tarleton, said Shaw, should emphasize, "A woman whom *you* bring into my house is my guest," and Summerhays should "Acknowledge." In *Pygmalion*, when Liza reclaims from Mrs. Pearce the handkerchief Higgins gave her, exclaiming, "He gev it to me, not to you" (4, 690), Pickering laughingly agrees with Liza. Shaw told Liza, "Give him an appreciative wink."[106]

Sometimes, his desire for realistic give and take between characters led him, during rehearsals, to add not only business but also exclamations and lines. In *Getting Married*, Lesbia asks the General, "Have you no imagination? Do you think I have never been in love with wonderful men? heroes! archangels! princes! sages! even fascinating rascals! and had the strangest adventures with them? Do you know what it is to look at a mere real man after that?" (3, 559). A rehearsal note suggested that on "even fascinating rascals," the General should say "Lesbia!" in a tone of "remonstrance." In the second act of *Pygmalion*, when Higgins tells Liza, "If youre good and do what youre told, you shall sleep in a proper bedroom, and have lots to eat, and money to buy chocolates and take rides in taxis. If youre naughty and idle [. . .]" (4, 697), rehearsal notes indicated Liza's response: on "chocolates," her "Mouth waters," and on "taxis," she says, "Aw *should* lawk to take a taxi." Even for *Macbeth*, Shaw provided verbal responses to help achieve a sense of interplay among the characters. When Ross tells Macduff, "Your castle is surprised; your wife and babes / Savagely slaughter'd" (IV,iii), Shaw noted in parentheses Malcolm's responses: "Your castle is surprised (not) your wife & children savagely slaughtered (Oh)."[107] The responses, of course, build to Malcolm's "Merciful heaven!" which follows Ross's speech. As a critic, Shaw delighted in ensemble acting. As a director, he tried to produce ensemble playing. Helping his actors motivate their actions and words, making them aware of the tension between text and subtext, prompting them to respond to other characters—occasionally with business, exclamations, or lines—assisting them in dissecting their speeches into small and clearly differentiated units, Shaw tried to create a moment-to-moment reality, an illusion that the events were occurring for the first time, and a sense of realistic interplay among characters.

Mechanical Technique

Shaw's concern with the internal, motivational aspects of acting did not lead him to neglect the external, mechanical aspects. When a mechanical problem confronted him, he usually tried to solve it by technical means—emphasis, tempo, or tone of voice, for example—though sometimes he added explanations regarding characterization, motivation, and the like.

Of course, rehearsal notes, written hurriedly in a dark theater as actors go through an entire scene or act without interruption, frequently use technical, mechanical terms as reduced cues because it is more convenient for the director to jot down "slower" or "angrily" than to compose an explanation of why a passage should be delivered more slowly or why a character is angry.

His letters to actors often combined explanatory statements with technical instructions. In the examples used in the previous section, the stress was on the former; here, the emphasis is on the latter. After a rehearsal of *John Bull's Other Island,* Shaw wrote to John L. Shine (Larry Doyle): "In the last scene you say to Keegan 'In heaven, I suppose.' The exact words are 'Oh, in heaven, no doubt,' which sounds more sceptical. [. . .] Then there is 'Yes, yes: I know that as well as you do.' The 'Yes, yes' gives a much better effect of nervous irritability than an improvised substitute. Today you said 'undersell England in the EYES of the world' instead of 'markets of the world,' which is bad political economy."[108] Not only did Shaw give the correct lines, but he analyzed the differences in meaning between these lines and Shine's substitutions. On some occasions, he wrote such explanations during rehearsals—telling Higgins, for example, that he should not change "'I'm devilish sleepy'" to "Devilish tired," because "He is never tired: he's sleepy." Usually, Shaw's rehearsal notes on line readings are entirely technical: they give the incorrect version and the correct one. Rummy Mitchens (*Major Barbara*) should say "'at the other gate in Cripp's Lane,' not 'in the other lane at C's gate'"; Sir Patrick Cullen (*The Doctor's Dilemma*) should not change the verb in "'His brother-in-law extirpated tonsils for two hundred guineas'" to "exterminated" and the Inquisitor (*Saint Joan*) should say, "'vain and ignorant persons setting up their own judgments against the Church'" instead of "setting themselves up."[109]

Shaw insisted on both the correct line and on what he considered to be the correct emphasis. Sometimes he gave reasons for this emphasis. Matt Haffigan asks, "Fadher Dempsey: wouldnt you think well to ask him what he manes about the lan?" Larry Doyle answers, "I'll tell you, Matt" (2, 961). Shaw's rehearsal note gave both the emphasis and the explanation: "'*I'll* tell you, Mat'—that is, *I,* not Father D." Postcards to Ellen Terry exaggeratedly stressed emphasis in Lady Cicely's lines:

Have you ever thought of the GRANDEUR of wickedness?
Grand! Thats the word. Something grandly wicked.
Not very wicked, not dreadfully wicked, not shockingly wicked,

but

GRANDLY WICKED.
GRANDIOSO
SOMETHING Grandly WICKED to their enemies.

and

That's what English people are like, Captain Kearney.
Yes, positively.
That's what English people are like.
No use your contradicting it, Captain Kearney. I tell you THAT'S
what English people are like.[110]

Usually, Shaw's rehearsal notes concerning emphasis indicated only the
emphasis he wanted—as in various lines of Hypatia (*Misalliance*): "Jerry
would drive me MAD," "Well, what *would* you call a man proposing to a
girl who might be—," "They never *do* anything"—or else the desired and
undesired emphasis, such as Undershaft's "'The fourth had no *literary*
turn,' not '*had* no literary turn,'" Dubedat's "'Do you mean *operate* on
me'—not 'operate on *me*,'" Baudricourt's "'You think the girl can work
miracles, do you?' not 'the *girl* can work' &c."[111]

Shaw was also meticulous about phrasing and pauses. According to
Dame Sybil Thorndike, "He disliked that awful habit of pausing after a
conjunction, illogically ('I don't know why, but—I love you') rather than
before it, logically ('I don't know why—but I love you')."[112] On Doolittle's
(*Pygmalion*) "I cant carry the girl through the streets like a blooming
monkey, can I?" (4, 709), Shaw indicated that there should be no pause
before "blooming monkey." Summerhays, trying to prevent Hypatia from
describing her experience in the woods with Percival— "Please dont tell us
this. It's not fit for old people to hear" (4, 240)—should "Mind the full
stop" after the first sentence. When Bluntschli tells Raina, "you recognize
my uniform? Serb!" (1, 396), Shaw admonished the actor not to say the
last two words like "UniformSerb" but to "divide them."[113] Clearly, he
used punctuation to indicate pauses.

Precise about movements as well as about lines, Shaw sometimes explained why the actor should or should not move on a particular line. He
instructed Annie Russell, who played Major Barbara, that when Undershaft says, "'neither reason, nor morals, nor the lives of other men,' turn
away; but do not leave your place. I think it would be better not to move
until, on the line 'It is no use running away from wicked people' you can

emphasize your refusal to go with your mother by going right over to her chair, and standing behind it for a while. This avoids the risk of masking Lomax when he makes his speech. Afterwards, when he jumps up at the cue 'Mr Lomax is sitting on them,' keep the line of sight open for him." For the same reason, the Devil (*Man and Superman*) should "get RC" and not "mask Ana" on his line, "Don Juan: shall I be frank with you?" However, explanations do not usually accompany Shaw's mechanical blocking notes, which concern such matters as sitting and rising, or movement from one part of the stage to another. Ellie Dunn, for example, should not cross to stage center, but should "Keep RC" on "But why did you do that, Hesione?" While planning these movements, Shaw kept motivation in mind. In his prompt script for *Pygmalion*, he noted in the margin that Higgins "Finally sits down on the piano bench to escape Doolittle's caresses."[114]

One of Shaw's mechanical directorial responsibilities was checking sight lines. In the first act of *Arms and the Man*, he observed, "3d row of stalls cut off—ottoman too far up[stage]." In *Misalliance*, Gunner pokes his head out of the Turkish bath, so the director must "test visibility of head in Turkish bath from stalls."[115] In blocking his plays, Shaw kept in mind, as most directors do, the fact that all members of the audience should be able to see the action.

Shaw occasionally wrote reminders to himself and to the actors about the difficulties they would encounter in making adjustments from rehearsal conditions to performance conditions. Because movements in ancient Egyptian clothes differ from those in modern English clothes, Shaw indicated that some scenes of *Cæsar and Cleopatra* required special rehearsals with costumes and slippers. Because the rehearsal area was smaller than the stage, he reminded Catherine (*Arms and the Man*) that in performance her walk to the electric bell would be longer.[116] Preparing a revival of *John Bull's Other Island*, he implored Barker to let the cast use the Court Theatre's stage and scenery, reminding him that on a previous occasion the scenery "knocked [Louis] Calvert to pieces."[117]

Directions concerning the actor's emotions or attitudes were often written not in motivational terms but in what actors call result terms—that is, a statement of the feeling that the actor should convey, but not the cause of that feeling. Marchbanks was told that he should appear "more lost" when he confesses, "She said I'd understand; but I dont," and "more imposing" when he says, "Either the truth or a lie" (1, 539, 546). Tanner should be "more joyous" on "It's agreed that we all stand by Violet" (2,

561) but is "not grave enough" on "I trust, Enry, that, as between employer and engineer, I shall always know how to keep my proper distance, and not intrude my private affairs on you" (2, 610).[118]

Shaw's notes frequently directed the actor in such mechanical techniques as where to look or how to deliver a line (as opposed to why). In the opening scene of *Major Barbara,* Stephen was instructed not to "look as much at" Lady Britomart. Cusins was advised to "lift" the passage beginning, "Homer, speaking of Autolycus" (3, 81). Shaw sometimes gave stage directions in terms of speed. Lady Britomart's speeches in the opening scene were delivered "too quick[ly] for an exposition," and she must "Slow down the explanation about U[ndershaft]'s queer morals." "Tumble this out," he told Marchbanks about one line; "slow slow," he warned Candida about another.[119]

On some occasions, Shaw's instructions were in musical terms. One recalls his "musical" interpretations of Shakespeare, for example, his advice to Mrs. Patrick Campbell to consider Shakespeare's music rather than his characterization:

> if you get the music right, the whole thing will come right. And neither he nor any other musician ever wrote music without fortissimi and thundering ones too. [. . .] It is not by tootling to [Macbeth] con sordino that Lady Macbeth makes Macbeth say "Bring forth men children only." She lashes him to murder.
>
> And then you must modulate. Unless you can produce in speaking exactly the same effect that Mozart produces when he stops in C and then begins again in A flat, you cant play Shakespear.[120]

According to Shaw, Shakespeare achieves his effects by "word music" — that is, by doing with words, rhythms, rhymes, and the like, what Mozart does with music. Replace one of Shakespeare's poetic passages by a prose paraphrase and "you have nothing left but a platitude that even an American professor of ethics would blush to offer to his disciples." If you speak the poetry unmusically, "you will make your audience wince as if you were singing Mozart out of tune."[121]

Shaw discussed his own plays in musical terms: "I [. . .] wrote long rhetorical speeches like operatic solos, regarding my plays as musical performances [. . .] ." When Robert Loraine played Don Juan in *Man and Superman,* Shaw annotated his script like a symphony. "The margin in the book," said Winifred Loraine, "twinkled with crotchets, crescendoes and minims; with G clefs, F clefs, and pianissimos [. . .]."[122] According to G. W. Bishop, Shaw performed a similar service for Scott Sunderland when he acted Cain in *Back to Methuselah.* Cain's first long speech, in which he asks whose fault it was that he killed Abel, should be delivered, "say, in C Major." When he confesses that he envied Abel's happiness and freedom, Shaw asked him to "drop without modulation to A flat, and abandon all affectation. He is now *talking about himself,* and much more serious than when he was talking about Abel." When protesting that he does not want to kill women, he was to "begin at a low pitch and drag the time a little; then take the whole speech as a *crescendo—p.* to *ff.*" Beside the words "fighting, fighting, killing, killing" is the musical direction "*martellato,*" and next to "burning, overwhelming life," "*meno mosso.*" When he declares that he revolts against the clay, he should reach "his top note; it is the climax—and indeed the end—of this part. His style in this speech is large and grand and harmonious, in longer bars, a little restrained in speed, but otherwise all out." Bishop adds that Shaw was able to do this because the actor understood Mozart.[123] Dame Sybil Thorndike reports that Shaw treated his dialogue almost like a musical score. At times, he would even give the actor a musical tune for a line reading. "He would say something like, 'No, no, not this:

but this:.'

He worked to get the right *sound.*"[124] His rehearsal notes contain many examples of musical direction. When Ana asks, "Has even death failed to refine your soul, Juan?" (2, 640), she should "sing it like a dirge." For the first London production of *Pygmalion,* Shaw freely used directions in musical terms for Beerbohm Tree and Mrs. Patrick Campbell: "The crescendo accelerando is softened away," "Tenor register," "Dont go back to *Tannhauser,*" "Andante tranquilo," "f."[125]

In a frequently quoted story of a conversation between Shaw and Arnold Daly,[126] the playwright tells the actor, "All that it is necessary for you to do is to say my lines so slowly and clearly that the audience can hear every word." "What about my acting?" asks Daly. "As long as they can hear my lines," replies Shaw, "you can act or not, as you please." The story may be—as I suspect it is—untrue, but the moral is valid: speech was very important to Shaw. Emphasizing this aspect of Shaw's directing technique, Dame Sybil Thorndike declared that although "he minded character, he paid more attention to the reading of the lines than to anything else.

Speech was the main concern. One would get the thought through the language. The reality and the sincerity came from the voice and personality. His actors have to be good public speakers."[127] Sir Lewis Casson agrees: "To Shaw, careless speaking was as unpardonable as careless singing in opera—or careless dancing in ballet."[128] The accuracy of these statements is evidenced by the importance which Shaw himself explicitly attached to good speech. Lillah McCarthy, he wrote admiringly, "was saturated with declamatory poetry and rhetoric from her cradle, and had learnt her business out of London by doing work in which you were either heroic or nothing." In the fashionable London theaters, the "art of acting rhetorical and poetical drama [. . .] became a lost art [. . .]. Rhetoric and poetry vanished with it. But when I dragged rhetoric and poetry back its executive technique became again indispensable." Lillah McCarthy "combined the executive art of the grand school with a natural impulse to murder the Victorian womanly woman; and this being just what I needed I blessed the day when I found her [. . .]."[129]

Even before he was a regular theater critic, Shaw was adamant about good speech. "I am alive to the necessity of perfect diction when an attempt is made at realism in the pitch of conversation," he wrote to William Archer in 1889 and then complained of Charles Charrington's production of *A Doll's House*: "I was in the fourth row of the pit, which is not unreasonably far back; but I lost several lines, and was conscious of a great relief when [the actors] spoke out or made their words tell."[130] As a theater critic, he continually discussed voice and diction—reminding Lena Ashwell, for example, that "there are short vowels in the dictionary as well as long vowels," and that the first vowel in "fascination" should not be so long as to necessitate the omission of the second; and praising Mabel Terry's ability to "speak beautifully, without the slightest trick or mannerism of any sort [. . .]."[131]

As a director, he worked for audibility and good diction. Such reproofs as "not audible," "indistinct," and "quite inaudible" appear in rehearsal notes of every production he either directed or supervised. He frequently noted sloppy diction, warning Lady Macbeth, for instance, that "milk of human kindness" (I,v) sounded like "milkahumankindness," that "nature's mischief" (I,v) sounded like "naycher's mischief," and that "the owl that shriek'd" (II,ii) sounded like "Yowl that shrieked."[132] Bad diction sometimes inspired him to compose extravagant lectures to the erring actor. When Cedric Hardwicke was playing Magnus in *The Apple Cart*, Shaw reprimanded him for having tried the extraordinary experiment of delivering your big speech, and a great deal of the rest of the play, without a single article, definite or indefinite, a single preposition, a single conjunction; in short, without any grammatical structure except an occasional interjection and a precarious supply of verbs. There was not a solitary *but* from one end to the other; yet "but" is the most important conjunction in the English language. "Be not faithless believing" may sound well; but it doesnt made sense, and bewilders where it should impress. [. . .] In the pantomime of Robinson Crusoe, which I saw as a boy, Man Friday delivered a stump speech; and whenever he said "But," the goat went for him. If that goat had been on the stage on Monday you would have cut his part clean out. Any good Catholic will tell you how important first and last words are (see "The Garden of Jesus" and other devotional works); but you always omit the firsts and drop the lasts. It is a tragic thing to see you wrecking a great career by despising words of less than three syllables, and shortening the three into two [. . .]. Take care of your buts and though and fors and first syllables at the beginnings of the sentences and definite articles, and a great career is within your grasp. Neglect them, and your doom will be obscurity, poverty, ruin, despair, disgrace, and damnation.[133]

Shaw's rehearsal notes for his plays comprise a textbook of good and bad speech practices. Guard against dropping the end of a line, he told the actor: when Ramsden commands Octavius, "dont call him Jack under my roof" (2, 538), Shaw noted, "'roof' not heard." Do not run words together, he warned: Hypatia's "You may kiss me if you catch me" (4, 205) sounded like "youskissmMatchy." Do not add *r* to a vowel, he advised, as he told Bentley not to call Hypatia "Hypasher." Alert to the necessity of sounding initial vowels, he pointed out that Raina's "After—after" sounded like "after rafter." Since words beginning in *h* create pronunciation problems similar to those in words beginning with vowels, he urged Captain Shotover to sound this letter: "Dont swallow your articulation. 'Now before *H*igh *h*eaven.'" He called for distinct articulation of consonants: Shotover should pronounce the word "'Rum m m m m' not 'ru*b*'" and Cusins's "'evangelical sects'" must not sound like "evangelical sex."[134]

Shaw's preoccupation with diction led to a joke about mispronunciation in *Cæsar and Cleopatra*. Caesar, unable to pronounce Ftatateeta's name, calls her "Teetatota" or "Totateeta." Since Cleopatra and Ftata-teeta herself must pronounce the name perfectly, Shaw indicated that they may learn to do so by practicing it "as Aftatateeta" and later drop the *A*. "It will then be as easy as saying 'left a message' or 'laughed to scorn' or 'lift a suitcase' or any other phrase with an ft in it."[135] *Misalliance* contains a diction lesson: Lina Szczepanowska teaches Tarleton how to pronounce her Polish name.

> LINA. Say fish.
> TARLETON. Fish.
> LINA. Say church.
> TARLETON. Church.
> LINA. Say fish church.
> TARLETON (*remonstrating*) But it's not good sense.
> LINA. (*inexorably*) Say fish church.
> TARLETON.Fish church.
> LINA. Again.
> TARLETON. No, bu—(*resigning himself*) fish church.
> LINA. Now say Szczepanowska.
> TARLETON. Szczepanowska. Got it, by Gad. (4, 193)

Since dialect is so important in *John Bull's Other Island,* Shaw composed for future directors of the play a set of instructions in which he warned that unless they exercise "the most unsparing vigilance," the entire company would assume that "mean is pronounced mane, sleep slape &c. by Irish people of all classes." Although Larry Doyle "must be an unmistakable Irishman [. . .] his speech is that of a refined and educated man" and his father's "pronunciation is no better and no worse than the text indicated." Although Father Keegan "jocularly affects a brogue in his talk with the grasshopper and Patsy, [he] is a man of ascetic refinement and distinction, compared with whom an English Archbishop would seem only a respectable family butler." Hodson should "not drop his aitches except when he is excited: as indicated," nor should Aunt Judy "mispronounce any worse than the text indicates."[136]

Shaw's efforts to have the actors in productions which he did not superintend pronounce the dialogue precisely as the character would took the extreme form, in *Major Barbara,* of writing out Bill Walker's cockney dialect quasi-phonetically, with traditional orthography. Thus, Bill says: "Aw did wot Aw said Aw'd do. Aw spit in is eye. E looks ap at the skoy and sez, 'Ow that Aw should be fahnd worthy to be spit upon for the gospel's sike!' e sez; an Mog sez 'Glaory Allelloolier!'; an then e called me Braddher, an dahned me as if Aw was a kid and e was me mather worshin me a Setterda nawt. Aw ednt jast nao shaow wiv im at all. Arf the street pryed; an the tather arf larfed fit to split theirselves. (*To Barbara*) There! are you settisfawd nah?" (3, 126). The translation is: "I did what I said I'd do. I spit in his eye. He looks up at the sky and says, 'Oh that I should be found worthy to be spit upon for the gospel's sake!' he says; and Mog says 'Glory Hallelujah!'; and then he called me Brother and downed me as if I was a kid and he was my mother washing me a Saturday night. I hadnt just no show with him at all. Half the street prayed; and the tother half laughed fit to split theirselves. (*To Barbara*) There! are you satisfied now?" In *Pygmalion*, written seven years later, he abandoned this practice shortly after the beginning of the first act: "*Here, with apologies, this desperate attempt to represent [Liza's] dialect without a phonetic alphabet must be abandoned as unintelligible outside London*" (4, 671). Shaw's efforts to find a way to transcribe pronunciation with accuracy led him to set aside in his will a certain amount of money for a new alphabet that would do the job. The result of this provision is an edition of *Androcles and the Lion* with parallel texts of the old and new alphabets.[137]

As an acting coach, Shaw's resources were astonishingly varied. He drew on a wide range of techniques, motivational and mechanical, internal and external as they are often called, to help the actor create the illusion of actuality. Concerned with the individual actor, Shaw was at the same time aware of the ensemble. He aimed at realism, but he also wanted theatrical effectiveness. Several aspects of a director's dealings with actors—pace, building, and timing—will be discussed in the next chapter, which deals more directly with theatrical effectiveness.

5 Stage Effects and Stage Effectiveness

Shaw arranged each stage picture so that it contributed to the impact of the play, but he was also careful to see that the play did not become a mere pretext for lively scenic effects. This does not mean that he opposed scenic effects or stage machinery: he resisted them only when they threatened to become more important than the text. The play should not stop, he believed, in order for the scene technician to display his skill. When William Faversham was about to present *Misalliance* in the United States in 1917, Shaw warned him against overdoing the airplane crash. To create the illusion of the crash, Shaw insisted, all Faversham needed was a hamper filled with broken glass and actors who would look up and shout.[1] When Leon Schiller directed *Heartbreak House* in Poland in 1930, he wanted to introduce a Piscator-like motion picture at the end, showing two flying airplanes. Shaw opposed the idea, and he advised Floryan Sobieniowski, his Polish translator, to tell Schiller to write a program note explaining that at the conclusion of the play "there will be a cinema show by Mr S. whilst the audience is leaving the theatre." Emphasizing that "The aeroplanes are not dramatic characters in the play," Shaw urged Schiller to forget about an airplane film and instead "devote himself to producing an illusion of their sound in the air. The best imitation is produced by a vacuum cleaner."[2]

If special effects were essential to a theatrical effect, however, or if they enhanced the dramatic action, Shaw used them. Codirecting *Heartbreak House* in London, he carefully attended to sound effects. When Mangan and Billy Dunn are blown up, he noted, "Explosion no good."[3] In *Arms and the Man,* Bluntschli's entrance is preceded by a burst of bullets. Rather than have a series of rifle shots ad lib, Shaw timed the effect, calling for a fusillade of exactly five shots.[4] He even tried to get a believable sound effect for the grasshopper in the second act of *John Bull's Other Island:*

"The grasshopper will not do in the provinces with that silly ginger beer bottle. We must go to Tisley & Spiller or some other maker of laboratory apparatus, and get one of the little whistles with which they test how shrill a note you can hear. Tiny brass things, with pneumatic blowers attached. We ought to have used one all through at the Court, but I did not think of the device until too late."[5]

When a stage effect did not overwhelm or get in the way of the play but instead reinforced the dramatic point that the author intended, Shaw tried to make the most of it. To Forbes Robertson, he described in detail how he would stage the final scene of *Richard III*. Declaring that "No actor has ever done the curious recovery of Richard of his old gaiety of heart in the excitement of the battle," which "whirls him up out of his vulgar ambition to be a king" and makes him once more an "ecstatic prince of mischief," Shaw suggested how Forbes Robertson, as Richard, might realize the effects of this last scene: "he should have a bucket of rose pink thrown in his face, and then reel on; all cut to pieces, killed already six times over, with a broken sword and his armor all in splinters, wrenching off the battered crown which is torturing his poor split head. Being hunted down just then by the Reverend Pecksniff Richmond & his choir, he is just able, after an impulse to hold on to the crown tooth & nail, to pitch it gaily to him & die like a gentleman." Rose pink, splintered armor, and battered crown notwithstanding, Shaw's major emphasis—here as elsewhere—was on the actor, and in his staging of crucial scenes he tried to help the actor achieve the maximum effect. When Robert Loraine was playing the title role of *Cyrano de Bergerac*, Shaw suggested that he stage the final scene differently:

> I dont think Cyrano should fall. The whole point of the death is that he dies on his feet and he ought to stiffen there and be visibly a dead man. To make this clear, Roxane, not realizing that he is dead, should go to his assistance; and then the statue should fall, and fall stiff. To save your bones, one of the men, seeing what is happening, should catch him as he is falling away from her, and the two should let him down, still stiff as a poker at full length. Just try it in one or two ways. As it is, it is too obviously a stage fall; and the effect of the scene is so very fine that it is a pity to mar it by the slightest touch of artificiality.[6]

Not only was Shaw trying to help Loraine stage the scene more effectively, he was also aiming to nullify a stagey moment so artificial that the audience could not believe that a real thing was happening to a real person.

Shaw's own plays contain stage effects that imaginative directors can exploit. Music, dancing, and colorful masquerade costumes enliven the final act of *You Never Can Tell*. At the end of the second act of *Major Barbara*, a loud band blares forth a marching version of the Wedding Chorus from Donizetti's *Lucia di Lammermoor* as the heartbroken heroine repeats Christ's last words on the cross. The last scene of *The Devil's Disciple* has a melodramatic reprieve from the gallows at the eleventh hour. Scenery changes before our eyes in *Androcles and the Lion*, and an angel drops from the sky in *The Simpleton of the Unexpected Isles*.

However, Shaw was not content to let these effects, in theatrical terminology, play themselves. An imaginative director himself, he took considerable care to enhance the effects written into the text. During the first act of *Pygmalion*, the text calls for "*Torrents of heavy summer rain*" (4, 669). His rehearsal notes entreat, "More horrible, finer rain! Cant we get the clouds to move & a moon to come out when the rain stops [later in the act]?"[7] Joan of Arc, entering the Court of the Inquisition in chains, creates a striking impact, but Shaw advised Joan on how to make it more forceful: "When you come on in the trial scene, kick the chain from step to step instead of dragging it. Let the kicks be heard before you come on [. . .]."[8] Bluntschli's entrance from the balcony onto the pitch-black stage in the first act of *Arms and the Man* was made more vivid as Shaw the director, following through the implications in the text, asked for five rifle shots, and then told Bluntschli not to enter until their noise has died away.[9] For a split second, Bluntschli stands with the curtains apart, silhouetted against the dark blue sky.[10] Following this, he closes the curtains and pauses ominously before he speaks his first line in the dark: "'Sh!' (dead silence) 'Dont call out or youll be shot.'"[11] Then Raina lights a candle.

A former art critic, Shaw did not neglect the stage picture, though he derided compositional effects that sacrificed credibility, motion, and life to "living pictures" with obviously posed models.[12] When Mrs. Patrick Campbell was playing in Björnstjerne Björnson's *Beyond Human Power,* he told her that George Titheradge's determination to die parallel to the footlights "with his heels O. P. and his head P, whilst you occupy the corresponding position P & O. P. rather spoils the picture. After all, it is not natural that he should die unassisted, especially after gurgling; and it would be a great improvement if he would breathe his last in the arms of Horatio—say the sceptical parson who wants the miracle."[13] By placing the actors in positions suggested by the situation in the play, Shaw achieved both a more natural effect and a more interesting composition.

As a director, he tried to prevent awkward or pedestrian groupings.

Seeing that Higgins, Liza, and Mrs. Pearce were lined up in an evenly spaced row, which is a monotonous arrangement, he noted: "Not XXX up at the door." Later in the play, when he observed Doolittle, Pickering, and Mrs. Higgins similarly lined up, he told Doolittle, "get with Pick. ●● ● not ● ● ●." With only two characters on stage, such as Raina and Bluntschli in the first act of *Arms and the Man*, he varied their relative positions so that they would "open up" to a three-quarter position, the other one-quarter, rather than face each other in profile throughout the scene.[14] But even though Shaw tried to avoid clumsy or dull groupings of actors, he eschewed beautiful compositions when they called attention to themselves as pictorial effects, for such effects distract from the situation in the play. When Joan of Arc assumes leadership of the army, he told Lawrence Langner, "she should be in front of all the rest, in command of the stage in the good old fashioned way from the point of view of the audience, and not beautifuly composed in the middle of the picture with all the other people turning their backs to the spectators. Why dont you carry out my directions and get my effects instead of working for pictorial effects [?]."[15] His own plays indicate stage pictures that visualize important thematic content. Probably the most obvious illustration of this is the final curtain of *Candida*, when the poet rushes out, leaving the parson and his wife as part of a stage picture of bourgeois bliss: in a comfortable parlor, with the fire going in the fireplace, they embrace. This sort of cozy, domestic scene is uncongenial to the poetic temperament, and though audiences are not told this verbally, they are told it visually.

As a director, Shaw attempted at every opportunity to tell the story and convey the theme in a visual manner. In rehearsal for *Man and Superman*, Robert Loraine, as Tanner, "wanted to deliver the great speech about the tyranny of mothers enthroned in the motor car, with Lillah [McCarthy as Ann] somewhere under the wheels with her back to the audience. I immediately saw the value of the idea, and put Lillah in the car in a fascinating attitude with her breast on the driving wheel and Loraine ranting about on the gravel."[16] Thus, the audience *sees* the windbag pontificating and the controlling woman seated womanly at—appropriately—the driver's wheel.

In trying to illuminate the play visually, Shaw frequently made use of stage business. When Tarleton sneaks back from an exhausting session at the gymnasium with Lina, Shaw asks him to feel his biceps as he enters. At a stroke, the audience remembers where he has been, sees the effects on him, and notices both a counterpoint and comic punctuation to the end of the previous scene: after young Hypatia dashes off in pursuit of Percival, enter her father, exhausted from his encounter with the object of his desires. In *Arms and the Man,* Bluntschli estimates Raina's age as "[not] much over seventeen." She corrects him: "Next time, I hope you will know the difference between a schoolgirl of seventeen and a woman of twenty-three." Bluntschli is *"stupefied"* and exclaims, "Twenty-three!" Raina then snatches the photograph from his hand, tears it up, and throws the pieces at his face (1, 468–69). At rehearsal, Shaw added stage business to help motivate the tear-up. He told Bluntschli to be "more stupefied" when he exclaims her age, to "[look] at her, then at the photo to see if it is retouched." *Then,* Raina snatches it and tears it up. The tear-up is made more effective by the rational Bluntschli examining evidence and thus further infuriating the already angry Raina. In *Pygmalion,* the director's additional business underscores the desires and reactions of the characters. When Liza urges Pickering to buy a flower from her, Shaw suggests, "Try to put the flower into his buttonhole." The physical business points up Liza's sales technique and also Pickering's growing annoyance and ultimate surrender, as his response to the flower girl alters from the apologetic "I'm sorry. I havnt any change"—following which comes Liza's business with the flower—to the reprimand, "Now dont be troublesome: theres a good girl" and perusal of his pockets (4, 673). Shaw's stage business aims to increase the naturalness of a character's behavior. When Higgins opens the second act with "Well, I think thats the whole show" (4, 685), Shaw has him "Pull a drawer out & recollect" before speaking. After the Porter has admitted Macduff and Lennox (*Macbeth*), Shaw suggests that he deliver the line, "remember the Porter," which should prompt one of them to throw him a coin.[17]

Shaw, who admired stage business that illuminated the play, abhorred it as a substitute for what the playwright was trying to achieve. While admitting that Beerbohm Tree had "some telling stroke" in each of his Shakespearean characterizations, he also pointed out that "it is never one of Shakespear's strokes." Tree's Caliban catches flies to stop them from teasing Stephano, his Richard II stifles a sob when Richard's dog turns from him to lick Bolingbroke's hand, and his Benedick sits in a tree "shying oranges at the three conspirators, and finally shaking the whole crop down on them when they accuse him of [being] 'a contemptible spirit,' quite content to exploit the phrase in its modern sense, though Shakespeare means, not contemptible, but contemptuous." Some of these bits of business, Shaw conceded, were "strokes of genius"; others, though, were "inconsiderate tomfooleries (for you should really not, like Crummles's comic countryman, catch flies when another actor is trying to hold the audience); but they are all pure original Tree and not Shakespear."[18] Shaw wanted stage business to bolster the playwright's work, not to compete with it.

Making certain that the action and plot are intelligible to the audience is part of the director's job. When Charles Charrington directed *A Doll's House,* the situation in the second act, Shaw wrote, was "not made clear. The audience does not understand [Nora's] idea that Helmer will take the forgery on himself. When she exclaims 'He will do it' they dont know what it means."[19] But when Charrington directed *The Wild Duck,* Shaw rejoiced that he clarified the situation and ideas. "The same insight which enables Mr Charrington, in acting Relling, to point the moral of the play in half a dozen strokes, has also enabled him to order the whole representation in such a fashion that there is not a moment of bewilderment during the development of a dramatic action subtle enough in its motives to have left even highly trained and attentive readers of the play quite addled as to what it is all about."[20] As a director, Shaw saw to it that important points "carried" to the audience. When Gunner drew his pistol and examined it, Shaw directed him to turn in profile so that the audience could see what he was holding. At the very beginning of the fifth act of *Cæsar and Cleopatra,* Apollodorus appears on a stage crowded with extras, and calls, "Hullo! May I pass?" (2, 284). Shaw warned him to pause after "Hullo" until the audience has seen and recognized him, and only then ask whether he might pass. Otherwise, the audience would be confused as to who was speaking and why.[21] Since the intelligibility of dramatic action sometimes depends upon statements and motives that are made or revealed earlier in the play, Shaw was careful to emphasize the "plants," as they are called. In the first act of *The Doctor's Dilemma,* Ridgeon asks Blenkinsop whether he can do anything for him; Blenkinsop replies, "Well, if you have an old frock-coat to spare? you see what would be an old one for you would be a new one for me; so remember me the next time you turn out your wardrobe" (3, 351). Blenkinsop, Shaw noted, must not speak confidentially but be "Quite frank about the coat—Paddy must hear," for in the next act, when Walpole is about to take Blenkinsop home in his automobile, Sir Patrick asks Blenkinsop whether he has a sufficiently thick overcoat to wear in the motor car. After Higgins tells his mother, "Ive had to work at the girl every day for months to get her to her present pitch. Besides, she's useful. She knows where my things are, and remembers my appointments and so forth" (4, 734), Shaw jotted down, "'Besides, she's useful, finds all my things'—emphasize this."²² This passage, from the third act, needs emphasis because the audience must understand the reason for Higgins's despair in the fifth act: after his mother remarks that Liza has a right to leave him if she wishes, he complains, "But I cant find anything. I dont know what appointments Ive got" (4, 758).

Part of the directorial problem of making the action intelligible to the spectators is focus: ensuring that they see what the director wants them to see, and guarding against distractions. Shaw tried to prevent actors from performing business or movements that would divert the audience's attention from the dramatic point being made by another actor. "Dont fiddle about during BB's speech," Shaw warned Dubedat. "Dont get up until 'Keep discipline,'" he told Raina, as "it takes attention off B[luntschli]. Have a pause." As director of the first London production of *Pygmalion,* he was constantly on the alert against scene-stealing by the two principals, Beerbohm Tree and Mrs. Patrick Campbell. "Dont destroy Doolittle with the business of the hat on the piano" while Doolittle is speaking, Shaw told Tree. And "Dont spoil the exit of Mrs E[ynsford] H[ill]" by tomfooling with her coat." To Mrs. Patrick Campbell, he gave similar notes, asking her not to toy with her handkerchief while Pickering is talking, not to move on Higgins's line, and not to talk through a speech by Doolittle.²³

Pace, Shaw believed, is an essential preoccupation of the director: the play's rhythm must not falter because of movement, business, or failure to pick up cues. He advised the director: "*Never have a moment of silence on the stage except as an intentional stage effect.* The play must not stop while an actor is sitting down or getting up or walking off the stage. The last word of an exit speech must get the actor off the stage. He must sit on a word and rise on a word; if he has to make a movement, he must move as he speaks and not before or after; and the cues must be picked up as smartly as a ball is fielded in cricket. This is the secret of pace, and of holding an audience."²⁴ Shaw's rehearsal notes reveal that he followed his own advice. "Take up this cue sharply," he told Soames (*Getting Married*). When Macbeth says, "yet let that be, / Which the eye fears, when it is done, to see" (I,iv), Shaw told him to start moving offstage on "when it is done, to see," rather than after the line.²⁵

Although the director may purposely break this "rule," and all technical rules, in order to create a special effect, he must nevertheless be sparing in such special effects if they are to have any impact. Shaw recalled having seen "a fine play of Masefield's prolonged by half an hour and almost ruined because the actors made their movements in silence between the speeches."[26] His suggestions to Ellen Terry on playing Imogen contained advice on the subject of pace:

> In playing Shakespere, play *to* the lines, *through* the lines, *on* the lines, but never between the lines. There simply isnt time for it. You would not stick five bars rest into a Beethoven symphony to pick up your drumsticks; and similarly you must not stop the Shakespear orchestra for business. Nothing short of a procession or a fight should make anything so extraordinary as a silence during a Shakesperean performance. All that cave business wants pulling together: from the line about "'tis some savage hold" to "Such a foe! Good Heavens!" you ought to get all the business of peeping & hesitating & so on packed into the duration of the speech, spoken without a single interval except a pause after the call. Otherwise it drags. Mind, I dont propose that you should omit or slur anything, but only that you should do it with the utmost economy of time.[27]

The last sentence is crucial. Business should not be omitted or rushed through, but it should not hold up the dialogue. How this might be accomplished in his own plays is seen in the fifth act of *Pygmalion,* when Doolittle says, "I, as one of the undeserving poor, have nothing between me and the pauper's uniform but this here blasted three thousand a year that shoves me into the middle class. (Excuse the expression, maam; youd use it yourself if you had my provocation.)" (4, 763). Shaw's rehearsal notes directed Higgins to "kick him" when he says what was then a minor obscenity, "blasted."[28] The realization of the meaning of that kick motivates Doolittle's parenthetical remark to Mrs. Higgins, but the play does not stop for this business, since it is accomplished on the lines, not between them.

Although pace involves such practices as picking up cues and not stopping the dialogue for business, it is not merely a question of speed. When people complain that a scene is "too slow," they mean that it bores them. The reason for the boredom, said Shaw, is not that the scene is paced too slowly, but that it is "'too fast to sink in,' or 'too empty of action & significance of playing.'" The remedy, most of the time, is not for the actors to go faster, but for them "to go slower and bring out the meaning better by contrasts of tone and speed."[29] Contrast gives the illusion of pace, for a particular scene will seem to be moving quickly when the scene that has preceded it is played in a slower tempo. Nor will the slower tempo necessarily seem to be too slow, for it will relieve the other scene. Variety of tempo helps achieve pace.

Shaw advocated many types of contrast. The play should be divided into smaller units, each with its own mood, tone, and tempo that contrast with the surrounding units. *Hamlet,* he said, is a long play which can seem short "only [. . .] when the high mettled comedy with which it is interpenetrated from beginning to end leaps out with all the lightness and spring of its wonderful loftiness of temper." In a review of *As You Like It,* he used a musical analogy, suggesting that the director divide the play "into movements like those of a symphony. [He] will find that there are several sections which can be safely taken at a brisk *allegro,* and a few that may be taken *prestissimo* [. . .]."[30]

As director, Shaw tried to provide contrast between individual scenes. In *Misalliance,* Lord Summerhays's scene with Hypatia is followed by one between him and Tarleton. With Hypatia, the subject is sex; with Tarleton, parents and children. "Make this speech brighter," Shaw told Summerhays about his first speech to Tarleton, "to shake off the previous scene." After an all-male scene in the second act of *The Doctor's Dilemma,* Jennifer enters. Shaw noted that her "pride—gentle pride all through the part" should provide "the relief after the men."[31] He sometimes discussed scenic contrasts in musical terms. In the final act of *Man and Superman,* he told Lillah McCarthy, "when Malone, Ramsden & Tanner go off making a great cackle & fuss, do not begin the scene with Tavy until the noise is over and the audience's attention has quite come back to you. Just wait, looking provokingly at Tavy, until there is a dead silence & expectation & then say, without the least hurry, 'Wont you go with them, Tavy?' Otherwise you will not get the new key and the slow movement."[32] Each scene has its own "key" and "movement," which the director must find and have the actors play.

Vocal contrast is equally necessary. The voices of the actors "should not all have the same pitch nor gabble away at the same speed."[33] "The director must accordingly take care that every speech contrasts as strongly as possible in speed, tone, manner, and pitch with the one which provokes it"; and he should try to "prevent the actors from taking their tone and speed from one another, instead of from their own parts, and thus destroying the continual variety and contrast which are the soul of liveliness in comedy and truth in tragedy."[34] During rehearsals, Shaw took many notes for this purpose. "Dont catch [Joan's] speed as she comes in," he told Dunois (*Saint Joan*); "keep [your] curiosity about the stranger." Keep "cool against BB's fuss," he cautioned Dubedat. Reginald, about to describe Hotchkiss as a man with a face like a mushroom, should deliver his lines more slowly in order to contrast with the preceding speech by the General.[35]

Shaw also wanted each actor to achieve vocal variety. In Petkoff's long speech about the absurdity of washing every day, he noted, "Speed not varied—all snapped out at the same rate." When Ariadne compliments Hesione on her husband (*Heartbreak House*), Shaw pointed out that her speech should show "extreme self-possession in contrast to excitement before." For *Getting Married,* which is subtitled *A Disquisitory Play,* variety is essential in order to prevent the discourse from becoming monotonous. In Shaw's rehearsal notes, such entries as "change of speed" appear frequently.[36]

Realizing that physical variety is as necessary as vocal variety, Shaw the director tried to vary the positions, business, and movements of actors. Higgins should advance closer to Liza on the line, "the streets will be strewn with the bodies of men shooting themselves for your sake before Ive done with you" (4, 693), for he should "not always [keep] the same distance from [her]." After the Russian Officer gives Raina a military bow, as the text indicates, he should "Salute Catherine" (the text indicates that he bows to her as well). When Bluntschli interrupts Louka's scene with Sergius, in which she behaves independently, she should, "On entry of Bluntschli, get up at once, like a servant."[37] The principle of contrasts was designed to "hold an audience" by creating variety and was in Shaw's mind from the process of casting through the final stage of rehearsals.

Pace and variety, while necessary to create and maintain theatrical excitement, are by themselves insufficient. Another essential element is building toward climaxes. As director, Shaw tried to prevent the action from proceeding on a single level. Within individual speeches, among groups of speeches, in scenes, and in the play as a whole, Shaw aimed—through increases and decreases in volume, tempo, intensity, and so forth—to create crescendos and diminuendos, climaxes and resting places. Small units within each speech received Shaw's attention. In the first act of *Major Barbara*, Lady Britomart tells Stephen of his father's defiance of conventional social and moral attitudes. Two-thirds of the way through the long speech, she says, "I asked Gladstone to take it up. I asked The Times to take it up. I asked the Lord Chamberlain to take it up" (3, 72). Although the climax occurs at the end of the speech, and the climax of that particular portion of dialogue occurs two speeches later, Shaw understands the necessity of a smaller build within the passage: his notes ask the actress to build in pitch from "Gladstone" to "Times" to "Chamberlain," thereby enhancing the comedy in the text that goes from the very important (the former prime minister) to the important (a major newspaper) to the relatively trivial (the duties of the Lord Chamberlain's office included stage censorship). However, Shaw did not lose sight of the larger units. Whatever its components, a long speech has a climax that requires preparation. In *John Bull's Other Island*, Larry talks of giving tenant farmers a pound a week. When Father Dempsey replies that some of the landlords do not even make that much from the land, Larry retorts, "Then let them make room for those who can. Is Ireland never to have a chance? First she was given to the rich; and now that they have gorged on her flesh, her bones are to be flung to the poor, that can do nothing but suck the marrow out of her. If we cant have men of honor own the land, lets have men of ability. If we cant have men with ability, let us at least have men with capital. Anybody's better than Matt, who has neither honor, nor ability, nor capital, nor anything but mere brute labor and greed in him. Heaven help him!" (2, 963). Shaw warned Larry that "If we cant have men of honor" should "not [be] too high" since it is "before a climax." In the same way, Shaw tried to create crescendos and climaxes in dialogue that extended through several speeches. For example, there is an exchange between Larry Doyle and Matt Haffigan:

> MATTHEW (*sullenly*) What call have you to look down on me? I suppose you think youre everybody because your father was a land agent.
> LARRY. What call have you to look down on Patsy Farrell? I suppose you think youre everybody because you own a few fields.
> MATTHEW. Was Patsy Farrll ever ill used as I was ill used? Tell me dhat.
> LARRY. He will be, if he ever gets into your power as you were in the power of your old landlord. (2, 961–62)

Shaw's rehearsal notes for this dialogue call for:

Matt	What call have you	
&	What call have you	} a row — crescendo.
Larry	Was Patsy Farrll	
	He will be	

Dubedat, arguing with the doctors for a full page, has a series of speeches beginning "Oh bigamy! bigamy! bigamy!" and ending, "Oh, go and do whatever the devil you please. Put me in prison. Kill Jennifer with the disgrace of it all. And then, when youve done all the mischief you can, go to church and feel good about it" (3, 390–91). Shaw called the actor's attention to the fact that he must not reach his peak too soon, for the climax is in the last speech.[38]

The largest unit, of course, is the entire play. Shaw understood that the actor must marshal his energy and grade its expenditure from act to act. He must become more rather than less powerful in each succeeding scene and prevent the audience from being bored by a sameness in his performance. Because Laurence Irving, in the title role of *Captain Brassbound's Conversion,* failed to build his performance in this manner, Shaw wrote to him:

> You are at present like a soldier who can do nothing but win the Victoria Cross, an astronomer who can do nothing but observe the transit of Venus, or the fabled American doctor who could not cure measles, but was the death on fits. You began the first act in the middle of the second, to the intense astonishment of the spectators. I am far from grudging Brassbound a certain sense of injury even in the first act; but you were a volcano smouldering with unutterable wrongs from your first step on the stage. When the right moment for the eruption came, the audience had acquired a Neapolitan indifference to lava, because there was such a lot of it from the commencement that they had become used to it.[39]

By failing to become more powerful, Irving did not succeed in remaining *as* powerful.

Pace and building are among the director's paramount concerns during the "polishing" phase of rehearsals. Trying to increase the theatrical effectiveness of each scene, Shaw intensified his already scrupulous attention to detail, expending a great deal of attention on another aspect of polishing, timing. On many occasions, he recorded that a character made an entrance too late, or too early. He had actors pick up their cues more sharply, or, on the other hand, more slowly — but the slow pick-up was timed for effect. For example, Lina's removal of her goggles, which reveals that she is a woman, prompts the other characters to respond verbally: "Well I never !!!" "Oh, I say!" and so forth (4, 192). Shaw timed the effect, telling the cast, "ALL. Count two of dead silence when the goggles come off." Movements, too, were precisely timed. In *Candida,* Prossy accuses Lexy of imitating Morell. A stage direction reads, "*coming at him,*" as she says, "Yes, you do: you imitate him. Why do you tuck your umbrella under your left arm instead of carrying it in your hand like anyone else? Why do you walk with your chin stuck out before you, hurrying along with that eager look in your eyes? you! who never get up before half past nine in the morning. Why do you say 'knoaledge' in church, though you always say 'knolledge' in private conversation!" (1, 524). As director, Shaw coordinated Prossy's "*coming at him*" to coincide with the repetitions of "Why" in her speech, stopping after each movement to let the audience and Lexy take in what she says: "Why—why—why—step step step & shove him to the sofa." The rhythm of the movement reinforces that of the words, emphasizes the meaning of the speech, and helps to get a laugh on the last line. In *Arms and the Man*, Bluntschli's movement is timed with his speech. He tells Raina, "My dear young lady, dont let this worry you" (1, 445), and Shaw notes precisely, "'My dear young lady'—cross—'dont let this worry'—sit—'you.'"[40] Since movement and speech are executed simultaneously, rather than alternately, the scene's rhythm does not falter or its pace flag.

Business and gestures were also coordinated with the lines. Cusins should not give Undershaft the trombone until he begins to speak the line, "Blow, Machiavelli, blow" (3, 135). Only on "What the—" (3, 323) does Redpenny (*The Doctor's Dilemma*) throw down his pen. Dubedat is not to lift his hand until he starts speaking the artist's creed, "I believe in Michael Angelo" (3, 419). And in Lady Macbeth's sleepwalking scene, she puts her hands to her nose and makes a wry face *on* the line, "Here's the smell of the blood still" (V,i).[41]

As some of the previous notes reveal, Shaw was especially aware of the importance of timing in comedy. On several occasions, he warned actors to hold for laughs. In the fifth act of *Pygmalion,* he devised specific activities for the actors in case a laugh came during a speech, so that they would not be left simply standing on stage waiting for the laughter to subside in order to continue. In the middle of Doolittle's long speech about the good old days is the statement that he once needed a solicitor when some people "found a pram in the dust cart" (4, 762). Telling Doolittle that he would "probably [get] a laugh" on the line, Shaw directed Pickering to "unclasp hands" when he heard the phrase, and told Higgins and Mrs. Higgins to "Play to 'pram in the dust cart.'"[42] The reactions can adequately cover the duration of the laugh and keep the actors behaving in character. If there is no laugh, the responses need not delay the remainder of the speech.

But before the actor can hold for a laugh, he must first get it. To help him, Shaw used several devices, including pauses. When Undershaft, visiting his family for the first time in many years, is told by his wife, "This is your family," he replies, "(*surprised*) Is it so large?" (3, 84). During rehearsals, Shaw noted that the reply was "too quick." If Undershaft pauses before he speaks, perhaps looking at the five young people (including the fiancés of his two daughters) during that pause, the line would probably get a laugh. In *Arms and the Man,* Sergius tells Raina and Catherine the story of how Bluntschli escaped after the battle of Slivnitza and concludes with the episode of the borrowed overcoat. A note told him to have "More fun on the story." Another note advised Raina, before speaking her next line, to "Leave a pause for the story to fall dead flat." When Tanner first enters in *Man and Superman,* he goes directly to Ramsden

> *as if with the fixed intention of shooting him on his own hearthrug. But what he pulls from his breast pocket is not a pistol, but a foolscap document which he thrusts under the indignant nose of Ramsden as he exclaims*
>
> TANNER. Ramsden: do you know what that is? (2, 541)

"Dont speak," Shaw told Tanner, "until the will is directly under Ramsden's nose." To point the laugh, Shaw also used the device of looking at someone before speaking. When Collins introduces Mrs. George to Mrs. Bridgenorth, Mrs. Bridgenorth is directed to "Look at Lesbia, [then] at Mrs. George!—then—'Do you mean that Mrs G. is a real person' more abruptly."[43]

For comic purposes, Shaw contrasted what is said and how it is said. In *Arms and the Man,* Catherine explains the use of an electric bell:

> CATHERINE. You touch a button; something tinkles in the kitchen; and then Nicola comes up.
>
> PETKOFF. Why not shout for him?
>
> CATHERINE. Civilized people never shout for their servants. (1, 417)

In rehearsal, Shaw told Petkoff to "howl" his question and Catherine to "deafen" him with her reply. Here, the manner of delivery provides a comic comment on the words delivered, a subtext that contrasts with the surface text. For comic effect, Shaw also used the device of a sudden change in volume. In *Misalliance,* Lord Summerhays reprimands his son, "Bentley: you are not behaving well. You had better leave us until you have recovered yourself." Shaw's rehearsal notes record the first word as "Bentley!!!!" Then "With quiet severity," Lord Summerhays should deliver the remainder of the speech. Like father, like son. Immediately after the father's instant change of volume, Shaw had Bentley use the same device. Bentley "*throws himself on the floor and begins to yell.*" Responding to this action, everyone starts to talk at once. "Leave him to me, Mrs

Tarleton," says Lina, who appears at the door. "(*Clear and authoritative*) Stand clear, please." She lifts Bentley, throws him across her shoulders, and leaves with him, as Bentley says, "(*in scared, sobered, humble tones as he is borne off*) What are you doing? Let me down. Please, Miss Szczepanowska—(*they pass off out of hearing*)" (4, 233). Shaw told Bentley, "Keep yelling & stop suddenly with a change of tone for Lina."[44] The key word, which helps achieve the comic effect, is "suddenly."

Movement and gesture contrasting with the lines also increase the comic potential of the dialogue. When Bill Walker declares to Barbara that he is not afraid of Todger Fairmile—who is a professional fighter and who outweighs him—Shaw asked him to "look outside" on the line. As Leo self-righteously labels as "simple immorality" Lesbia's assertion that a woman should be allowed to leave a man if she wants to, Shaw told her to "put her arm round Hotchkiss's shoulders" (Hotchkiss is the man for whom she left her husband).[45] And he explained to Boanerges that Magnus "cannot get the effect on his 'Shall we sit, ladies and gentlemen' after B. sits down on [the previous line] 'you might as well call me Bo-Anner-jeeze.' You must make it by hastily rising and sitting down again."[46]

Shaw observed the actor as part of the total stage picture and at the same time attended to minute details of execution. The grouping of actors on stage, mechanical devices, stage business, pace, contrast, building, timing: to enhance the theatrical effectiveness of the scene and the play, Shaw used all of these. But he employed these techniques as means of illuminating thematic aspects of the play, not as substitutes for the effects intended by the author.

6 The Technical Elements of Production

The prevalent view of Shaw's attitude toward the various technical or
mechanical elements of production—such as scenery, lighting, and costumes—is summarized by Sir Lewis Casson: "In his whole history of a
producer of his own or anyone else's plays, I never knew Shaw [to] take
any serious practical interest in anything beyond the casting and the acting. All the rest, including scenery, costumes, lighting and grouping, was
of very minor importance, and personally, as a director, I sympathize with
him."[1] Apart from Sir Lewis's sympathy, the statement is simply not true.
We have already witnessed Shaw's concern with the grouping of actors.
As we shall see, he also took great interest in scenery, lighting, costume,
make-up, and music.

Scenery

As noted earlier, Shaw wanted the actor to make the audience believe that
real things were happening to real people. In 1890, he implied a similar
aim for the scene designer when he cited with approval the singer Victor
Maurel's insistence that the scene designer produce "an appropriate illusion as to the place and period assigned by the dramatist to the action of
the piece [. . .]."[2] Later, Shaw tended to modify this opinion, for he
became more interested in the scenery creating the illusion of the world of
the play, than in mere representationalism or pictorial realism.

When Shaw approached the scenic aspect of production, he combined
his knowledge of art with his understanding of the drama and the stage.
Condemning as an idiot the scene painter responsible for the settings of
Cymbeline, he told Ellen Terry that the scenic environment of her discovery of the headless man should be "a land of lions, murderers and hobgob-
lins, with dreadful lonely distances and threatening darknesses. [. . .]

Great Lord, if I were a scene painter I'd have painted such an endless valley of desolation for you that at your appearance in its awful solitudes, lost and encompassed by terrors, everybody would have caught their breath with a sob before you opened your mouth." In *Hamlet,* he would "make such a scene of 'How all occasions do inform against me!'—Hamlet in his travelling furs on a heath like a polar desert, and Fortinbras and his men 'going to their graves like beds'—as should never be forgotten." Recognizing the importance of scenery, he advised Ellen Terry that if ever she played Shakespeare again, she should consider the scenery before she considered anything else, for "art is one and indivisible" and the scenery is a vital part of the total picture.[3]

As a music and theater critic, he was constantly aware of the scenery. He scorned such gross improbabilities as the mountains in the second act of *Die Walküre* "being provided with flights of stairs and galleries exactly like the hall of an old manor house [. . .]." Abhorring scenic clichés, he reported that "nobody could help laughing" at the collection of supernatural effects that Sir Augustus Harris assembled for *Der Freischütz:* "illuminated steam clouds from Bayreuth, and fiery rain from the Lyceum Faust," plus the "red fire, glowing hell-mouth caverns, apparitions, skeletons, vampire bats, explosions, conflagrations, besides the traditional wheels, the skulls, the owl, and the charmed circle." Since one of the owl's eyes was larger than the other, it seemed to be looking at the audience through a monocle. "To appeal to our extinct sense of the supernatural by means that outrage our heightened sense of the natural is to court ridicule." He objected when scenery or properties called attention to their unreality or remoteness from the world of the play. In *Rosmersholm,* for example, "the Conservative paper which attacked the Pastor for his conversion to Radicalism was none other than our own Globe; and the thrill which passed through the house when Rebecca West contemptuously tore it across and flung it down, far exceeded that which Mrs Ebbsmith sends nightly through the Garrick audiences [when, in *The Notorious Mrs. Ebbsmith,* she hurls the Bible into the fire]." Aware of the need to utilize stage space to produce an impression of largeness or smallness, he remarked that Forbes Robertson had not yet mastered the problem of disguising the spaciousness of the Lyceum stage when he had to show interiors. He deplored the makeshift scenery of a production of *John Gabriel Borkman.* In the first act, a hodgepodge of a Norwegian stove, a painted staircase, a few old chairs, and "a faded, soiled, dusty wreck of some gay French salon" represented the Borkman home. The second-act gallery was not a gallery but an ugly, square box. In the third act, two back cloths of a snowy pine forest and a mountain at midnight used the same set of wings and were placed upon an obviously wooden floor. "When I looked at that," said Shaw, "and thought of the eminence of the author and the greatness of his work, I felt ashamed."[4]

The art critic's eyes perceived ugliness and lack of harmony. Augustin Daly's textually mutilated production of *Two Gentlemen of Verona,* Shaw wrote, displayed a sense of color that was "cognate with Mr Daly's theory of how Shakespear should have written plays." After diagnosing what was wrong with the scenery of *A Man about Town* ("an attempt at harmony in two shades of terra cotta, carried out in the wallpaper, curtains, and upholstery, is murdered by a ceiling, a carpet, and a conservatory, of such horribly discordant colors that it is difficult to look at them without a shriek of agony"), he suggested a remedy ("Why not repaint the ceiling, change the carpet, and fill the conservatory with a bank of flowers of the right color?").[5]

Illusion, beauty, and appropriateness are the triadic principles that underlie many of Shaw's statements on stage scenery. In 1895, he reviewed a biography of the comedian John Hare. That same year, Adolphe Appia published *La mise en scène du drame Wagnérien;* five years later, Gordon Craig designed Purcell's *Dido and Aeneas,* and not until ten years later did he publish *The Art of the Theatre.* Shaw's review of the Hare biography contains a plea for atmospheric and poetic scenery that is in harmony with these aspects of Appia's and Craig's ideas for scenic reform: "It is one thing to banish vulgarity and monstrosity from the stage and replace them by conventional refinement and scrupulous verisimilitude. It is quite another to surround a real drama with its appropriate atmosphere, and provide a poetic background or an ironically prosaic setting for a tragic scene. There are some rooms in which no reasonable person could possibly commit suicide [. . .]."[6] Gordon Craig's demands that scenery have beauty, simplicity, atmosphere, and suggestiveness fell in line with Shaw's ideas. As expected, Shaw consistently praised Craig's art, though, also as expected, he condemned Craig's unwillingness to grapple with the practical problems of theater.[7]

Shaw's fondness for atmospheric beauty and his distaste for prosaic verisimilitude were partly reactions against exhibitions of Shakespeare that he witnessed. The nineteenth-century pictorial stage mangled Shakespeare's texts and framed what was left of them in two-dimensional scenery whose tawdry ugliness contrasted harshly with the poetic beauty of the dialogue. In 1895, Shaw complained that *All's Well That Ends Well* was "pulled to pieces in order that some bad scenery, totally unconnected with

Florence or Rousillon, might destroy all the illusion" that the language creates. "Briefly, the whole play was vivisected, and the fragments mutilated, for the sake of accessories which were in every particular silly and ridiculous. If they were meant to heighten the illusion, they were worse than failures, since they rendered illusion almost impossible. If they were intended as illustrations of place and period, they were ignorant impostures. I have seen poetic plays performed without costumes before a pair of curtains by ladies and gentlemen in evening dress with twenty times the effect [. . .]." On 13 July of that year, in a review of *A Midsummer Night's Dream,* he condemned Augustin Daly's failure to realize that his scene painter could not possibly compete with Shakespeare's verbal descriptions, and called Daly's "'panoramic illusion of the passage of Theseus's barge to Athens' [. . .] more absurd than anything that occurs in the tragedy of Pyramus and Thisbe in the last act." A week later he reviewed the Elizabethan Stage Society's production of *Twelfth Night* on a platform stage. This method of staging, in sharp contrast with Daly's method, led Shaw to conclude, "I do not, like the E. S. S., affirm it as a principle that Shakespear's plays should be accorded the build of stage for which he designed them. I simply affirm it as a fact, personally observed by myself, that the modern pictorial stage is not so favorable to Shakespearean acting and stage illusion as the platform stage." Recalling a production of Browning's *Luria* that was "acted — not merely read — in a lecture theatre at University College, against a background of plain curtains, by performers also in evening dress," he described its scenic effect as "so satisfactory in comparison to the ordinary pictorial stage effect that I have ever since regarded the return to the old conditions of stage representation for old plays as perfectly practical and advisable." A year later, when William Poel directed Marlowe's *Doctor Faustus* for the Elizabethan Stage Society, Shaw was even more enthusiastic:

> The more I see of these performances by the Elizabethan Stage Society, the more I am convinced that their method of presenting an Elizabethan play is not only the right method for that particular sort of play but that any play performed on a platform amidst the audience gets closer home to its hearers than when it is presented as a picture framed by a proscenium. Also, that we are less conscious of the artificiality of the stage when a few well-understood conventions, adroitly handled, are substituted for attempts at an impossible scenic verisimilitude. All the old fashioned tale-of-adventure plays,

with their frequent changes of scene, and all the new problem plays, with their intense intimacies, should be done in this way.

In a review of Poel's 1897 production of *The Tempest,* Shaw praised his technique of creating illusion without illusionistic scenery. When Poel frankly told his audience, "'See that singers' gallery up there! Well, lets pretend that it's the ship,'" the audience agreed, willingly using its imagination to transform the gallery into a ship. "But how could we agree to such a pretence with a stage ship? Before it we should say 'Take that thing away: if our imagination is to create a ship, it must not be contradicted by something that apes a ship so vilely as to fill us with denial and repudiation of its imposture.'" Similarly, a superstitious person will see a ghost in a ray of moonlight on an old coat hanging on the wall but will not be deceived by an elaborate, picturesque ghost. "The reason is, not that a man can a l w a y s imagine things more vividly than art can present them to him, but that it takes an altogether extraordinary degree of art to compete with the pictures which the imagination makes when it is stimulated by such potent forces as [. . .] the poetry of Shakespear."8

However, Shaw pointed out, what is true for Shakespeare is not necessarily true for every playwright. A director who stages a modern realistic drama in verisimilar prose dialogue and asks us to imagine that the singer's gallery is a locale that is familiar to us would be refused, said Shaw, modifying his suggestion that "all the new problem plays" be staged in the Poel manner. As Shaw realized upon reflection, to know just how much help the imagination needs requires precise judgment. Not only is there no general rule for all dramatists, there is no general rule for any individual playwright. Bare-stage productions of *The Tempest* and *A Midsummer Night's Dream* are better than productions with the best scenery, which destroys the illusion that the poetry creates; but it does not follow that scenery will not improve *Othello.* Shaw concluded that "the manager who stages every play in the same way is a bad manager, even when he is an adept at his own way."9 Shaw's eclecticism in regard to stage scenery is typically linked to practicality. "The wise playwright, when he cannot get absolute reality of presentation, goes to the other extreme, and aims at atmosphere and suggestion of mood rather than at simulative illusion" (4, 840).

Practicality informs Shaw's scenic techniques. In the review of *John Hare, Comedian,* in which Shaw said that a drama should be surrounded with an appropriate atmosphere, he makes an equally revealing point about his relationship to the scenic conventions of the theater of his day: "I do not say that the stage drawing rooms of the old Court and the St James's were better than 'four boards and a passion'; but they were worlds above flats, wings, sky borders, and no passion, which was the practical alternative." He always considered the practical alternative, and in 1926 he frankly admitted, "I am tied down to what can actually be done with the theatre as it stands; and if you perform my plays in any sort of theatre but the one they were written for, you may have to mutilate them more or less horribly to make them practicable." If a theater company "can give me another sort of theatre I can write another sort of play, quite as good as, and fresher in form than the old ones, but impossible of performance in the old XIX century theatres." He praised Ibsen for asking—in *When We Dead Awaken*—that the scenic possibilities of the theater expand themselves to his requirements, instead of the other way around, which was Ibsen's custom. Shaw himself was no such innovator. He adapted his own scenic requirements to the theater of his time, but he was quick to seize upon the scenic innovations of others—even, at one point, suggesting that Granville Barker play Hamlet, with Gordon Craig reproducing the scenery he had designed for the Moscow Art Theatre production, and possibly playing the ghost of Hamlet's father as well.[10]

The stage directions in Shaw's plays are notable for their detail. However, not all of the detail describes what the audience sees on stage. The three pages of stage directions that introduce *Candida,* for instance, tell about the appearance of the neighborhood as well as the room on stage. While more than five pages of stage directions introduce *The Man of Destiny,* only nine lines describe the room we see. The rest concern mainly the history of Napoleon and the impact of a French army of occupation on an Italian village. *Widowers' Houses* and *Mrs. Warren's Profession,* dealing with slum landlordism and prostitution, respectively, fit the category of "social problem play" more closely than any of his other plays, and the scenic descriptions are unexpectedly sparse. Shaw describes the seven settings of these two plays with little more than instructions for the relative placement of furniture and properties—in short, ground plans. Can this be reconciled with his detailed description of scenery in other plays: the very books in Morell's library in *Candida,* or the busts, portrait, and photographs in Roebuck Ramsden's study in *Man and Superman*? I think so. Shaw rightly considered himself "A Dramatic Realist" (1, 485). As a realist, he was concerned with the influence of social environment upon his characters, and the influence of his characters upon their social environment. When the homes of his characters could establish a milieu and re-

veal an environment, Shaw used them for that purpose. The settings for
the first two acts of *The Devil's Disciple*—the homes of Mrs. Dudgeon and
Mrs. Anderson—contain the same scenic elements, yet their different arrangements reveal the distinct characters of these women. Since the social
questions that are the subjects of *Widowers' Houses* and *Mrs. Warren's
Profession* concern environments that lie offstage, Shaw did not pay great
attention to the scenic environment that the audience sees.

When the environment is abstract, as in the dream of Hell in *Man and
Superman,* Shaw described no scenery at all. We see *"a man in the void [
. . .] seated, absurdly enough, on nothing"* (2, 632). If an objection be
raised that since the act was written with no thought of performance, this
scenic description should not be taken into account, it could be answered
that the author could then write *precisely* the type of scenic description he
wanted, for he was not constrained to limit himself to the exigencies of the
theater as he knew it. Significantly, when the Court Theatre produced the
Hell scene under Shaw's supervision in 1907, the scenery aimed to simu-
late the void indicated in his stage direction: it consisted of stools covered
with black velvet draperies of the same material.[11]

Shaw's realistic framework contains elements of symbolism. *Arms and
the Man,* for example, deals with the shedding of romantic idealism and
the acquisition of a realistic point of view. The first act shows religious
icons and other paraphernalia of romantic idealism in an aura of romantic
moonlight. The second act, by contrast, presents newly cleaned linen dry-
ing in the sun. The third act takes place in an unromantic library; properties utilized in the opening action are papers and a pen, to compose businesslike, prosaic, military orders.

A symbolic progression also occurs in *Major Barbara,* in which Barbara
and Cusins shed their illusions and acquire a realistic point of view. The
first act takes place in Lady Britomart's home in fashionable Wilton Cres-
cent—an actual London street, whose stately town houses reflect the un-
ostentatious luxury to which the Stevanages are accustomed. In this environment, characters enjoy the benefits of romantic idealism. The second
act takes place in the Salvation Army shelter in West Ham, a slum neighborhood. Here, characters suffer from the economic and political inequi-
ties that allow the characters in the first act to enjoy themselves. The third
act moves to a new location, the factory town of Perivale St. Andrews. It
is a place where work can be done; Undershaft offers Cusins a job, and
Barbara sees that this is where she must work. Clean, efficient, without
frills, the scenery features formidable instruments of power: a cannon, a
shell, and an explosives shed. In this setting, Barbara and Cusins embrace

Undershaft's offer of "reality and [. . .] power" (3, 181). These three scenes, moreover, embody—respectively—Don Juan's descriptions of Hell, earth, and Heaven in the third act of *Man and Superman*. He calls Hell "the home of the unreal and of the seekers for happiness," earth "the home of the slaves of reality," and Heaven "the home of the masters of reality [. . .]." The inhabitants of Hell are insulated against social and political problems. "Here you call your appearance beauty, your emotions love, your sentiments heroism, your aspirations virtue, just as you did on earth; but here there are no hard facts to contradict you [. . .]." Earth is a place "in which men and women play at being heroes and heroines, saints and sinners; but they are dragged down from their fool's paradise by their bodies: hunger and cold and thirst, age and decay and disease, death above all, makes them slaves of reality [. . .]." In Heaven, "you live and work instead of playing and pretending. You face things as they are; you escape nothing but glamor; and your steadfastness and your peril are your glory. If the play still goes on here and on earth, and all the world is a stage, Heaven is at least behind the scenes" (2, 650).[12]

During the second decade of this century, Shaw was still writing realistic plays, but he also began to write fantasies—a practice he continued with greater frequency during the next three decades. Shaw's scenic descriptions show an increasing tendency toward simplification and suggestiveness, although he never completely abandoned realism in scenery or in playwriting. While the décor in the prologue to *Androcles and the Lion* is described simply as "*A jungle path*" (4, 585), other plays have considerably more detail. If it is important for us to understand the environment of the character who lives in the house, Shaw provides realistic scenic descriptions: for example, Captain Shotover's boat-like home in *Heartbreak House* is described in detail; Higgins's laboratory and Mrs. Higgins's drawing room in *Pygmalion* have detailed, contrasting milieus, which provide appropriate visual backgrounds for these characters.

Other plays, however, employ suggestive, simplified scenery. Shaw cited with approval William Morris's contention that "no more was necessary for stage illusion than some distinct conventional symbol, such as a halo for a saint, a crook for a bishop, or, if you liked, a cloak and dagger for the villain, and a red wig for the comedian."[13] In *Saint Joan,* Shaw created a fifteenth-century milieu through scenery as well as dialogue, but he did so by suggestion rather than by naturalistic means. The first scene uses "*a plain strong oak table,*" with chair and stool, and a "*mullioned thirteenth-century window*" with a wooden chest beneath it, to suggest the castle at Vaucouleurs (5, 81). The second scene begins in front of a curtain, which Shaw does not describe. When the curtain is opened, two chairs of state on a dais, a curtained arch behind the dais, and a door evoke the throne room in the castle at Chinon. The third and fourth scenes have still less description: a pennon in the wind indicates *"a patch of ground on the south bank of the silver Loire"* (5, 117), and a table and leather stools suggest *"A tent in the English camp"* (5, 124). In the fifth scene, Shaw uses what he later referred to as "a single pillar of the Gordon Craig type" to evoke the ambulatory in Rheims Cathedral.[14] In the trial scene, a row of arches stands for the *"great stone hall in the castle"* (5, 156), and the Epilogue uses one property to suggest Charles's bedchamber: a canopied bed on a dais. In each of these scenes, one or a few scenic elements symbolize an environment of which they are a part. Shaw's practice in *Saint Joan* harmonizes with the precepts of simplified, suggestive scenery enunciated by the theorists of what was called "the New Stagecraft." His practice in *The Millionairess*, on the other hand, contrasts sharply with these precepts: Sagamore's office and The Pig & Whistle Inn are described in realistic detail. The practices in both plays, however, are consistent with the precept Shaw gave in his review of *The Tempest:* that one should not stage every play in the same way. Although he used simplified scenery more frequently in his later plays, he varied his practice with the requirements of the individual work.

When Shaw directed his own plays, or was at hand when they were produced, he closely supervised their scenic preparations. He drew sketches and plans of the opening act of *Pygmalion,* with detailed instructions. For the 1906 revival of *Captain Brassbound's Conversion,* he sent J. E. Vedrenne photographs to be used as models by the scene painter. One photograph, he instructed, "would do for the missionary's house in Act I. Of course it is a mosque, and impossible for such a purpose; but it is very Moorish; and nobody would know, especially if the decorations were planed off." Another had "the sort of divan seat that is wanted for Act II" as well as "a simple & characteristic design for the tiling, and a good sample of a floor." A third photograph "gives the Koran inscriptions pretty plainly and a very good decorative arch. The window compartments also shew what the smaller door in Act II would be like."[15]

He had sufficient objectivity, however, to recognize when the results were bad. The scenery for the 1912 revival of *John Bull's Other Island,* which he supervised, turned out to be "grotesque: such an orgie of red lengths and pink lines and impossible rostrums covered with obvious old yacht sails died scarlet, such penny theatre wings, were never seen in any theatre." After saying that the sky was "beyond all description," he described it: the scene painter, "stimulated to insane excesses by me, first covered it with flaming vermilion clouds. When he realized that they wouldnt move as at Bayreuth and that the sky had to do for Acts III and IV he tried to paint the clouds out, and now they look like claret stains."[16]

During rehearsals, Shaw took notes on scenery and properties. He reminded the property master that Ramsden's copy of *The Revolutionist's Handbook* should be new; that Ridgeon (*The Doctor's Dilemma*), whose discovery is based on an actual discovery of Sir Almroth Wright, should have for stage use "a real pamphlet from Wright"; that the dummy soldiers which Undershaft kicks aside "must be left more obviously in U's way" and that the shell upon which Sarah sits should have a red band; that in *Fanny's First Play* the piano stool was filthy, the piano needed polishing, and the carpet was too small.[17] As a director, he wanted scenery and properties to be credible, to be appropriate to the character and to the practical needs of the dramatic action, and to have beauty.

When he was not at hand for productions of his own plays, he still tried to supervise the scenery. For the French production of *The Devil's Disciple*, he sent Augustin and Henriette Hamon, his French translators, floor plans and sketches of the scenery, with accompanying instructions in French, explaining how to accomplish quick scene shifts (see Figures 1–5). He also drew (probably on another occasion) a detailed sketch of the fireplace used in Acts I and II, with instructions in English. When the Berlin première of *Cæsar and Cleopatra* was planned, Shaw wrote to Siegfried Trebitsch, "Will you find out for me *at once* what the mechanical resources of the Neues Theater are. All I want to know is, 1 Have they an electric turntable? 2 Have they hydraulic bridges? 3 Have they hydraulic clutches—that is, ropes to draw up weights from above—or is everything pushed up by a piston from below? 4 What is the depth of the stage from the footlights to the back wall & what is its width from side to side? Promise them drawings. I cannot draw; but I can make the painters & carpenters understand what I mean."[18] Since the first act of *Cæsar and Cleopatra* has scene-shifting problems similar to those of the last act of *The Devil's Disciple,* Shaw composed a set of practical instructions for future productions of the play:

> In this act the scenes must be planned so as to enable the changes to be made without any interval, or at most very brief ones with tableau-curtains and continuous music. The sphinx and pyramid, with a back cloth representing the desert, can be ready behind the first scene. In the third, the desert cloth can be taken up; the wall of

the square bay in which the throne stands can be shifted on in front of the Sphinx; the pyramid can be shifted off and the pillar wings on; and the throne and its platform, which should move on castors, can be pushed on. In this way the changes will be found quite practicable on old fashioned stages, where nothing but hand labor is available and the Sphinx cannot be shifted.

When hydraulic or electric machinery is available, the scenery can be improved accordingly; but the stage business should not be altered in such a way to make the dialogue ineffective.

In a similar set of instructions for future directors of *John Bull's Other Island,* he explained that the same back cloth could be used for the three scenes of Acts II and III, and the same raked piece (the hill) for both scenes in Act II, "but in the second scene the stone must be removed, the round tower pushed [on] as a wing, and the scene disguised by the change in the lighting." Since scene changes *"must not occupy more than one minute at the very outside,"* the first scene of Act IV must be shallow and the second scene set behind it. He also warned the scene designer that an Irish round tower does not resemble a ruined medieval castle and that an Irish land agent's house is not a thatched hovel.[19]

When he was in personal communication with the director or the designer, he sent pictures and wrote comments on the scenery. To William Faversham, who directed the United States première of *Getting Married* in 1916, Shaw sent photographs of the original production, commenting that he himself had designed the scenery.[20] Faversham also directed the United States première of *Misalliance* the following year. Since Shaw had no photographs of the original production, he drew and sent a ground plan and perspective sketch to Faversham (see Figures 6 and 7).

Like his blocking instructions, Shaw's scenic instructions were detailed, but they left room for the designer's creativity. Although he gave scene designer Lee Simonson minute instructions on Captain Shotover's home, including a sketch, he also pointed out, "So long as you do not alter or mask the positions of my people on the stage, or cut out an essential effect like the cutting off of the light and leaving the group in the dark, you may do the job in your own way. The more of your own you put in, the richer the play will be. [. . .] [L]et yourself rip. Artist and author are co-equal and co-eternal—see the Athanasian creed." Simonson complimented the scenic instructions in Shaw's stage directions for this play. The entrances, exits, and furniture, he said, "are perfectly placed for the playing of the entire first act. The movements and the groupings of actors take place

Figures 1–5. Sketches, plans, and instructions sent by Shaw to Augustin Hamon, his French translator, on five cards, in 1922, for a French production of *The Devil's Disciple*; the play was not produced in Paris until 1926. Except for the word "buanderie" (washhouse) (Figure 1), the writing is in Shaw's hand.

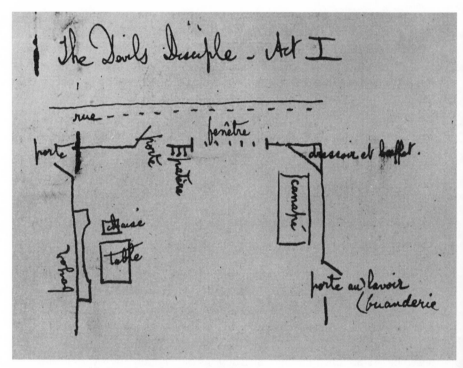

Figure 1. Ground plan of Act I, *The Devil's Disciple*. On stage right, left of the drawing of a fireplace, is "foyer" (fireside), before which are a "chaise" (chair) and a "table." Upstage right is the "porte" (door). On the upstage wall is another "porte," leading outside to the "rue" (street), seen through the "fenêtre" (window). Between them is a "patère" (a block on the wall with pegs for hats and coats). Upstage left contains a "dressoir et buffet" (sideboard and cupboard). Further downstage is a "canapé" (sofa), and below it a "porte au lavoir" (door to the scullery).

Figure 2. Perspective sketch of Act I, *The Devil's Disciple*.

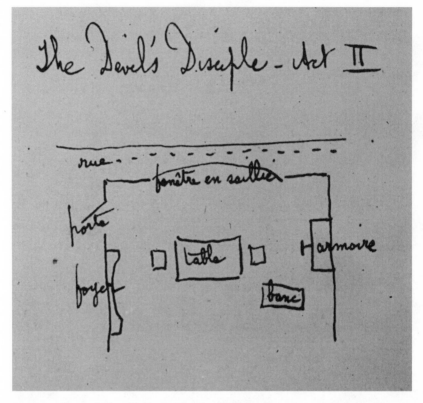

Figure 3. Ground plan of Act II, *The Devil's Disciple.* Stage right has a "foyer," upstage of which is a "porte." The upstage wall has a "fenêtre en saillie" (bay window), through which we see the "rue." Stage left has an "armoire" (wardrobe). Chairs flank both sides of the "table" at stage center, downstage left of which is a "banc" (settle).

The Devils Disciple. Act II

Figure 4. Perspective sketch of Act II, *The Devil's Disciple.* On stage right is the fireplace, upstage the bay window, and on stage left the "armoire avec Anderson's [*sic*] habit noir suspendu a [*sic*] la cheville" (wardrobe with Anderson's black clothes hanging on the peg [Shaw draws a coat]).

- The 'Devil' Disciple'. Act III —

— grande chaise pour le Président .

— chaises (les bancs sont pour les officiers de l'état major).

→ décor final — De marche , avec marcan , église etc .

porte

banc — table pour le conseil de guerre — banc

couleur

☑ ☑

→ Troisième décor - rideaux drapés de velours rouge avec monogramme R.R.
(Georges Rex) en ... Montez les rideaux et écartez les meubles au plus vite possible .
L'intervalle ne doit excéder 45 secondes .

→ Premier décor , un couleur . Un simple rideau suffira . Sans meubles . Monter
un escalier a la fin sans intervalle .

Il faut absolument avoir les trois décors en place avant le lever de rideau , et jouer l'acte entier
d'un seul trait sans intervalles .

A. HAMON

TY AN DIAOUL

Figure 5. Plan of Act III, *The Devil's Disciple*. Scenes 1, 2, and 3 are separated by curtains. Beneath the plan, Shaw writes, "Il faut absolument avoir les trois décors en place avant le lever de rideau, et jouer l'acte d'un seul trait sans intervalles" ("It is absolutely necessary to have the three sets in place before the curtain rises, and to play the act in one stretch, without breaks).

Downstage is the first set, a "couloir" (lobby). To the side of the plan, Shaw writes, "premier décor, un couloir. Un simple rideau suffice. Sans meubles. Montez ou écartez a [*sic*] la fin sans intervalle" (first set, a lobby. A simple curtain will suffice. Without furniture. Raise or separate [the curtain] at the end without a break."

Above this, writes Shaw to the side, is the "deuxième décor—rideaux drapés de velours rouge avec monogramme G.R. (Georges Rex) en or. Montez les rideaux et écartez les meubles au plus vite possible. L'intervalle ne doit excède 45 secondes" (second set—red velour curtains with monogram G.R. [George Rex] in gold. Raise the curtain and strike the furniture as quickly as possible. The time break should not exceed 45 seconds). On the set, stage right has a "porte." At stage center is a "table pour le conseil de guerre" (table for the court martial), each side of which has a "banc" (bench). Above the table is a "grande chaise pour le president [*sic*]" (large chair for the presiding officer)." On stage left are two "chaises (les bancs sont pour les officiers de l'etat [*sic*] major [*sic*]" (chairs [the benches are for the officers of the general staff]).

Upstage, Shaw writes on the side, is the "décor final . . . la marché, avec maisons, église &c." (final set . . . the procession, with houses, church &c). At upstage right and left are "Maisons." Up right center is the "potence" (gallows).

Figures 6 and 7. Ground plan and perspective sketch of *Misalliance,* sent by Shaw to William Faversham for his 1917 production in the United States. The writing is in Shaw's hand.

Figure 6. Ground Plan of *Misalliance.*

At the top of the page, partly torn, is "[BACK CLOTH]," "SURREY HILL LANDSCAPE IN SUM[MER]." At the foot of the page is "Misalliance. Plan of Scene."

The upper left corner has: "The gramophone (invisible) is supposed to be here, and the track of the aeroplane is supposed to be from P. to O.P. [stage right to stage left]." Behind the "GLASS WALL OF PAVILION," which contains a "GARDEN DOOR," are three clusters of "Rhododendrons." Below the glass wall, in addition to the what the capital letters make clear, the small script says, "Gramophone" and "Flamboyant Crockery or statues ad lib. (not necessary)." Both wicker chairs are "afterwards moved to Y."

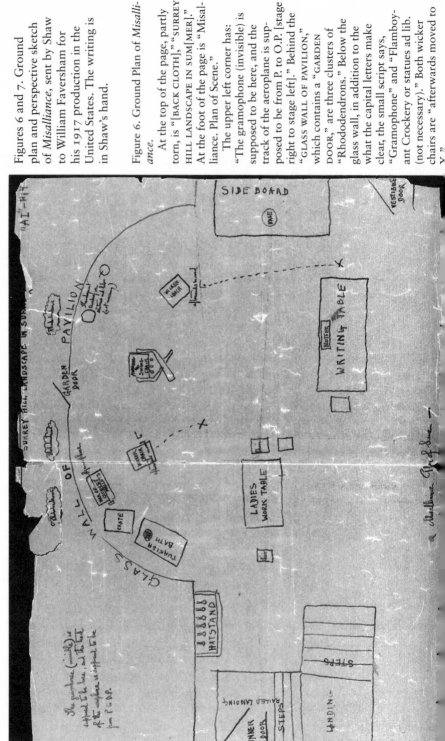

(by Shaw) of *Misalliance*.

At the foot of the page, below a drawing of the bottom of a curtain, Shaw writes, "Misalliance. Scene in perspective, shewing the doors."

Upstage center: "GREAT GLASS PAVILION through which is seen a distant landscape of fir clad Surrey hills, and, in the foreground, a garden—not a formal terraced garden, but 'A [illegible] garden,' with clumps of rhododendrons in flower. This is the centre of light and must make a pretty picture. The interior must be quiet in tone and not fussy, to give the necessary relief." The center aperture is a "garden door."

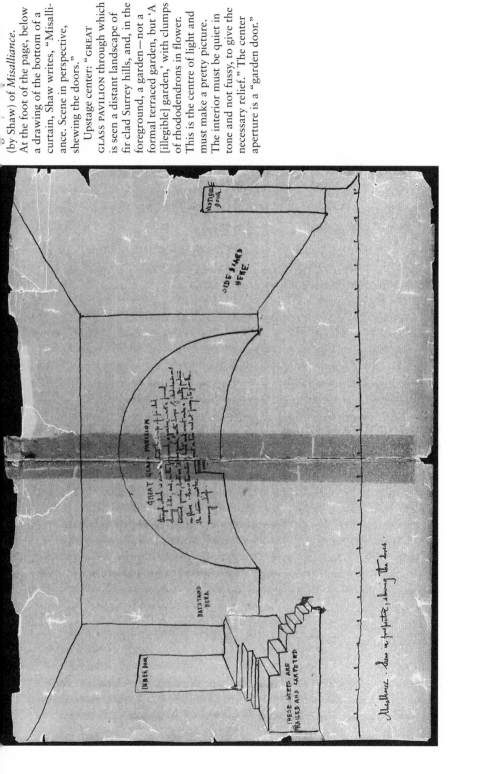

easily, naturally, almost inevitably, as I realized when the play was put into rehearsal. The two window seats specified seem mere interior decoration until the second act, when for the scene with the burglar the cast of ten fills the stage. The window seat with its nautical lockers below takes the place of all the additional chairs or a couch that would otherwise have to be lugged on for this single scene or clutter up the stage and get in the actors' way for the rest of the time." Shaw, Simonson continued, had "made the setting, with its galleon windows and its nautical beaming—an enlarged captain's cabin—a symbol of the meaning of the play, which is itself a symbol of the fate of a floundering ship of stage. This is exactly what an imaginative designer should have done if the stage directions had been nothing more than 'Captain Shotover's study in his Sussex county home.'"[21]

Lighting

"If I had never been taught to use my eyes as a critic of pictures," Shaw wrote in his review of *The Prisoner of Zenda* in 1896, "I might, perhaps, have been satisfied with the sunset scene in the forest of Zenda [. . .]." Shaw had more than an art critic's eyes: he had a practical knowledge of stage lighting techniques. As early as 1894, he was able not only to diagnose what was wrong but to prescribe a remedy as well. Reviewing *Die Walküre* that year, he suggested blowing up the person responsible for lighting the stage because "a rock in the foreground, supposed to be illuminated by the sun overhead, throws a strong black shadow *upwards* on a rock behind which is higher than itself; and [. . .] this system of black shadows is carried out through the whole scene, destroying all effects of distance, and making the stage look like a mere store room for dingy canvases"; instead, this person should have "seen that there were sufficient lights placed on the floor between each set of rocks to overcome the shadow from the footlights and to make the back of the stage looks five miles away from the front." Throughout his theater reviews, Shaw attacked old fashioned lighting practices—berating one director, for instance, for modeling his technique on a style of scene painting based on gas illumination instead of making full use of the electric lighting facilities at his disposal.[22]

Shaw kept abreast of developments in stage lighting. In 1905, he called Gordon Craig's design of Ibsen's *The Vikings in Helgeland* "very instructive as to the possibility of doing away with the eternal [. . .] footlight illumination which [is] so destructive of stage illusion [. . .]." That same year, he said that the dream scene of *Man and Superman* should be staged "with top lighting in the manner of Craig [. . .]." A dozen years later, he commented that footlighting and top lighting were equally bad and suggested that the main source of illumination should be the front of the house. In an article supporting the Theatre Guild's fund drive for a new theater, he urged that "the stage lighting should be modern, and if possible planned by persons who have never seen footlights and wonder what on earth they can have been when they read about them in books."[23]

In his own plays, Shaw used lighting to enhance both theme and theatricality. During the second act of *Mrs. Warren's Profession,* after Mrs. Warren has won Vivie over with her story of what poverty means, Vivie "*opens the cottage door, and finds that it is broad moonlight.*" Enchanted by the beauty of the night, "*She draws aside the curtains of the window. The landscape is seen bathed in the radiance of the harvest moon rising over Blackdown.*" The act ends with this beautiful, romantic moonlight filling the stage, an ironic comment on the new comradeship between mother and daughter. The next act begins the following morning, "*with the sun shining from a cloudless sky,*" underlining Vivie's new state of mind (1, 316–17). When the Devil takes the Statue below in the third act of *Man and Superman,* they stand on the grave trap. "*It begins to descend slowly. Red glow from the abyss.*" The Statue reminisces, "Ah, this reminds me of old times." Ana cries, "Stop!" The trap stops partway down, the red glow illuminating the three—as in the "old times"—while Ana talks to them briefly (2, 689). The Epilogue to *Saint Joan* uses projections to enhance the spectacle: "*A vision of the statue in Winchester Cathedral is seen through the window,*" and soon afterward, "*A vision of the statue before Rheims Cathedral appears.*" When Joan asks whether she shall rise from the dead and return, there is sudden darkness: only the bed and the figure are visible in silhouette against the light outside the window. At the end of the play, as the clock strikes midnight, "*The last remaining rays of light gather into a white radiance descending on Joan*" while she delivers the final lines: "O God that madest this beautiful earth, when will it be ready to receive Thy saints? How long, O Lord, how long?" (6, 205, 208). The aura illuminating Joan at the end of the play creates a beautiful stage effect and at the same time underscores the play's theme, for she is visually alone, set off even from the stage setting.

Shaw's rehearsal notes include the routine, mechanical details of lighting. During rehearsals of *Heartbreak House,* he observed that when the curtain rose the lights came up too late and came from the wrong source. A note for *You Never Can Tell* indicates that the front of the stage was too dark; in *Misalliance* there was "not enough light on the centre clump of flowers." For the first act of *Arms and the Man,* he wrote that the faces of Raina and Catherine were "absolutely in the dark," that when Louka opened the door the passage outside was lighter than the stage, that when Raina lit a candle the electrician should cheat on the light, sneaking up more illumination than the actual candle would give, and that he should not distractingly change light settings while a scene was in progress: "Dont fool with the lights: if they are not right, leave them so."[24]

When others produced his plays, Shaw advised on the stage lighting. The arc light in the final act of *Heartbreak House,* he admitted to Lee Simonson, who was to design the play for the Theatre Guild, bothered him from the start. At first, he thought of having a white globe throw a circle of light on the stage floor, "so that the characters could, as directed, disappear into the surrounding darkness and emerge into the radiance. But, as you say, if you put even a candle in a dark scene the audience can see nothing else." Since the action called for a visible light that could be visibly extinguished, he thought that Simonson would have to shade the light by draping it ornamentally or putting a green shade around it so as to conceal the actual glare, but do the real lighting from offstage. "The flagstaff is only an excuse for something characteristic to attach the cable which feeds the arc light. All these things are suggestions and makeshifts."[25]

Costume

In a review of *Romeo and Juliet,* Shaw quoted a program credit that Mrs. Patrick Campbell's dresses "'have been carried out by Mrs Mason, of New Burlington Street,'" and commented, "I wish they had been carried out and buried. [. . .] I can only excuse the Lyceum Juliet costumes on the supposition that Mrs Campbell deliberately aimed at suggesting by them the tutelage of a girl of fourteen who is not yet allowed to choose her own dresses." This quotation is typical of his remarks on costume in his theater and opera reviews. In the same review, he enunciated one of his major dissatisfactions with costuming in the British theater: "I am [. . .] not surprised to find the dresses at the Lyceum, though handsome and expensive, chastened by the taste of a British gentleman; so that the stalls can contemplate the XIV century and yet feel at home there [. . .]." He denounced actors and actresses who were "little more than walking fashion plates. The actor, in particular, with his carefully ironed new trousers, and his boots conscientiously blacked on the sole underneath the arch of the foot, is a curiously uncomfortable spectacle. [. . .] I have gradually come to regard the leading man in a play as a set of applied tailor's measurements; so that [. . .] the clothes have usurped the men's place." It is pleasant, said Shaw, to look "at a woman who is characteristically dressed by herself, or affectionately and beautifully dressed by an artist; but fashionable ladies hung with the trophies of their tradesmen are among my strongest aversions [. . .]."26

Prudery in women's costumes was another aversion. It is "quite impossible to feel a ray of illusion," Shaw wrote on one occasion, while looking at a Bayreuth Brünhild (*Die Walküre*) climbing the mountains "with her legs carefully hidden in a long white skirt [. . .]." To ask the Rhine maidens (*Das Rheingold*) to dress like Rhine maidens might be going too far, he suggested on another occasion, for "The world is not decent enough for that yet." But he wondered whether it were necessary for them "to go to the other extreme and swim about in muslin *fichus* and tea-gowns?"27

Still another pet aversion was a hodge-podge, that is, an absence of artistic costuming. In a production of *Marta*, which takes place at the time of Queen Anne and has her as a character, the ladies were "in early Victorian Archery Club dresses, the Queen's retinue in the costume of feudal retainers of the Plantagenet period, the comic lord as Sir Peter Teazle, the noblemen in tunics and tights from Il Trovatore, and the peasants with huge Bavarian hats beneath their shoulders, reminding one of the men in Othello's yarns." In a production of *All's Well That Ends Well,* "The dresses were the usual fancy ball odds and ends, Helena especially distinguishing herself by playing the first scene partly in the costume of Hamlet and partly in that of a waitress in an Aerated Bread Shop [. . .]."28 Such rag-bag costuming was not uncommon.

The major considerations of the costumer, according to Shaw, should be appropriateness to character, social position, situation in the play, and atmosphere. Of a Bayreuth production of Wagner's *Siegfried,* he wrote that the costume of the title character "is hardly to be described without malice. Imagine an XVIII century bank clerk living in a cave, with fashionable sandals and cross garters, an elegant modern classic tunic, a Regent-street bearskin, and a deportment only to be learnt in quadrilles. Or, rather, do not imagine it; but pray that I, who have seen the reality, may not be haunted by it in my dreams. He needed only a tinderbox instead of a furnace, and a patent knife-cleaning machine instead of an anvil, to make him complete." Realistic costuming is mandatory in Ibsen's dramas, and when reviewing them, Shaw paid special attention to costuming. The "reckless garments" worn by Nora Helmer, he noted, were "impossible for a snobbish bank manager's wife." In *Rosmersholm,* by contrast, Kroll was not dressed well enough: "I know Kroll by sight perfectly well (was he not for a long time chairman of the London School Board?); and I am certain he would die sooner than pay a visit to the rector in a coat and trousers which would make a superannuated coffee-stall keeper feel apologetic [. . .]."[29]

Although Shaw attacked the absence of appropriateness and artistry in stage costuming, he did not neglect to praise them when they were present. In William Poel's production of *Doctor Faustus,* Baliol and Belcher "were not theatrical devils with huge pasteboard heads, but pictorial Temptation-of-St-Anthony devils such as Martin Schongauer drew. The angels were Florentine XV century angels, with their draperies sewn into Botticellian folds and tucks. The Emperor's bodyguard had Maximilianesque uniforms copied from Holbein. Mephistophilis made his first appearance as Mr Joseph Pennell's favorite devil from the roof of Notre Dame [. . .]." The Seven Deadly Sins were the most *fin de siècle* things in existence (*"tout ce qu'il y a de plus fin de siècle"*). "In short," Shaw concluded, "Mr William Poel gave us an artistic rather than a literal presentation of Elizabethan conditions, the result being, as always happens in such cases, that the picture of the past was really a picture of the future. For the which he is, in my judgment, to be highly praised." On another occasion, Shaw compared Poel's costuming with that of commercial directors who had more money and less imagination: "our ordinary managers have simply been patronizing the conventional costumier's business in a very expensive way, whilst Mr Poel has achieved artistic originality, beauty, and novelty of effect, as well as the fullest attainable measure of historical conviction."[30]

Although Shaw was certainly interested in costume, the printed editions of his plays do not have as much costume detail as one might expect. In *The Doctor's Dilemma,* Jennifer's first-act costume is not described at all: Shaw merely notes that Ridgeon *"has an impression that she is very well dressed; but she has a figure on which any dress would look well"*; in the second act, we are told only that she is *"wrapped up for departure"*; in the third, she wears a cardinal's robe and hat while modeling for Dubedat but then removes the robe to reveal *"a plain frock of tussore silk"*; in the fourth, *"She wears a nurse's apron"* and in the fifth she is *"beautifully dressed"* (3, 353, 361, 380, 410, 426). Shaw was not always so sparing of detail. See, for example, the costume of The Strange Lady in *The Man of Destiny: "She is not, judging by her dress, an admirer of the latest fashions of the Directory; or perhaps she uses up her old dresses for travelling. At all events she wears no jacket with extravagant lappels, no Greco-Tallien sham chiton, nothing, indeed, that the Princesse de Lamballe might not have worn. Her dress of flowered silk is long waisted, with a Watteau plait behind, but with the paniers reduced to mere rudiments, as she is too tall for them. It is cut low in the neck, where it is eked out by a creamy fichu"* (1, 622–23). With several costumes from which to choose, Shaw selected the most delicate and feminine, thereby ensuring the greatest contrast when The Strange Lady dons a soldier's uniform. Without the explicit stage direction, a costumer might select the businesslike *"jacket with extravagant lappels,"* a reasonable choice for a travelling costume, but less feminine than the low-cut, long-waisted, flowered silk dress, and less theatrically effective.

Shaw was equally adept at describing inelegant dress. In the first act of *Pygmalion*, Liza *"wears a little sailor hat of black straw that has long been exposed to the dust and soot of London and has seldom if ever been brushed. [. . .] She wears a shoddy black coat that reaches nearly to her knees and is shaped to her waist. She has a brown skirt with a coarse apron. Her boots are much the worse for wear."* In the second act, *"She has a hat with three ostrich feathers, orange, sky-blue, and red. She has a nearly clean apron, and the shoddy coat has been tidied a little"* (4, 671, 687). These costume descriptions reveal a great deal about the character and the situation. In the first act, we see the results of Liza's unhygienic habits and poverty: her coat is shoddy, her shoes worn out, and her filthy hat may never have been cleaned at all. Her notion of dressing up for a special occasion, we see in the costume description for Act II, consists of wearing cheap, gaudy accessories and cleaning up only somewhat. Her efforts to dress up are both comic and pathetic, for she knows no better. During the play, she learns not only diction but dress and deportment, and her later cleanliness is all the more striking because of the early dirtiness. Her costumes are visual accompaniments to the play's theme.

When it was appropriate, Shaw also described characteristic men's costumes. Marchbanks enters in the first act of *Candida* with apparel that Shaw called *"anarchic. He wears an old blue serge jacket, unbuttoned, over a woollen lawn tennis shirt, with a silk handkerchief for a cravat, trousers matching the jacket, and brown canvas shoes. In these garments he has apparently lain in the heather and waded through the waters; and there is no evidence of his having ever brushed them"* (1, 535). Apollodorus, in *Cæsar and Cleopatra*, is aestheticism personified, apparently as *fin de siècle* as William Poel's Seven Deadly Sins. He is *"dressed with deliberate æstheticism in the most delicate purples and dove greys, with ornaments of bronze, oxydized silver, and stones of jade and agate. His sword, designed as carefully as a medieval cross, has a blued blade shewing through an openwork scabbard of purple leather and filagree.*" Marchbanks's clothes indicate the Bohemian poet, Apollodorus's the devotee of "Art for Art's sake," which Apollodorus claims as his motto (2, 225–26).

While Shaw's textual commentaries were generally sparse, he made up for it in his personal dealings with actors, directors, and costumers. In *Fanny's First Play,* Count O'Dowda is described as wearing costumes "*a hundred years out of date*" and his nineteen-year-old daughter is in attire "*synchronous with her father's*" (4, 351, 361). Shaw explained his general idea to Charles Ricketts, who was designing costumes for this play.

> Now one of the Count's repudiations of modern civilization takes the form of refusing to wear modern dress because it is ugly. When he appears in the Induction simply in front of a black tableau curtain, he may wear any dress of any country and any period or of no country and no period, provided it dates before 1830. I vaguely conceived him as a Venetian eighteenth century *père noble*, somewhere between Guardi and Goya, but I was utterly unable to reduce this conception to anything definite. [. . .]
>
> Then there is the daughter. She is to be played by Christine Silver, who has a very slim pretty girlish figure of the Canova sort. I had an idea of making her one of those *fillettes* that one sees on French eighteenth-century crockery of the most elegant pre-revolutionary period; but though I rushed through the Wallace Collection and then through the Victoria and Albert Museum, from one end to the other, I could not find a single specimen of what I wanted.[31]

When directing a production, Shaw was compelled to be precise—even to the point of drawing costume sketches for *Arms and the Man* (see Figures 8–10). "Dont muddle about mid-Victorian costumes," he advised Molly Tompkins, who was to appear in *You Never Can Tell;* "take the exact year (1895?) and look up the volumes of *Punch* for that year: the DuMaurier pictures will give you the fashions."[32] In *Captain Brassbound's Conversion,* Lady Cicely dresses as she would in Surrey and does not wear a tailor-made tourist's costume because "she is too conventional to regard dress as a wholly adaptable-to-circumstances matter. She would wear petticoats & drawers, just as she would say her prayers, for half a century after all the working women in the country would have taken to knickerbockers & agnosticism." Shaw provided Granville Barker with a list of costumes and costume accessories for *The Admirable Bashville,* including "A gorgeous livery with tags, plush smalls, calves, and a heavily

powdered wig for Bashville. The wig is important, as when he says O
Bathos! in his great soliloquy he must strike his head & send up a cloud of
powder from it." He suggested that Barker borrow one of painter Neville
Lytton's thoroughly dirtied old painting smocks to wear as Dubedat in
The Doctor's Dilemma. The Beadle's costume in *Getting Married* "must
not be a comic one out of sketches by Boz. A modern Borough Council
Beadle is rather like a fashionable music hall chucker-out. The cocked hat
still exists; and there is a short caped Inverness with gold braid; but the rest
is an immaculate frock coat and trousers with gold braid and stripe down
the leg [. . .]. The mace may be ad lib." In the first scene of *Saint Joan,*
Baudricourt and Poulengey "should be in half armor and be obviously
soldiers and not merchants. This is important, as it strikes the note of
France in war time." Poulengey's "coat should not be belted [as it was
in the Theatre Guild production]. Baudricourt should be smart, a *beau
sabreur.*"[33]

Shaw's rehearsal notes regarding costumes sometimes merely expressed
dissatisfaction. For instance, he called Mrs. Clandon's costume "appal-
lingly wrong—dress contradicts her part." Sometimes, his notes either
explicitly stated or implied the remedy. Gunner should have a "celluloid
collar." Ann Whitefield must "have a hat—she looks too old. ?flowers
in hair or at waist." Bluntschli's uniform was "not torn enough." Liza's
dressing gown should have been blue and white, and smaller.[34]

Clearly, Shaw did not neglect costuming, but rather paid a great deal of
attention to it. He researched historical costumes and on some occasions
gave detailed descriptions of them. In a few instances, he carefully described modern costumes. Although his printed specifications on dress
are, for the most part, far less precise than his descriptions of scenery, they
are adequate guides to the costumer who must provide a specific actress
(or actor) with attractive or unattractive, but (in either case) characteristic
clothing, the selection of which can vary greatly from one actress to the
next, for what will enhance one actress's beauty may very well tear down
another's. As a director, however, with particular individuals to costume,
Shaw was exact.

Make-Up

As a director, Shaw scrutinized make-up (including wigs), for he knew its
value in convincing the audience of the reality of the character. Most of his
statements on this subject are characteristically pragmatic and concern the
make-up of an individual actor or actress. As an opera and theater critic,

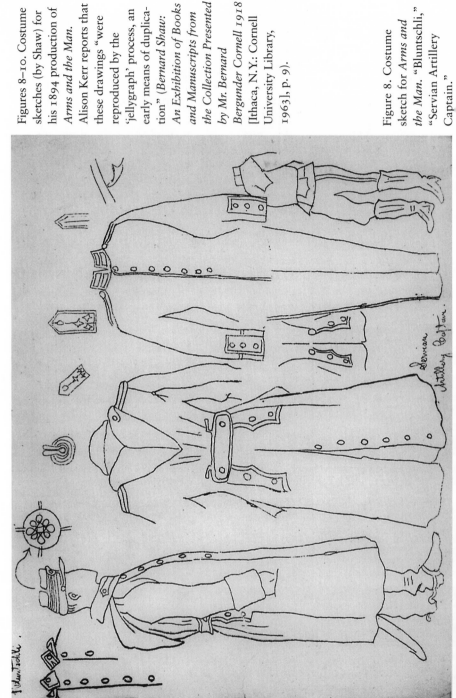

Figures 8–10. Costume sketches (by Shaw) for his 1894 production of *Arms and the Man*. Alison Kerr reports that these drawings "were reproduced by the 'jellygraph' process, an early means of duplication" (*Bernard Shaw: An Exhibition of Books and Manuscripts from the Collection Presented by Mr. Bernard Bergunder Cornell 1918* [Ithaca, N.Y.: Cornell University Library, 1963], p. 9).

Figure 8. Costume sketch for *Arms and the Man.* "Bluntschli," "Servian Artillery Captain."

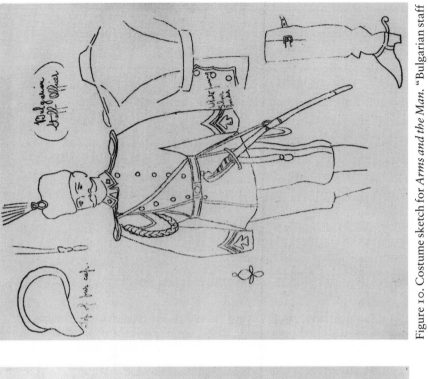

Figure 10. Costume sketch for *Arms and the Man.* "Bulgarian staff officer." Upper left: "Top of fur cap." To right of left arm: "White facing," "Silver border."

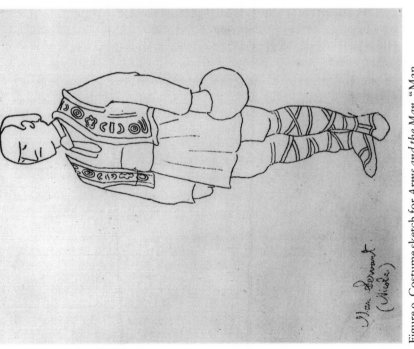

Figure 9. Costume sketch for *Arms and the Man.* "Man Servant (Nicola)."

Shaw pointed out those instances where the make-up spoiled the dramatic illusion. He recalled having seen Céleste "as the heroine of a melodrama in which she was eighteen in the first act, thirty in the second, forty in the third, sixty in the fourth, and eighty in the fifth; after which I came away wondering how old Madame really was, as she had looked like a made-up old woman in the early stages, and like a made-up young woman in the later ones, never by any chance presenting a convincing appearance of being near the age indicated by the dramatist." When Wilson Barrett appeared in *The Sign of the Cross,* he neglected to wear an appropriate wig. Instead of the cropped Roman hairdo, "he wears his own hair in his old familiar feminine fashion, with the result that when he first steps on the stage he presents such an amazing resemblance to Miss Victor that, instead of applauding him, I stared with a shocked conviction that I had that lady before me in the costume of a Roman warrior."[35]

During productions of his own plays, he attended closely to the make-up. He told Janet Achurch, who had recently become a blonde, that in order to play Candida she must immediately

> send for a barber, and have your head shaved absolutely bald. Then get a brown wig, of the natural color of your own hair. Candida with gold hair is impossible. Further, you must not be fringy or fluffy. Send to a photograph shop for a picture of some Roman bust—say that of Julia, daughter of Augustus and wife of Agrippa, from the Uffizi in Florence—and take that as your model, or rather as your point of departure. You must part your hair in the middle, and be sweet, sensible, comely, dignified, and Madonna like. If you condescend to the vulgarity of being a pretty woman, much less a flashy one [. . .] you are lost.

For Elder Daniels in *The Shewing-up of Blanco Posnet,* he suggested "an Abraham Lincoln get-up." For the Dauphin in *Saint Joan,* the wig should be modeled on a portrait of the real Dauphin, which demonstrates that "his hair was completely concealed by the fashion of the time, giving him a curiously starved and bald appearance that would be very effective on the stage."[36]

As a director of his own plays, Shaw realized that the make-up could assist or spoil the dramatic illusion. His rehearsal notes contain practical suggestions on make-up. When Higgins calls Liza "so horribly dirty," Shaw asked Mrs. Patrick Campbell, "How can [he] say that to such a make-up?" He noted that Broadbent's make-up was too young, and that Mrs. Higgins's was too old. Lord Summerhays, he suggested, needed a "touch of pink in the make-up." He advised the Raina of 1911 that her left eyebrow was ragged, and the Raina of 1919 that the rouge on her cheeks should continue up to her eyes.[37] Hairpieces, too, came under Shaw's scrutiny: he noted that in *Man and Superman,* "Malone's wig [was] too short," that in *Heartbreak House,* Shotover might have "whiskers like Ibsen," and that in *Cæsar and Cleopatra,* Britannus "must have Dundreary whiskers—yellow whiskers." His "wig, moustache, and whiskers can all be made on a frame which he can put on like a helmet: it cannot be stuck on with spirit gum."[38] In short, Shaw not only gave his attention to the make-up of the actors, he also had enough practical knowledge of make-up to be able to specify a remedy when he noted a shortcoming.

Music

As one would expect of a director who had been a music critic, Shaw was precise about the employment of music in plays. He deplored Augustin Daly's use of music in *Twelfth Night* as "a curious example of the theatrical tradition that any song written by Shakespear is appropriate to any play written by him, except, perhaps, the play in which it occurs." Insisting on the appropriateness of the music to the play, to the situation, and, if sung, to both the character who sings it and to his audience, Shaw derided as an "absurdity" the opening scene of the production: "the entry of all the lodging-house keepers (as I presume) on the seacoast of Illyria to sing Ariel's song from The Tempest, Come unto these yellow sands." "On the other hand," said Shaw, "the introduction of the serenade from Cymbeline at the end of the third act, with Who is Sylvia? altered to Who's Olivia? seems to me to be quite permissible, as it is neither an interpolation nor an alteration, but a pure interlude, and a very attractive one [. . .]." In Daly's production of *Two Gentlemen of Verona,*

> the most horribly common music repeatedly breaks out on the slightest pretext or on no pretext at all. One dance, set to a crude old English popular tune, sundry XVIII and XIX century musical banalities, and a titivated plantation melody in the first act which produces an indescribably atrocious effect by coming in behind the scenes as a sort of coda to Julia's curtain speech, all turn the play [. . .] into a vaudeville. Needless to add, the accompaniments are not played on lutes and viols, but by the orchestra and a guitar or two. In the forest scene the outlaws begin the act by a chorus. After their encounter

with Valentine they go off the stage singing the refrain exactly in the style of La Fille de Madame Angot.

Shaw called this "wanton absurdity."[39]

When he asked for music in his plays, he was exact, specifying such works as *Don Giovanni* and Gounod's *Faust* for the Hell scene of *Man and Superman,* "Keep the Home Fires Burning" as the bombs fall in *Heartbreak House,* "Oh, Won't You Come Home, Bill Bailey?" (sung by a chorus of angels) in *Passion, Poison, and Petrifaction,* and a march adapted from the Wedding Chorus in Donizetti's *Lucia di Lammermoor* as Barbara's heart is breaking in the second act of *Major Barbara.*

On a few occasions, he gave instructions regarding instrumentation. In the prefatory note to *Passion, Poison, and Petrifaction,* he specified an orchestra of "at least a harp, a drum, and a pair of cymbals" (3, 203). And he was precise in instructions to directors of *Cæsar and Cleopatra:*

> The sound of the bucina and the trumpet calls must not, even at hopelessly third rate provincial representations, be represented by hackneyed flourishes on the cornet. A trombone for the bucina and a couple of cavalry trumpets can always be procured with a little trouble. Where proper arrangements can be made, as in London, by the conductor of the orchestra, he should be empowered to specially engage a few players who can handle the long trumpet. [. . .] Perhaps the best instrument to represent the bucina is the ophicleide, which gives a peculiar bullock-like bellow, but as it is hard to find ophicleide players now-a-days, the bombardon (E flat tuba—or B flat, if one can be got) is likely to be the practicable alternative. A powerful low note from such an instrument, answered by a flourish on an alto trombone, and leading to several ringing high notes from the long trumpets, would be the sort of thing for the alarums. On no account should a cornet be heard on the stage.[40]

When Shaw prepared the first production of *The Dark Lady of the Sonnets,* he called for music at several points:

> 1. A prelude to take up the curtain and exhibit the sky and the warder. My notion is simply a long sustained mysterious note on the bassoon and the Westminster chimes presently played in single notes by the harp, which will finally strike the hour on its lowest E (I think Big Ben is in E). The music stops when the Warder challenges Shakespear. 2. A shimmering from the fiddles when the light heralds Elizabeth, continuing more or less until she wakes, when it stops abruptly.

3. I am not quite sure about this; but there might be some music when the Dark Lady enters, rising rapidly to a climax and breaking off when she boxes their ears. 4. The Westminster chimes again as at first at the end, as Shakespear is led off by the Warder. [. . .] I shall get the Warder on to lead Shakespear off whilst Elizabeth retires in to her original ray of light. In short, a very quiet "Exeunt severally" — stealing off to mysterious music.[41]

When Shaw used an orchestra, he took care that it did not alter his plans. After attending a performance of *Annajanska,* he asked Lillah McCarthy, who played the title role, "What is the matter with the band? [. . .] [W]hy on earth dont they give the last 13 bars of the overture at the end full crash instead of piffling as they do?"[42]

In summation, to say that Shaw did not pay much attention to the technical side of play production is inaccurate. Vitally concerned with this aspect of theater, he knew that obvious make-up, inadequate lighting, makeshift scenery, inappropriate music, and the like, could destroy any illusion of reality that the author and actors might otherwise create. Detesting clichés, shoddy execution, and lack of credibility in stage scenery, lighting, and costuming, Shaw aimed for beauty, harmony, illusion, and appropriateness to the play's themes, moods, and characters. Moreover, he kept up with new developments in scene design and lighting, drawing upon those that he found useful. "Art is one and indivisable," he said to Ellen Terry when he tried to impress upon her the importance of stage scenery. The statement might serve as a Shavian maxim. For Shaw the director, art was indeed a unified, indivisible entity. He worried about the lighting plot and the eyebrow pencil as he worried about a line reading, for he understood that all are components in the total art of the theater, and all are the province of the director, who employs them in his efforts to realize the play on the stage.

7 The Business of Theater

Shaw was a complete "man of the theater," a director and playwright who involved himself in every aspect of theatrical activity—including finances, promotion and publicity, and even front-of-house operations. Our study should therefore consider him in relation to these aspects.

In his preface to William Archer's *The Theatrical "World" of 1894,* Shaw wrote that "the art of the theatre is as dependent on its business as a poet's genius is on his bread and butter."[1] Shaw himself was an astute businessman. According to Lawrence Langner, every time Shaw and the Theatre Guild had a difference about a business matter, "he almost invariably turned out to be right."[2]

Shaw's wealth (by the time of his death he had amassed over a million dollars) was partially a result of his absolute refusal to sell or assign his copyrights. To producers and publishers, he granted only licenses for fixed periods of time. If he suspected his rights were being violated by surreptitious performances of his work, or by pirated editions, he ascertained whether this were the case, and, if so, retaliated with every legal means at his disposal.

His first job—for the Dublin firm of Uniacke Townshend and Company—included handling large sums of money and keeping accounts of receipts and expenditures. The business skills acquired there served him throughout his life. He kept careful records of all his financial transactions and the laws relating to these transactions—no small undertaking, since national boundaries were crossed. He maintained records of weekly and sometimes daily gross receipts, as well as his author's share, on all of his plays that were being performed on several continents. These figures were in pounds, shillings, and even pence. After Charlotte Payne-Townshend married Shaw, she took charge of his ledgers, and later a secretary performed this task, but Shaw carefully examined the ledgers.[3] "An author should always have these [box office] returns," he explained to Siegfried Trebitsch, "not only to check the accounts, but to be able to follow the history of his play—whether it is getting more or less popular, whether it is gaining with the gallery and losing with the stalls (so as to shew the class of people it appeals to), and also to be able to shew them to managers in making fresh contracts as proof of the previous success of the author."[4]

To protect themselves against the unscrupulous business practices of German publishers, Shaw suggested that he and Trebitsch might do their own printing of the German editions of Shaw's works and have Cotta or another publisher sell them on a commission basis; in this case, Trebitsch must stipulate that *he* would order and pay for the printing: "Otherwise the publisher will produce receipts from the printer and bookbinder for sums on which he has been allowed a discount of 20 or 30 per cent, and we will be cheated. It is worth while fighting out these details as it will save you a great deal of time and trouble afterwards. When Cotta learns that you know the tricks of trade, he will not waste your time trying them on you." Aware of the tricks of trade, even of international trade, Shaw urged Trebitsch, after World War I, to keep the money for Shaw's royalties in a Vienna account until the rate of exchange improved. He was also aware of the tricks of copyright. A chapter in *The Irrational Knot* had been "purposely so altered in the new edition that an attempt to pirate the new edition under cover of the old [which was out of copyright] can be immediately detected and proved [. . .]."[5]

He drove a hard bargain and demanded royalties on a sliding scale geared to the gross receipts of each performance. The figures in the scale varied, changing in Shaw's favor as his plays became more popular.[6] In the United States, he often did business at a straight 10 percent, but, he said, "this may be regarded as a minimum," and "a good deal depends on the manager with whom I am dealing."[7] In order to prevent managers from taking a play in order to keep someone else from producing it, Shaw stipulated that if the play were not produced by a specified date, or if it were immediately withdrawn before the total payments amounted to a certain sum, that amount was forfeited to him. In 1916, the amount was five hundred pounds (or twenty-five hundred dollars).[8]

Shaw had a reputation for being inexorable about his sliding scale. Lawrence Langner complained that since it cost at least fifteen thousand dollars per week to run one of Shaw's plays, the author's 15 percent royalty was too high. Shaw promptly offered his plays royalty-free up to fifteen thousand dollars, with a fifty-fifty split over that sum. Of course, Langner refused, for the author's share would come to much more on that basis.[9] Although Shaw fostered the impression that he was absolutely intractable on the subject of author's royalties, this was not actually so. When Mrs. Patrick Campbell toured *Pygmalion* in the United States, he worked out a kickback arrangement whereby he would remit half of his fees to her when receipts fell to eight hundred pounds a week.[10] His motive might have been friendship or a desire to keep his play running even if it meant playing to only moderately sized houses, or possibly both. It was certainly worth more to him in the long run to keep the Court Theatre in operation than to squeeze as much as possible from a single play, for he was that company's chief playwright and the company had actors sympathetic to and proficient in performing his plays. He therefore gave them every possible concession.[11] When the Court seasons ended in June 1907, Shaw helped to arrange for a season at the Savoy Theatre, guaranteeing £2,000, to be repaid on net profits, which were to be reckoned after charging Vedrenne's and Barker's salaries (£1,000 a year each). His own salary, he said, would "be taken out in moral superiority."[12] In America three decades later, after the Federal Theater Project was inaugurated during the Depression, as part of President Franklin D. Roosevelt's Works Progress Administration, to give socially useful jobs to the unemployed, Shaw placed all his plays at its disposal on condition that the highest price it charged for admission was, as it announced, fifty cents (then the equivalent of two shillings).[13] On other occasions, Shaw reasonably agreed to a 5 percent royalty in places where the higher percentages would prevent the play from being done.[14] And he sometimes made arrangements for weekly or fixed fees.[15]

For amateurs, there were different terms. The "old style" amateurs—that is, the nonprofessionals who would get up a performance for a charity benefit—had to pay five guineas (five pounds, five shillings) per performance, or eight guineas for two performances. But if amateurs decided to compete with professionals—for example, taking a major Dublin theater to present premières of Shaw plays—Shaw refused them amateur terms: to take Dublin's Gaiety Theatre, "present a play which has not been judged in that city by a professional performance, and claim amateur terms, is absurd."[16] When a new type of amateur appeared, devoted to the art of the theater and trying to produce plays where professionals would not go, Shaw recognized this change and altered his fees accordingly. He sympathized with the new amateurs, who presented the new drama at a price the people could afford, perhaps taking in a total of fifteen shillings at the gate. Under such circumstances, he thought it unreasonable to demand five guineas. Instead, he charged them a percentage of the gate, and if that percentage came to sixpence, he would tip his hat, thank them, and sincerely ask for a renewal of their favors.[17] Still, he did not wish to have advantage taken of him. If these new amateurs organized theater clubs and charged nonmembers, Shaw demanded that his percentage include the seats occupied by the members.[18]

As a trade unionist, however, Shaw would not undersell foreign competitors, for he wanted all playwrights to have a decent minimum wage. Even though it was difficult enough for a dramatist to live on 10 percent, he explained to Trebitsch, a manager in a foreign country would, if he could, offer the native playwright 4 percent, telling him that if he did not take it the manager would get an English play for 4 percent. Shaw therefore ascertained the highest percentage paid to native authors and then demanded more. "In Denmark they told me that no Danish author ever got more than 6%; and they offered me 5. I said 7 1/2. They said it was utterly impossible. I stuck to it like a mule. They gave in; and now the Danish authors bless me for putting up prices."[19]

While Shaw drove a hard bargain, he was not rapacious to the extent of being unfair to his friends and supporters. Refusing to give rights for the United States première of *John Bull's Other Island* to anyone but Arnold Daly, Shaw told his agent: "Daly has done very well with my plays: why should I now wantonly throw him over & let the other fellows profit by his risk & his devotion? Tell your man to go away & write a play for himself if he wants one." When Robert Loraine had a success in *Cyrano de Bergerac* in 1919, he sent a check to Shaw for an outstanding debt on royalties from the Canadian tour of *Man and Superman*, seven years earlier. Shaw replied:

> The £600 or whatever it is is all nonsense. The play did not make the money. Now, if your acting had lost it, and I could contend that the money was there for you to make had you been equal to the occasion, I should claim it remorselessly. But the facts as compared with runs elsewhere prove that your acting made more money than the play, and of this surplus I had a very substantial whack.
>
> There is consequently no real human reason why I should exploit you and Rostand (or another) for money that the wretched *Superman* never earned. The Statute of Limitations which has already written off the item legally is for once right as well as convenient.

And when *Fanny's First Play* became, as Shaw put it, "the *Charley's Aunt* of the new drama," he told Charles Ricketts, who had designed costumes for the play, of the fortune he received in author's fees: "As this clearly

changes a desperate artistic enterprise into a sordid commercial speculation, I can see no mortal reason why you should design dresses for it for
nothing. I therefore, with the brutal indelicacy of a successful man, ask
you what is your tariff for designing dresses [. . .]. Tell me what I ought to
pay you, and I will give you 5 per cent of it, as, if you put it anywhere near
the truth, I shall not be able to afford any more." Ricketts, not to be
outdone, asked Shaw to accept the costumes as a "cheap *beau geste* [. . .]
the natural neighbourly act of one art to another."[20]

But Shaw did not use his business knowledge only to drive bargains for
royalties. Since he wanted his plays to get large audiences and to make
money for all concerned, he examined the numerous factors affecting
these objectives. *You Never Can Tell* had played six matinées at the Strand
Theater early in May 1900. When Frank Curzon, manager of the Strand,
proposed that Yorke Stephens (who had played Valentine) revive the play
at the end of May, Shaw refused. "Our profits," he told Stephens, "are
easily computed: there wont be any." He then instructed Stephens:

> Tell Mr Curzon that no play of mine is going into an evening bill
> at the end of May, under any circumstances whatever, short of an
> advance of £2,500 to the author. The 25th March is my latest date
> for a summer production, and the 1st of September my earliest for a
> winter one.
>
> If he cares to make a serious proposal for a regular production in
> September, with certain comparatively expensive changes in the cast,
> new scenery, and everything firstrate, I am open to that or anything
> else in the regular way of business, though I shouldnt advise him to
> do anything of the sort, because nothing but a very stylish produc-
> tion at a very stylish theatre, with handsome advertising, will give
> the play a chance. But in any case no fresh move can be made at the
> West End before September.

He urged Ada Rehan, who was contemplating a production of *Captain
Brassbound's Conversion* in the United States, to play it in London first,
for a success in one country may not mean a success in the other.

> Now the failure of a London success in America does nobody any
> harm except the manager, because it is always claimed that a play
> good enough for London is good enough for anywhere, and that the
> Americans ought to be ashamed of themselves for not appreciating
> it.

BUT—and this is important—the failure of an American success in London is bad for everybody, because it is attributed at once to the superior taste of London.

Moral: always try London first. If you succeed, no subsequent failure can discredit your success or lower your prestige in the part. If you dont succeed, the management has a far stronger interest in keeping the piece on and nursing it as an apparent success for America & the provinces than in the case of an American production. If you fail, you can still try America far more easily and hopefully than you could try London after an American failure. And you can win in London what is called a moral victory: that is, if your venture is recognized as aiming high, you can come out a financial failure with an enhanced reputation, whereas in America nothing succeeds but financial success.[21]

He informed Trebitsch that unless a star actress who was both extraordinarily popular and extraordinarily good were engaged for *Pygmalion,* failure would be certain, and he warned William Faversham that too many high-priced actors for *Getting Married* would mean financial ruin, since their drawing powers would overlap, and there were only so many people in New York willing to see this type of play.[22] The opening of *John Bull's Other Island,* he advised Barker, must not take place until after Parliament met in the fall, for the political people would fill the theater. The opening of *Heartbreak House,* he told the Theatre Guild, must be delayed until after the November elections in the United States:

> It would be far better to produce *H.H.* with the first cast you could pick out of the gutter on the 15th of Nov. than to produce it on the 15th of October with Sarah Bernhardt, the two Guitrys, Edwin Drew, Maude Adams, Charlie Chaplin and Mary Pickford.
>
> A running play may do very well, because people already know about it, and it needs no press. But a new production has no chance. The presidential candidates play the author and the cast off the stage: and the election crowds out the theatre. If you doubt me, try— but with somebody else's play. You will never try again.

Langner admitted that it took the Theatre Guild several years to learn how right Shaw was.[23]

Well aware of the fact that promotion and publicity affect the box office, Shaw often took charge of these matters. Sometimes, he composed journalistically factual press releases: "Please note that the forthcoming revival of Mr Bernard Shaw's Arms & The Man under Mr F. C. Whitney's management will take place at the Criterion Theatre on Thursday the 18th May," with the cast, the time of performance, and the theater's phone number.[24] At other times, his publicity releases were in the usual Shavian style: "This morning," he wrote to Trebitsch, "I sent an article to Die Zeit of the most Shawish description, full of the most insufferable egotism, and warning the Viennese against Candida. Also explaining that the Teufel-skerl [*The Devil's Disciple*] is all stale melodrama."[25] He was concerned that the audience know exactly when a play was being performed if it did not run on consecutive days. For Barker's matinées of *Candida,* Shaw insisted, "Unless every advertisement is headed TUESDAYS THURS-DAYS and FRIDAYS in colossal print the scheme will fail because people will get confused about the dates, which are perfectly idiotic." And he knew how to make use of popular clichés about himself. When the The-atre Guild produced *Jitta's Atonement,* which he adapted from the German of Siegfried Trebitsch, he wrote to Lawrence Langner, "I saw your press communication about the play; but I do not want it suggested that it is 95% Shaw and 5% Trebitsch. Novelty is always valuable; and novelty is the one quality that I have lost hopelessly with the affirmation of my reputation. The line to take is to boom Trebitsch [. . .] and to suggest that as what has been lacking in my plays is HEART, the combination of the emotional Trebitsch with the intellectual Shaw is ideal, and will make the most dramatic event of the season."[26]

Shaw was not only interested in getting an audience into the theater: he felt responsible for their comfort once they got there. During the run of *Candida* at the Court, he wrote to Vedrenne:

[William] Archer came into my box today because he couldnt stand the cold in the stalls. Four cases of frostbite were treated at the Chelsea infirmary—one stall & three pit. A man in the dress circle got so rhe[u]matic after the second act that he had to be lifted out by the attendants. The Morning Post has lumbago for life. The Daily Mail threatens to head his article "A Frost at the Court." The fire-man caught one man attempting to set fire to the theatre. You will have to warm the theatre and to announce the fact in the advertise-ments, or the Christmas piece is done for.

There is not a hook or a hat peg in the boxes. You can get excellent ones for threepence apiece. The man in Box B said that if there had been a hook he would have hanged himself to draw public attention to the frightful cold. My wife was affected to tears by the play; and her tears froze so that it took me five minutes to get her eyes open with the warmth of my hands, which are now covered with chilblains. My mother went to sleep; and we are still (6.15) vainly trying to wake her. I think you have done for her. You can get coals & blankets at the Parish Hall, I believe. Why not apply?[27]

Shaw's ideal theater would not only be adequately heated, it would have superior optics and acoustics. The seating accommodations would be comfortable, in contrast to the present state of affairs: "If criminals were crowded together in our prisons without proper ventilation and elbow room as playgoers are in our theatres there would be an agitation against the cruelty of the authorities." Each seat would be wide enough for comfort, and there would be enough space between rows so that one could walk through without falling into the laps of those seated. If a good play makes the theatergoer forget his discomfort, a bad play makes him remember it and hesitate to attend the theater the next time. In Shaw's ideal theater plush and velvety upholstery would be abolished in favor of cushions covered with woollen cloth. This theater, moreover, would be beautiful: "a theatre which is paneled, and mirrored, and mantelpieced like the first-class saloon of a Peninsular and Oriental liner or a Pullman drawing room car, is no place for Julius Cæsar, or indeed for anything except tailormade drama and farcial comedy." A theater should make the playgoer feel that he is in "a place where high scenes are to be enacted and dignified things to be done." Such "petty cadgings like charges for programs and cloakroom fees" would be eliminated. The audience would not be made to feel uncomfortable because they are not fashionably dressed but would be encouraged to wear what they wear to the cinema. This, Shaw believed, was one reason for the success of motion pictures.[28]

Shaw understood that some of these reforms were impractical within the contemporary economic framework. For one thing, the large amount of ground space required for the type of seating arrangement he would like was impossible in the West End because of high rents. But, he suggested, there was no reason for the theater to remain in the West End. If the Church could move from the center of the city to the suburbs, then so could the theater. "It is clear to me that we shall never become a playgoing people until we discard our fixed idea that it is the business of the people to come to the theatre, and substitute for it the idea that it is the business of the theatre to come to the people."[29] The theater, then, should be decentralized and made as easily accessible to the people as motion picture houses.

Shaw was indeed a "man of the theater"—writing plays, casting them, mounting and rehearsing them, putting them before an audience, and getting an audience to sit before them. Convinced that the art of play production was as much his business as the art of playwriting, he had a guiding hand in every aspect of play production. As director, he planned blocking, worked closely with actors during rehearsals, and helped them to polish their performances in order to achieve maximum stage effectiveness. But Shaw was a director, not only an acting coach. Sound effects, music, lighting, scenery, costumes, and make-up—all elements of play production fell within his directorial jurisdiction as he guided artists in each of these areas to express themselves in ways that would further the total effect of the play. Did he limit the other artists—the actor or designer, for instance? Certainly, inasmuch as any control designed to create a unified entity from disparate theatrical elements is limiting. And Shaw, who knew the effects he wanted to achieve, was a strong director. But many artists who worked under his supervision—Lillah McCarthy, Forbes Robertson, Sir Cedric Hardwicke, Joseph Harker, and Lee Simonson, among others—felt his guidance to be a help rather than a hindrance. In any case, Shaw supervised every area of production in trying to realize the play on stage. He had a vision of what the theater should be, and a willingness to wrestle with the theater as it was to help him fulfill this vision. Few were as completely immersed in the total theatrical mechanism as Shaw was. One thinks of Molière and Brecht in this regard: playwrights whose comedies reflect social realities, men engaged in the day-to-day theatrical activity of line rehearsals, budgets, blocking, scene painting, and the like. Molière, Brecht, and Shaw all involved themselves in the total production apparatus. It is clear that Shaw was a practical theater man, a director whose resources included every aspect of theater.

The Director as Interpreter: Shaw's *Pygmalion*

SHAW'S TWO MAJOR WRITINGS about play direction, usually titled "The Art of Rehearsal" (1922) and "Rules for Directors" (1949), say very little about interpretation. The first does not even use the word and the second uses it only once.[1] Yet Shaw's own plays abound in interpretive stage directions. For example, two successive pages of *The Apple Cart*, taken at random, include these interpretations of dialogue which are not necessarily self-evident from the dialogue: "*in a glow of gratification,*" "*remonstrating,*" "*struck by this view,*" "*graciously,*" and "*apparently much pleased*" (6, 296–97). In fact, the preface to this very play includes an admonition not to take Shaw's plays at their face value. To take them at other than face value, however, or for that matter even to determine their face value, involves interpretation.

My concerns here are first to analyze Shaw's concept of the question of directorial interpretation—employing the basic texts just mentioned, augmented by other relevant writings—and then to examine his own directorial interpretation of one of his most popular plays, *Pygmalion*. Evidence for the latter derives from the following sources, identified by small roman numerals: (i) chiefly, Shaw's rehearsal notes for the first London production, which opened on 11 April 1914;[2] (ii) and (iii) his rehearsal notes for the second London production, which opened on 10 February 1920;[3] (iv) his rehearsal notes for the Malvern production, which opened on 30 July 1936;[4] (v) his blocking and other notes in the printed 1913 rehearsal edition of the play used for the 1914 production (plus passages from this edition);[5] (vi), (vii), and (viii) his letters to Mrs. Patrick Campbell, who played Liza Doolittle in the 1914 and 1920 productions.[6] Except where indicated differently, quotations from the Definitive Text in the Bodley Head edition of Shaw's plays are identical in the 1913 rehearsal edition and the 1914 published edition. I will not treat such subjects as dealing with actors, picking up cues, clarity of diction, taking another actor's rhythm, or blocking—except, of course, as these relate to interpretation.

This essay divides into three parts: Shaw's general ideas about directorial interpretation, his own directorial interpretation of *Pygmalion,* and his revisions of *Pygmalion* to include his directorial interpretation for the guidance of future directors, actors, and readers.

Interpretation and the Shavian Director

Practicality is among the underlying bases of Shaw's statements about play direction. In "The Art of Rehearsal," he concentrates exclusively on the director's day-to-day business in the theater, including preparation of floor plans, blocking, stage business, line rehearsals, pace, and note-taking. He does almost the same in "Rules for Directors," where he explicitly states, using italics for emphasis: "*These pages are an attempt to supply a beginners' guide. They are not concerned with direction as a fine art; but they cover the mechanical and teachable conditions which are common to all productions* [. . .]."[7] By implication, interpretation is not mechanical and is therefore unteachable. Thus, his advice to Reginald Golding Bright, already cited, that to teach himself play direction he should, when a Shakespearean or Sheridan play is scheduled to be performed, buy a copy, mark the blocking and stage business in advance of seeing it, and then analyze not only his own mistakes, but also those of the actors.

Practicality informs the Shavian director's work with the actors, whose job, like the director's, is to make the audience imagine that real people are in real situations. In all likelihood, a director who discusses Kierkegaard's influence on Ibsen would leave most actors bewildered; even those actors familiar with Kierkegaard might be puzzled as to how to translate his alleged sway on a play into stage action. To discuss the Oedipus complex with the actress playing Queen Gertrude would be less productive of behavior that reveals real things happening to real people than, for instance, a note on contrast or on an action occurring too suddenly, if the contrast refers to a different attitude toward Hamlet than toward Polonius or if the sudden action refers to the beginning or termination of an embrace with her son—both directorial rather than literary interpretations. Fundamentally, then, the Shavian director's interpretation stresses not literary qualities, however valid they may be to a play's meaning, but performance activities applied to the play or scenic unit thereof.

Shaw's interpretation reveals itself through the dynamics of a scene and through characterization. Although he rules out discussions of philosophical or psychological theories as useful tools in dealing with actors, he does not rely exclusively on mechanical tools. As Sir Lewis Casson, who acted under his direction and who codirected *Saint Joan* with him, points out, Shaw was able "to analyze how effects were got, and to pass on the knowledge of *how* as well as why."[8] Sir Lewis may emphasize *how* because it would come as a surprise to his readers that Shaw the voluble literary figure could analyze *how,* but would come as no surprise to them that he could explain *why.* After all, the usual jibe, used by Shaw himself (in the epistle dedicatory to *Man and Superman*), is that he never did anything other than explain himself. In the present context, we may reverse the emphasis to point out that he could explain *why* as well as how.

In terms of acting, *why* often means motivation for saying or doing something. No matter how many times an actor has heard his cue, it must provoke him to respond verbally or physically in a distinctive way, as if he had never heard it before. Both handwritten rehearsal notes and printed stage directions stress motivation. Discussion between director and actor about why the actor says or does something is more productive of conveying the impression that real things befall real people than discussion about philosophy or literature. Thus, as the reader has noticed, Shaw's rehearsal notes include references to motivations about sitting or walking, and reminders that cause, such as the chimes of the church clock in Act I of *Pygmalion,* precedes speech and action, in this case Higgins's recollection and subsequent gift of money to Liza. Also as mentioned previously, if spectators consider a scene too slow, which means boring, the remedy is usually for the performer to act more slowly in order to make the meaning clearer by contrasts of tempo and tone. Unsurprisingly, to bring out the meaning is a goal of the Shavian director. What is surprising is that Shaw did not say more about it.

But how much did he expect the actor to understand the play's meaning? On this subject Shaw was paradoxical. I have quoted him as advising Molly Tompkins not to confuse the ability to understand characters and plays with the capacity to act them, noting that Shakespeare was not a better actor than Burbage, that an actor is to an author what a carpenter or mason is to an architect, and that like a carpenter or mason an actor not only need not understand the entire design, he would also not necessarily fulfill his function better if he did understand it. I have not seen a similar statement by Shaw about Granville Barker, whose intellectual understanding of the drama is amply documented. Furthermore, Shaw explicitly praises Janet Achurch, Florence Farr, Elizabeth Robins, and Marion Lea (early interpreters of Ibsen's female characters) because they are "products of the modern movement for the higher education of women, literate, in touch with advanced thought, and [. . .] in contradistinction to the senior generation of inveterately sentimental actresses," who are "intellectually naïve to the last degree. The new school says to the old: You cannot play Ibsen because you are ignoramuses."[9]

In Shaw's advice to Tompkins, he does not say that the abilities to act and to understand the plays are mutually exclusive, but that they are different. The context of his admonition is an attempt to persuade her not to confine her roles to intellectually important plays, else she will not develop as an actress for want of sufficient experience. Frequently, context determines Shaw's statements about the value of an actor's intellectual abilities. Thus, he writes to Siegfried Trebitsch: "You tell me not to be anxious about my stage directions (Good God!) because your directors & actors are much cleverer than English ones. Madman: *all* actors are idiots: all 'directors' are imposters. [. . .] Do not be deceived by reputations: unless you tell people exactly what to do, as if they were little children, and persuade them at the same time that they have thought of it all themselves, you will never get anything done properly." Implicit in this letter is the insistence that the German actors follow, not ignore, his stage directions — thus, his demand that Trebitsch treat these idiots and imposters as children who must obey the author's dicta. By contrast, he tells Trebitsch only eight days later that he himself informs old actors who complain of his stage directions that "an actor is not a mechanic to be ordered to cross right or left, sit, stand, or exit left upper entrance, without understanding why, but an artist who is entitled to demand that an author shall address himself to his taste, fancy, intellect, imagination, wit &c &c &c &c. This crushes him utterly: his self-respect compels him to agree with you" about the stage directions.[10] Here too, context is important. Unless Trebitsch puts the actors in the position of conforming to his highest estimation of their capacities, Shaw adds in the same letter, they will put him in the position of a novice who lacks understanding of professional theater practice.

Shaw expected actors and actresses to understand plays to the extent of being able to understand the characters they would portray. Interpreting *Arms and the Man*, for example, he states that "Raina is never in a hurry, never frightened, after her first pop into bed after the shots, always disdainful, patronising, superior, queening it, until her collapse. Until then it never occurs to her for a moment to doubt her enormous moral superiority to Bluntschli, or Sergius's superiority."[11] Unless Bluntschli is careful, he says, the audience might consider him a coward. Bluntschli "must there-fore seize certain moments to shew that he is a brave man." Shaw then points out such moments.[12] Of *The Doctor's Dilemma*, he declares,

> What I call the climax is Jennifer's discovery that Ridgeon deliber-ately murdered Dubedat. The dramatic effect is built up rather elaborately, because there is first a misunderstanding and then a dis-covery. When Ridgeon first says "I killed him," the audience knows that he means "I murdered him"; but Jennifer thinks that her own frankness and sincerity has at last conquered his vanity, and that what he means is "Yes yes: I own up: I confess I was a duffer and made a mess of the case." And on this she is delighted and forgives him.
>
> [...] She has to arrive at the truth by arguing about the medicines, being a little stupid and off the track at first, because the truth is so inconceivable and so wildly remote from her first misunderstanding. But when the revelation does come, it really ought to be a blinding one. It has to be done on the line "It is only dawning on me, oh! oh!! you MURDERED him."[13]

In these ways Shaw the director interprets Shaw the playwright for his actors.

Shaw warned the director against the star actress who might try "to substitute a personal performance of her own for the character you want to make the audience believe her to be; and your trouble with her would be in direct proportion to her charms as a fashionable leading lady." The early success of the Abbey Theater, he said, was due largely to its company having no such actors and actresses. Instead, "They were held down [...] ruthlessly to my formula of making the audience believe that real things were happening to real people." They did this "by sticking to the point of securing a good representation" — that is, by portraying the characters the author had written, not fashionably popular stage personalities. Straight-forwardly, Shaw described the relationship between director and play-wright: "The playwright has to tell a good story, and the director to 'get it across.'"[14]

To Shaw, the director should regard actors "as fellow artists collaborat-ing with him," not "as employees on whom he can impose his own notions of acting and his own interpretation of the author's meaning."[15] As he recognized, "A part that is any good can be played fifty different ways by fifty different people [...]."[16] Yet as he also recognized, there are an additional fifty ways, to use his phrase, that have nothing to do with the author's meaning. In rehearsal for the role of Higgins in *Pygmalion,* Sir Herbert Beerbohm Tree apparently found many of the latter fifty ways. Among other suggestions, he proposed that Higgins might have a twitch, occasionally vault onto the piano, take snuff, and speak with a Scottish accent. To avoid such interpretations, Shaw pleaded with the actor to do no more than read the lines as written.[17]

While blocking his plays, director Shaw visually interpreted dramatist Shaw. In one production of *Man and Superman,* as I have mentioned, in order to convey visually the idea that while Jack Tanner may spout revolutionary rhetoric, the silent Ann Whitefield is in her womanly way in command of the action, Shaw had Tanner pontificate while standing on the gravel driveway while Ann sat provocatively in the car with her breast on the driver's wheel. In another production, as I have not mentioned, he staged their final dialogue as if "she were a magnet and he a rather reluctant needle": Shaw placed her at stage center and had Tanner trying to leave the garden, walk away from her, but then vacillate and return, at first going off resolutely, then more and more feebly, getting closer to her on every return, until he was no longer able to move away.[18]

Although Shaw opposed idiosyncratic interpretations of Shakespeare and others by directors and actors, since in practical terms these usually result in textual mutilation of the sort associated with Colley Cibber and Henry Irving, he actually approved such idiosyncrasies when he considered them justified by the test of production. On the one hand, he condemned John Barrymore not only for cutting the text of *Hamlet* but also for misinterpreting it along then-fashionable Freudian lines. In place of the recorders passage and "such speeches as 'How all occasions do inform against me!'"—which he discarded as "hackneyed" and "obsolete junk"—Barrymore offered "that very modern discovery called the Œdipus complex," changed Hamlet and Ophelia into Romeo and Juliet, and allowed Laertes and Ophelia "to hug each other as lovers instead of lecturing and squabbling like hectoring big brother and little sister: another complex!"[19] On the other hand, as cited earlier, he applauded William Poel for taking freedoms with Marlowe's *Doctor Faustus,* notably, making the devils Baliol and Belcher resemble those of Schongauer, the angels Boticellian, and the seven deadly sins exceptionally *fin de siècle.* Shaw also accepted certain controversial, inauthentic renderings of Shakespeare. For instance, Barry Sullivan "cured" Macbeth's "ranting and redundant" speech in Act V, Scene v: "'Hang out your banners on the outer walls. / The cry is still they come.'"

He entered at the back of the stage throwing an order over his shoulders to his subalterns, and then came down to the footlights to discuss the military situation. Thus we got the reading:

> Hang out your banners. On the outer walls the cry is still they come.

This, tested on the stage [. . .], is a convincing improvement. But the authority for it is not the text as it has come down to us, but Barry Sullivan's conjecture submitted to [the test of performance]. And Barry Sullivan went further than that. Instead of saying, as Hamlet, "I am but mad north-northwest: when the wind is southerly, I know a hawk from a handsaw," he said "I know a hawk from a heron. Pshaw." This may read strainedly; but when acted with appropriate business it is so effective that [a] stage test would favor its adoption.

For such readings, there is "no authority but [. . .] artistic instinct."[20]

What is good enough for Marlowe may be good enough for Shakespeare, but is it good enough for Shaw? In "Rules for Directors" he recognized the need to cut, add to, or otherwise alter a play for reasons that include improving it as a play and overcoming a theatrically mechanical or acting difficulty. On the basis of these considerations, he cut, added to, and otherwise altered his own plays. Furthermore, as we have seen, he often incorporated into printed editions of his plays cuts, changes, and business that he made, developed, or saw in rehearsal or performance. However, he rejected artistic instincts that were at odds with his own, such as those of Beerbohm Tree, who wanted, at the end of *Pygmalion,* after Liza's departure, to walk to the balcony and throw flowers to her.[21] In other words, he sought to ensure that his own interpretation of his plays prevailed, and he encouraged the interpretation of others only when they fell within the broad framework of his.

Director Shaw Interprets *Pygmalion*

Although few, perhaps no one, would dispute the contention that *Pygmalion* is a comedy, not all of its dialogue is obviously funny. As director, Shaw enhances the comedy. In Act II, after Mrs. Pearce tells Higgins that they must be particular about Liza's personal cleanliness, not slovenly or untidy, he agrees and pontificates, "It is these little things that matter, Pickering. Take care of the pence and the pounds will take care of themselves is as true of personal habits as of money" (4, 704). Shaw notes, "imply that Pick is careless of his person (ii) and "moral lesson to Pick" (iv). In the next act, Higgins tells his mother, "When Pickering starts shouting nobody can get a word in edgeways." "Be quiet," she says, and then addresses Pickering (4, 736). Director Shaw advises her, "Put your hand on H's mouth after 'no one gets a word in edgeways'" (i). When Higgins tells Doolittle, in Act V, that since he paid him for Liza, Doolittle has no right to take her, his mother tells him, "Henry: dont be absurd. If you want to know where Eliza is, she is upstairs" (4, 764). The director gives her comic business to top Higgins's comic line: "'Henry—dont be absurd'—pull him by the tail into his chair" (ii).

The play is realistic as well as comic. To make Act I as convincing as possible, Shaw the director calls for "More horrible, finer rain! Cant we get the clouds to move & a moon to come out when the rain stops" (i), and when Freddy rushes in Shaw notes that he is "too dry" (ii). Liza is not a quaint creature but a businesswoman who must sell her wares in order to live. Thus, when she pleads, "Oh do buy a flower off me, Captain" (4, 673), Shaw suggests, "Try to put the flower into his buttonhole" (i)—a credible sales technique. A lower-class woman, she fears the social consequences if members of professional or upper classes complain to the police about her, since the law is more apt to believe them than her. "[T]errified," she cries that she has done nothing wrong by speaking to a gentleman and "Hysterically" insists she is a respectable girl (4, 673). Trying to vivify this social realism, the author-director calls the actress's complaints "Still nothing to collect a crowd" (i) and prods her, "I give up in despair that note of terror in the first scene which collects the crowds and suddenly shews the audience that there is a play there, and a human soul there, and a social problem there, and a formidable capacity for feeling in the trivial giggler of the comic passages. But until you get it I shall never admit that you can play Eliza, or play Shaw" (vi, p. 224). When Liza insists she did no harm and pleads with Pickering not to charge her to the police, she should convey the "blind terror of a wounded animal" (i). Make-up also conveys social reality. After a dress rehearsal, Shaw observes, "Make-up quite right for Acts I & II—just the right anemia for the flower girl; but too white in III & V [. . .] wants a little color to shew the effect of the Wimpole St feeding" (iii).

The director helps the actors interpret character. When Liza says in Act II that she hung a towel over the mirror in the bathroom, Shaw insists that the statement reveals "prudery—not fun" (i)—which is also a reminder to play the role from the character's viewpoint rather than hint to the audience, tritely and from the actress's view, that since she enjoys the line they should too. In Act V, Liza explains that her real education began when

Pickering called her Miss Doolittle, rose when she entered the room, and opened doors for her. To the character, the words are not simply explanatory Shavian dialogue; rather, they proceed from emotional experience. Therefore, urges Shaw, their delivery should be "low, slow, normal, deliberate, tasting a grateful memory" (i); she speaks to him "affectionately" (iv).

Higgins is a bully. His command to Liza in Act I—"(*explosively*) Woman: cease this detestable boohooing instantly; or else seek the shelter of some other place of worship" (4, 679)—is a "magnificent outburst," a "big outburst—first taste of H's quality" (i). In Act II, his rage at one moment turns to sweet reasonableness the next. Yet the sweet reasonableness, Shaw tells the actor, has "no effect because he has not walked over everybody" just before (ii). One way to demonstrate Higgins is a bully is to emphasize people's response to him. On being introduced to Mrs. Eynsford Hill in Act III, he gives her an order: "Youd better sit down" (4, 724). Shaw notes, "Mrs EH sit down at once" (ii).

He attends to minor as well as to major characters. In Act I, Clara berates Freddy for having failed to find a cab. Shaw directs her to "fly out," then to "bully" her mother about making Liza give change for a sixpence (i).

Unquestionably, the major interpretive issue concerning *Pygmalion* revolves around romance. While it is indisputable that Freddy loves Liza, it is by no means uncontestable that she loves him rather than Higgins, as Shaw maintains, and that Higgins does not love her, as he also maintains. As a theater historian aptly puts it, Sir Herbert Beerbohm Tree, who first played Higgins in England, "was a romantic and an incurable sentimentalist: it seemed to him natural and inevitable that if a play had a hero, he should love and eventually marry the heroine of it."[22] Director Shaw did what he could to convey the interpretation of author Shaw. He told Tree, concerning Higgins's boast about what he could do for Liza in three months, "Oh God, dont look at her too much when talking about the garden party" (i)—i.e., Higgins is interested in the job, not the woman. To him, Pickering's question about sexual impropriety regarding Liza is "irrelevant" and his response to the demand that he not take advantage of her is "Surprise—not tragedy" (i). Shaw stresses a reason other than romance for Higgins's attachment to Liza: "'Besides, she's useful, finds all my things'—emphasize this"; and, after her departure from Wimpole Street, "'But I cant find anything'—dont forget this" (i). When he pulls her up from the floor in Act IV, he should say "'Get up'—more brutally. 'Anything wrong?' not fatally sympathetic" (ii); and on his statement "'Youre not bad looking'—*dont* attend to her. Go to the fire & dont make a sympathetic point on '[youre what I should call] attractive'" (i).

When Higgins expresses admiration for Liza's independence in Act V, Mrs. Patrick Campbell should "throw his arm away" (ii). When she recognizes how to do without him=teaching what he taught her: phonetics=she should be "torrential-dont make pansies" (i). As Shaw more explicitly told the actress, "When Eliza emancipates herself=when Galatea comes to life=she must not relapse. She must retain her pride and triumph to the end. When Higgins takes your arm on 'consort battleship' you must instantly throw him off with implacable pride; and this is the note until the final 'Buy them yourself'" (vii, p. 155). Director Shaw pointed out that "On the grand finish 'I could kick myself' you retreat. The effect last night was 'Now Ive spoke my piece; anitz your turn, Srerbert.' You must plant yourself in an unmistakeable attitude of defiance, or in some way or other *hold* him for his reply" (vi, p. 224). "At the end, when Higgins says 'Oh, by the way, Eliza,' bridle your fatal propensity to run like Georgina to anyone who calls you, and to forget everything in an effectionate tête à tête with him. Imagine that he is the author, and be scornful. All that is necessary is to stop on the threshold. If you find it impossible not to come back, at least dont look obedient and affectionate" (vi, pp. 224–25). When she disregarded such directives and behaved differently, he denounced her: "Final scene rotten=no delicacy or pathos—hugging Higgins at end—serve you right, you ungrateful devil!" (iii).

Although Freddy is not onstage for very long, Shaw tried to make the most of the young man's infatuation while he was there. When he is introduced to Liza, he should "Lean over eagerly" (ii). After he says goodbye to Mrs. Higgins:

> MRS HIGGINS (*shaking hands*) Goodbye. Would you like to meet Miss Doolittle again?
> FREDDY (*eagerly*) Yes, I should, most awfully.
> MRS HIGGINS Well, you know my days.
> FREDDY. Yes. Thanks awfully. Goodbye. (4, 732)

Shaw directs her to "Hold Freddy when he turns away" (ii)=very likely after she says "Goodbye," so that the following dialogue would receive greater emphasis through pointed movement=and tells him to "Gush—on 'awfully'" (ii), thereby receiving emphasis as a presence.

By interpreting both the speeches and the responses of characters who do not speak, director Shaw enriches the play. In his view, when Higgins tempts Liza by means of a fanciful account of the glorious things that will befall her under his tutelage, she should respond as he wants her to. The story itself is a "fairy tale [that] must be recited" (iv) — i.e., spoken as if to a child. Her reaction should be "Dreamy for 'officer in guards'" (i). When he says she will have money enough to buy chocolates and ride in taxis, her "mouth waters" at the first and she interjects "'Aw *should* lawk to take a taxi'" at the second (ii). Upon his statement that if she is discovered she will be decapitated in the Tower of London, Mrs. Pearce and Pickering "look at one another" (ii).

As Shaw interprets Doolittle's first scene, Higgins consistently disconcerts Liza's father. After Doolittle "*menacingly*" asserts that he wants his daughter, Higgins replies, "Of course you do. Youre her father, arnt you? You dont suppose that anyone else wants her, do you? I'm glad to see you have some spark of family feeling left. She's upstairs. Take her away at once" (4, 706). Shaw notes, "'Of course you do.' surprise. 'Youre her father, arnt you' — prompt — jump down his throat" (i) and tells Doolittle to react to "'*some* spark'" (ii). When Higgins asks, "Have you any further advice to give her before you go, Doolittle? Your blessing, for instance" (4, 715), Doolittle should show "Suprise at 'your blessing'" (ii).

Reaction is particularly important in the beginning of Act IV, since it makes Liza's subsequent actions credible. Thus, Shaw calls for her "Surprise at 'Thank God it's all over' — take it in gradually," and demands, a "gradation — 'Thank God' [is] the first shock" (i). Mrs. Patrick Campbell's failure to react and to act appropriately provoked Shaw to call her performance in this act "a failure. [. . .] You looked like the loveliest of picture postcards blinking there at the piano whilst Higgins was talking daggers — 'Thank God it's over' — 'the whole thing has been a bore' etc., etc., etc. — without turning a hair, making your eyes twinkle like stars all the time — no shadows, no spasms of pain, no stabs, nothing but Stella. How carefully you avoided hurting him with the slippers; and how tenderly he raised you and reciprocated your gentleness! I almost slept" (viii, pp. 675–76). When he throws her into the easy-chair, she should sit "broken in the chair, not proud. [G]et to the proud attitude when he becomes sympathetic" (i); and she should "flinch frightfully when he touches [her]" on the shoulder (ii).

In Act V, Shaw worked for contrast in the different exchanges between Higgins and his mother. As he enters, he is, as the parlormaid says and a stage direction reiterates, "in a state," but she "*calmly*" writes (4, 757–58). The director tells Higgins, "Still not excitement enough at the beginning" (i), "More momentous" (i), "Much more injured, explosive" (i), and "more alarm" (ii). According to Shaw the director, Mrs. Higgins's account later in the act of Liza's accomplishment, feelings, and response to the way her son and Pickering treated her is a reprimand rather than a quietly dignified explanation. For the actress, he notes, "get up & harangue at them," "not indignant enough," "Get up the stage & bully down at them," "command the stage," and on "'[*I* should have thrown the] fire irons at you,' sit with a bounce—throw the paper about" (i).

From Stage to Page to Future Stages

When Shaw revised *Pygmalion* for new editions, he often incorporated interpretive movement, dialogue, and stage business developed during rehearsals. In new printings, these revisions became guides for directors and actors of future productions. For example, the 1913 rehearsal edition contains no stage direction before Higgins's thematically important statement that he is and is likely to remain a confirmed old bachelor. During rehearsals of the first London production, Shaw emphasized the line by having the actor change position immediately before it: "why not [sit on] the piano bench?" (i). Revised, the query becomes a stage direction that precedes the statement: "*He sits down on the bench at the keyboard*" (4, 702).

In Shaw the director's interpretation, Liza's fright in Act I sparks a commotion from the bystanders in general, not indifference from all but a few speakers. In the 1913 rehearsal edition, no stage directions indicate responses from the crowd when Liza cries in terror that she has done nothing wrong and pleads hysterically that she is a respectable girl. During rehearsals in 1914, Shaw wrote dialogue for members of the crowd—"'Dont holler.' 'Dont talk on.' 'Easy, Sally, easy'"—and he noted that there should be a "row—[at present,] crowd not much use" (i). The revised text makes use of the crowd:

> *General hubbub, mostly sympathetic to the flower girl, but deprecating her excessive sensibility. Cries of* Dont start hollerin. Who's hurting you? Nobody's going to touch you. Whats the good of fussing? Steady on. Easy, easy, etc., *come from the elderly staid spectators, who pat her comfortingly. Less patient ones bid her shut her hand, or ask her roughly what is wrong with her. A remoter group, not knowing what the matter is, crowd in and increase the noise with question and answer:* Whats the row? What-she do? Where is he? A tec taking her down. What! him? Yes: him over there: Took money off the gentleman, etc. (4, 673–74)

Motivational business and dialogue, developed at rehearsal, made their way into print for future productions. Initially, after Liza deposits

Higgins's slippers before him in Act IV, he says, "(*looking down at the slippers as if they had appeared there of their own accord*) Oh! theyre there, are they?" (v, p. 54). At rehearsal, Shaw recognized that Higgins needs a reason to look down. He therefore provided one: "Unlace your boots" (i). The published passage now reads: "(*yawning again*) Oh Lord! What an evening! What a crew! What a silly tomfoolery! (*He raises his shoe to unlace it, and catches sight of the slippers. He stops unlacing and looks at them as if they had appeared there of their own accord*). Oh! theyre there, are they?" (4, 745). Initially in Act V Liza agrees to attend her father's wedding as soon as he asks, "Wont you put on your hat, Liza, and come and see me turned off? Dont be afraid: she never comes to words with anyone now, poor woman! respectability has broke all the spirit out of her" (v, p. 73). At rehearsal, it became clear that Doolittle required a response to his question in order to have a reason to explain why Liza need not fear. Shaw therefore suggested that Liza "Play to [i.e., react to] 'Wont you come & see me turned off'=he needs a cue" (i). As published later, her reaction to his question becomes a line of dialogue: "If the Colonel says I must, I—I'll (*almost sobbing*) I'll demean myself. And get insulted for my pains, like enough" (4, 771). At rehearsal, Shaw may have felt that she required still more motivation before she rises and joins her father: "Dont go up=keep within reach of Pick" (i). In print, he adds a line for Pickering before she agrees: "(*squeezing Eliza's elbow gently*) Be kind to them, Eliza. Make the best of it" (4, 771).

Elements of characterization refined during rehearsals become printed interpretations for future directors and actors. For instance, the 1913 text has:

> HIGGINS. Pickering: shall we ask this baggage to sit down, or shall we throw her out of the window?
> THE FLOWER GIRL (*amazed*) Ah-ah-oh-ow-ow-ow-oo! (*Suddenly wounded and whimpering*) I wont be called a baggage when Ive offered to pay like any lady.   (v, p. 15)

Preparing the 1914 production, Shaw noted, "Run to piano. Turn at bay there" (v, p. 15); told the actress, "run to the piano like a hare=make the point of the fright" (i); and sketched a floor plan showing Liza by the piano at stage left, Higgins and Pickering at stage right, with a notation that the men are "staring at her" (v, p. 15). In the revised text, stage directions have Liza "*running away in terror to the piano, where she turns at bay*" and "*Motionless, the two men stare at her from the other side of the room, amazed*" before Pickering asks her what she wants (4, 688).

In the 1913 rehearsal edition, when Liza first enters the Wimpole Street flat, Higgins says, "(*brusquely, recognizing her with unconcealed disap-pointment*) Why, this is the girl I jotted down last night. She's no use: Ive got all the records I want of the Lisson Grove lingo; and I'm not going to waste another cylinder on it" (v, p. 14). Director Shaw coached the actor, "Not brusque enough on seeing Eliza" (i). Then writer Shaw added to the stage direction: "*and at once, babylike, making an intolerable grievance of it*" (4, 687). He also added descriptions that more clearly interpret this aspect of Higgins's character: "*He is [...] careless about himself and other people, including their feelings. He is, in fact, but for his years and size, rather like a very impetuous baby [...]. His manner varies from genial bullying when he is in a good humor to stormy petulance when anything goes wrong; but he is so entirely frank and void of malice that he remains likeable even in his least reasonable moments*" (4, 685). Furthermore, "*the only distinction he makes between men and women is that when he is neither bullying nor exclaiming to the heavens against some feather-weight cross, he coaxes women as a child coaxes its nurse when it wants to get anything out of her*" (4, 687).

Exemplifying Higgins's sudden, childlike change from stormy petu-lance to innocence is his response to Mrs. Pearce's admonitions not to eat breakfast while wearing his dressing gown and not to use the gown as a napkin. He protests, then tries to put her on the defensive by accusing her of using too much smelly benzine on his gown. She starts to point out that if he insists on wiping his fingers on it she must use enough benzine to clean it, he cries that in future he will wipe his fingers in his hair, she inquires whether she has offended him, and he replies that she has not. The 1913 rehearsal edition contains no stage directions for Higgins. During rehearsals, Shaw wanted him to reach a "climax on 'hair,'" told Mrs. Pearce "'I hope Ive not offended you' = dont catch his shout" = implicitly revealing that this is how Higgins delivered his dialogue = and demanded that Higgins's response be "polite when she says 'I hope youre not of-fended'" (i). In future printings, Higgins speaks "*Angrily*" when he men-tions the benzine, is "*yelling*" when he proposes to wipe his fingers in his hair, and when he responds to Mrs. Pearce's question as to his possibly having taken offence at her suggestion, he is "*shocked at finding himself thought capable of an unamiable sentiment*" (4, 704).

When Doolittle begins his attempt to extract money from Higgins, Shaw directed the actor to "take him by the elbow" (i) and noted, "D. is very intimate & confidential. Higgins finally sits down on the piano bench to escape his caresses" (v, p. 30). In addition, he warned Liza, who enters later, that her "'Dont e smell orrid?' is bad because Higgins has already got all the fun possible out of the dustiness of Doolittle. If [that question or attitude] had been needed I should have supplied [it]" (viii, p. 676). The present text contains a stage direction that conveys the basic points of these instructions: "*Higgins [. . .] takes refuge on the piano bench, a little overwhelmed by the proximity of his visitor; for Doolittle has a professional flavour of dust about him*" (4, 710).

Stage business reveals character. Initially, after Higgins in Act II thunders at Liza to sit, Mrs. Pearce more quietly tells her to do so and turns the chair for her; then Liza sits. For the 1914 production, Shaw added dialogue and movement in the margin of his rehearsal copy of the play:

> PICK: Wont you sit down?
> LIZA: (coy to Pick) Downt mawnd if a-de-oo.
> P. back to fire. (v, p. 16)

Subsequent printed texts reflect the new speeches and movement. But while Mrs. Pearce still fetches the chair in the 1914 edition, the present Definitive Text has Pickering do so—a further improvement that interprets his character and reveals to Liza how different it is from Higgins's.

The published texts of the play also reflect business that vividly interprets Higgins's bullying of Doolittle. The 1913 rehearsal edition contains this sequence:

> HIGGINS. [. . .] (*bullying him*) How dare you come here and attempt to blackmail me? You sent her here on purpose.
> DOOLITTLE (*protesting*) No, Governor.
> HIGGINS. You must have. How else could you possibly know that she is here? This is a plant—a plot to extort money by threats. I shall telephone for the police.
> DOOLITTLE. Dont take a man up like that, Governor. Have I asked you for a brass farthing? I leave it to the gentleman here: have I said a word about money?
> HIGGINS. What else did you come for? (v, p. 28)

During rehearsals, stage business with a telephone developed. Before the line about the telephone, Shaw told Higgins, "Dont take up the telephone—look out Scotland Yard in the book'; and on the last speech, 'drop the telephone' (i). After Doolittle's first speech, the text, incorporating and augmenting this business, now reads:

> HIGGINS. You must have. How else could you possibly know that she is here?
> DOOLITTLE. Dont take a man up like that, Governor.
> HIGGINS. The police shall take you up. This is a plant—a plot to

extort money by threats. I shall telephone for the police (*he goes resolutely to the telephone and opens the directory*).
DOOLITTLE. Have I asked you for a brass farthing? I leave it to the gentleman here: have I said a word about money?
HIGGINS (*throwing the book aside and marching down on Doolittle with a poser*) What else did you come for? (4, 707)

Stage business that developed during rehearsals visually interprets the relationship between Higgins and his mother. At the start of Act III, the 1913 rehearsal edition has the door open violently, Higgins enter, and his mother ask, "(*dismayed*) Henry: what are you doing here to-day? It is my at-home day: you promised not to come. Go home at once" (v, p. 39). Shaw's 1914 notes state "hat biz" for them and "Entry too cool" (i). Later texts clarify the business and the heat desired by the director. Higgins enters "*with his hat on.*" Then:

MRS HIGGINS (*dismayed*) Henry! (*Scolding him*) What are you doing here today? It is my at-home day: you promised not to come. (*As he bends to kiss her, she takes his hat off, and presents it to him*).
HIGGINS. Oh bother! (*He throws the hat down on the table*).
MRS HIGGINS Go home at once. (4, 721)

In rehearsing *Pygmalion*, Shaw the director interpreted Shaw the playwright. He avoided literary methodology in favor of performance activities that interpreted the dramatic text through characterization, the changing dynamics of a scene, illustrative stage business, and visual imagery. In practical rather than theoretical terms, he helped the actors to elucidate themes, characters, motivations, and interrelationships and to enhance the play's comedy. Analyzing and explaining both how and why something should be said or done, he guided actors to create theatrical effects and evoke the play's meaning. His directives at rehearsals aimed to convince audiences at performances that real things were happening to real people. While he recognized that there are a variety of appropriate ways to interpret any well-written role, he rejected what he considered inappropriate interpretations, since the real people in whom director Shaw wanted audiences to believe were the people whom playwright Shaw had created. To extend his directorial influence beyond the particular productions he directed, playwright Shaw often revised the texts of his plays so that new editions incorporated what director Shaw had done, thereby preserving for future directors and actors the interpretations of director Shaw.

The Theater in Bernard Shaw's Drama

Dedicated to my children:
Sam and Lucy,
who are young enough to keep me on my toes,
and Joan,
now a mature young woman,
who dances on her toes

IN "THE AUTHOR'S APOLOGY" (1902) to *Mrs Warren's Profession,* Bernard Shaw's third play, he berates critics who accuse him of "cynicism and inhumanity" because his "characters behave like human beings, instead of conforming to the romantic logic of the stage," and he protests that when reviewers "with completely theatrified imaginations" say that no girl would treat her mother as Vivie Warren does, they mean that "no stage heroine would in a popular sentimental play." He "burlesques them" by having the "sentimental artist" Praed expect that the feelings of the other characters are "logically deducible from their family relationships and from his 'conventionally unconventional' social code." According to Shaw, his parody is lost on these critics, who think Praed "the sole sensible person on the stage." Shaw pretends to chastise himself, "[F]ool that I was not to make him a theatre critic instead of an architect!" (1, 252).

Why did Shaw not make him a theater critic? From the start, as Shaw's handwritten first draft shows, he thought of Praed as an "architect by profession,"[1] perhaps to provide a rough parallel between the failed restoration of old churches in Victorian times with Mrs. Warren's failed efforts to restore a maternal relationship with her daughter. Perhaps, too, since a prominent character in his second play, *The Philanderer,* is a theater critic, the fledgling dramatist, consciously or not, selected a different profession connected with the arts.

Recognizing the latter likelihood creates an awareness of how often Shaw uses aspects of theater in his plays, including characters whose professions are connected with the theater, characters who behave like such people as actors and directors, stage settings, theatrical devices (chiefly, the play-within-a-play), allusions to the theater (including theatrical genres, and the play's spectators who are watching it in the auditorium). A cursory review of the Shavian canon reveals that not one but four critics appear in *Fanny's First Play*, plying their trade, as do a theater producer and a dramatist, whose untitled titular work is a play-within-a-play. The chief character of *The Dark Lady of the Sonnets* is a real dramatist, Shakespeare, who reappears in *Shakes versus Shav*, along with Shaw, and the second work has two plays-within-a-play. This theatrical device, as well as similar contrivances, like a concert-within-a-play, occurs in several other works, including *The Devil's Disciple, The Music-Cure*, and *Back to Methuselah*, which also has a theatrical multimedia effect. Related to plays-within-plays, onstage audiences both mirror and cue audiences of Shaw's plays. Other uses of the theater abound. In *Pygmalion*, Higgins coaches Liza in speech and in a performance at his mother's home. In *Cæsar and Cleopatra*, Caesar teaches Cleopatra costuming and acting. A scene in *Androcles and the Lion* takes place backstage at the Coliseum in Rome. In various plays, characters deliberately play roles, acting so that others will believe them to be different from what they are. Destroying illusionistic realism, some characters break the fourth wall and directly address the audience; one character exits by way of the auditorium. Furthermore, Shaw deliberately invokes theatrical tradition, such as the harlequinade and the pantomime. Also characteristic of his theatrical use of the drama is metatheatricality, in which the drama is conscious of itself as a play being performed, conscious too of its author and of dramatic and theatrical tradition.

As these illustrations and generalities demonstrate, theatrical elements in Shavian comedy, spanning half a century, are more prevalent and more consequential than is generally realized. In the preceding sentence, the key word, which is repeated, is *more*. After Shaw's preface (1900) to *Three Plays for Puritans* pointed out that his "characters are the familiar harlequin and columbine, clown and pantaloon" (2, 46), critics sometimes note that his characters derive from traditional theatrical personages, which they do, and occasionally quote this passage.[2] When critics go further, they do so only occasionally and confine themselves to one or a few plays. On the centenary of Shaw's birth, for example, two books appeared. Archibald Henderson observes that *Androcles and the Lion* is "a Shavian species of Christmas pantomime" and that *Fanny's First Play* "is on the plan of *The Taming of the Shrew*—consisting of an Induction, the encysted plan, and an Epilogue." The work goes no further, not even mentioning the harlequin and columbine of *You Never Can Tell*. St. John Ervine's book quotes Count O'Dowda's prediction that his daughter's play will contain a columbine, a harlequin, and a pantaloon. It too goes no further and does not mention the harlequin and columbine of *You Never Can Tell*.[3] Seven years later, Martin Meisel published a groundbreaking and still enormously valuable study of Shaw's indebtedness to the theater of the century in which he was born. He goes into far greater detail in describing the pantomime and harlequinade aspects of *Androcles and the Lion,* but he too says nothing of the harlequinade figures in *You Never Can Tell.* Like his predecessors, he cites O'Dowda's prediction about Fanny's play and indicates that Shaw's play frames her drama with an induction and epilogue. He also mentions that it is in the tradition of *The Rehearsal* and *The Critic,* but he does little more.[4] Later critics analyze individual plays in greater depth—Margery Morgan and A. M. Gibbs, for instance, are particularly illuminating about *You Never Can Tell*—but in harmony with the different aims and themes of their books, they do not explore Shaw's widespread use of the theater in his dramatic corpus.[5]

Unlike these other works, the aim here is to analyze Shaw's pervasive employment of theatrical elements in his plays. Examples will include but not be limited to the works just cited. In addition, this analysis will determine their consequentiality: the dramatic and thematic relevance of the theater in his drama.

On occasions when Shaw treats theater incidentally or inconsequentially, this study will not discuss them, except to illustrate the point here. In Mrs. Warren's first duologue with Vivie, for example, she "*[throws] herself on her knees*" and "*buries her face in her hands,*" ploys recognized as such by Vivie, who makes her stop using them (1, 307–8). Neither will it treat plays in which a character behaves theatrically but not for an onstage audience. Thinking himself alone, Hector Hushabye practices theatrical swordplay and love-making, but the moment someone who might be a spectator enters, he pretends he is doing gymnastic exercises. Although Lina Szczepanowska is an acrobat and a juggler, *Misalliance* dramatizes neither profession onstage—in contrast to *The Music-Cure,* which has Strega Thundridge playing the piano onstage. Whereas *The Man of Destiny* uses the Strange Lady's dressing as a man to invoke practices and techniques familiar to the drama and the stage, *Press Cuttings* does not use General Balsquith's wearing women's clothes to make people think he is a female suffragist, except offstage. In the latter play, cross-dressing does not refer to the theater. This principle holds for futuristic costumes (*Back to Methuselah, The Apple Cart*), songs (onstage in *The Apple Cart,* offstage in *On the Rocks*), personages whose characters may be theatrical but who do not consciously play for theatrical effect (Morell in *Candida*, Tanner in *Man and Superman*), and role-playing in daily life (He in *How He Lied to Her Husband*, Proteus in *The Apple Cart*).

Let us now examine Shaw's use of the theater in his drama, in the order in which he wrote each play or, in the case of *The Ra Prologue* to *Caesar and Cleopatra*, a new scene.

Widowers' Houses (1892)[6]

In the first act of Shaw's first play, Cokane gives an impromptu performance with Trench. Without the foggiest notion of what Cokane is up to, he becomes an unwitting actor in an exchange of which Cokane, improvising his dialogue, intends Sartorius to be an audience. "By the way, Harry," asks Cokane, "I have often meant to ask you: is Lady Roxdale your mother's sister or your father's?" Sartorius "*is perceptibly interested.*" "My mother's, of course," says Trench. "What put that into your head?" Cokane explains, for Sartorius's benefit, "She will expect you to marry, Harry: a doctor ought to marry. [. . .] She looks forward to floating your wife in society in London." When Cokane addresses Sartorius, Sartorius is more amenable to conversing with the strangers than he was moments before, when he turned his back on them (1, 51).

By making Cokane an improvisatory actor, Shaw conveys exposition to the audience as well as to Sartorius, he provides a way for Trench and Blanche to meet formally, and he establishes a reason for Sartorius to become interested in Trench. One reason Shaw gets away with this obvious stratagem is that it is part of the motivation of a character who is not a playwright or actor. Thus, the gambit registers as Cokane's, not Shaw's. Another reason is that because Trench has no clue what Cokane is doing, his stagey questions, those of an interlocutor in a well-made play, emerge not as an expository device, but as an expression of character, which parodies the stale gimmick of questions by a character who knows or should know the answers, in order to elicit answers from another character for the audience's benefit.

In the play's final act, Trench and Blanche assume roles to influence each other. When she catches him admiring her portrait, she "*shrewishly*" taunts him and stands in his way while declaring she does not want him to stay. As they face each other, "*quite close to one another,*" she provocatively defies and invites him to come closer. Recognizing her "*undisguised animal excitement,*" he performs a role different from what she expects. Stage directions convey the attitude of the character he plays: a "*cunning expression comes into the corners of his mouth*" and "*with a heavy assumption of indifference he walks straight back to his chair, and plants himself in it with his arms folded.*" She continues to abuse him verbally. "*At the end of every sentence she waits to see what execution she has done.*" She acts the role of dominatrix. Because he does not respond but plays a different role, the silent master, she fails to rule him. He "*maintains his attitude*" until her reprimand that her father ordered him out of her house. When she notices his reflex, "*her eyes gleam*" and she "*softens her tone a little as she affects to pity him.*" Once she calls him by his first name (in 1892, her use of his first name signified intimacy), "*he relaxes the fold of his arms; and a faint grin of anticipated victory appears on his face.*" Resuming the role of dominatrix, she resumes taunting him. After he continues his performance, showing that her acting has had no effect on him, she plays a different attitude, "*affectedly polite.*" He does not respond. She moves behind his chair and becomes the first to make physical contact, which he recognizes as sexual. She seizes his cheeks and twists his head to face her, demanding that he look at her. He closes his eyes and smiles. "*She suddenly kneels down beside him with her breast against his shoulder.*" This more overtly sexual maneuver is the response he hoped for. After he opens his eyes, now "*full of delight,*" she "*flings her arms round him, and crushes him in an ecstatic embrace*" that makes her words ironic: "How dare you touch anything belonging to me?" (1, 119–21).

The acting by a character in Act I results in the onstage audience wanting to learn more about his friend. The realistically seductive acting by two characters in Act III, whose subtext differs from their text, results in their becoming engaged to marry. Their mutual goal, sexual domination of the other, is genuinely dramatic. Whether either actually achieves this goal is ambiguous. What is unmistakable is that, ultimately, both get what they really want, which is each other. In addition, Trench's mastery of the art of realistic acting reveals his growing maturity, which is thematically relevant. In this play, whose subjects include mastery and submissiveness, control and manipulation of human beings and the body politic, a realistic view of sex and society marks an ability to function and prosper.

The Philanderer (1893)

Shaw's Opus Two contains direct references to theater. Cuthbertson, Grace Tranfield's father, is an anti-Ibsenite critic whose old-fashioned dramatic tastes inform his views of reality. He has told Craven that his life was spent "witnessing scenes of suffering nobly endured and sacrifice willingly rendered by womanly women and manly men" (1, 159). Craven asks if he works in a hospital. "Nonsense!" replies Charteris, "he's a dramatic critic. Didnt you hear me say he was the leading representative of manly sentiment in London?" Craven considers his views ridiculous and is astonished that he takes what he sees on the stage seriously. Charteris breezily concludes, "thats why he's a good critic" (1, 163–64).

Because Cuthbertson believes that what he sees on stage depicts reality, he applies playhouse stereotypes to real life. His expression of heartfelt sentiment at being reunited with his old friend is stagey: "*Cuthbertson goes to Craven and presses his hand silently; then returns to the sofa and sits down, pulling out his handkerchief, and displaying some emotion*" (1, 158). He uses a hackneyed theater term for Craven: an "old man, grown grey in the honored service of his country" (1, 176). He tells a bust of Ibsen, whose plays he considers cold and unfeeling, that his emotions "would do y o u good too" (1, 192). Since Charteris is an Ibsenite, "The only use he can find for sacred things is to make a jest of things. Thats the New Order." He is "*outraged*" when Charteris dismisses his speech as symbolic. "Symbolic! That is an accusation of Ibsenism. What do you mean?" "Symbolic of the Old Order," explains Charteris (1, 226).

"Symbolic," which to Cuthbertson means enigmatic or inscrutable, applies not to conventional drama, but to such Ibsenite plays as *The Master Builder*, which opened in London on 20 February 1893, the month before Shaw began to write *The Philanderer*. Cuthbertson's reaction recalls that of British theater critics to *The Master Builder*, such as Clement Scott's mockery that it has "infinite depths in the matters of symbolism and allegory," and an unsigned reviewer's dismissal, "Allegory, mysticism, and symbolism are all very well in their place, but I submit that they are not in their right place on the stage. On the stage I want lucidity, and if I dont get it I am angry."[7]

When Dr. Paramore asks if Julia is attached to Charteris, Cuthbertson's reply, reflecting the values of conventional drama, is that "he's not man enough for her. A woman of that sort likes a strong, manly, deep throated, broad chested man." Paramore infers that sportsmen attract her. "Oh, no, no," Cuthbertson responds. "A scientific man, perhaps, like yourself. But you know what I mean: a MAN. (*He strikes himself a sounding blow on the chest*)." Since Paramore finds the illustration inadequate, Cuthbertson becomes exasperated: "Pah! you dont see what I mean" (1, 169). What he cannot explain or comprehend is his belief that a pretty young woman can be attracted only to a man who resembles a leading actor in a play, and that since Charteris, who dresses unconventionally and behaves cleverly, imaginatively, and wittily, does not fit the role on stage, he cannot fit it in real life. Paramore, who as a scientist is serious and humorless, would qualify.

Shaw places Cuthbertson in dramatic circumstances like those of plays Cuthbertson admires. His meeting with Craven derives from a coincidence, which is a staple of such plays. They had not seen each other for many years but met at the theater "by pure chance" (1, 157). Their entrance interrupts an altercation between Charteris and Julia after Grace has left them. He pleads with Julia to "invent some thumping lie." She throws her outer garments on a table, *"darts to the piano, at which she seats herself,"* and commands him to sing. As he is about to do so, the fathers enter. Delighted by this tableau, Cuthbertson urges Julia to continue playing. He misses the irony of Charteris's refusal, "No, thank you. Miss Craven has just been taking me through an old song; and Ive had enough of it" (1, 155-56). After Cuthbertson has spoken to his daughter Grace, and after Craven and Julia leave, he asks Charteris what is the matter. Charteris explains in playhouse terms: "Ask your theatrical experience, Cuthbertson. A man, of course. [. . .] Julia wants to marry me: I want to marry Grace. I came here tonight to sweetheart Grace. Enter Julia. Alarums and excursions. Exit Grace. Enter you and Craven. Subterfuges and excuses. Exeunt Craven and Julia. And here we are. Thats the whole story. Sleep over it. Goodnight. *(He leaves)*." Aptly, Shaw gives Cuthbertson a stagey curtain line: "Well I'll be—" (1, 165).

Shaw recognizes that no human being can entirely base his life on theatrical formulas. Reality intervenes. Although Cuthbertson deplores how "everything is going to the dogs through advanced ideas in the younger generation" and how "the whole modern movement [is] abhorrent" to him, he belongs to the Ibsen Club. To qualify, one "must be nominated by a man and a woman, who both guarantee that the candidate, if female, is not womanly, and if male, not manly." Charteris, who calls him "the leading representative of manly sentiment in London," joined his daughter in guaranteeing his unmanliness (1, 159-61). He objects to the club on principle, but since it exists, he might as well benefit from its advantages. "When youre at home, you have the house more to yourself; and when you want to have your family about you, you can dine with them at the club." While women there "smoke, and earn their own living, no one really misbehaves, so theres nothing actually to complain of" (1, 172).

In marriage, too, Cuthbertson separates the real from the theatrical. Despite his belief in a happy home and a wholesome fireside, he admits that his marriage fell short of these ideals. His wife was "not bad. She might have been worse." They could not tolerate each other's relatives. She disliked living in the city and his work prevented him from living in the country. "But we hit it off as well as most people until we separated." While he accepts reality, he is incapable of questioning the conventional ideals reality contradicts. Instead, he sentimentalizes, "Some day the world will know how I loved that woman. But she was incapable of valuing a true man's affection." Learning that Craven married for money, not love, he does not condemn his friend: "We cant get on without it, you know" (1, 171).

Faced with real problems, Cuthbertson behaves not in line with trite theatrical views, but realistically. Charteris pleads with him to dissuade Craven from leaving immediately for Paramore's home, where Julia has gone, but to give Paramore a half hour to propose: "You know you're a kindly and sensible man as well as a deucedly clever one, Cuthbertson, in spite of all the nonsense you pick up in the theatre. Say a word for me." The critic carefully separates ideals from reality: "I am now going to speak as a man of the world: that is, without moral responsibility. [. . .] Therefore, although I have no sympathy whatever with Charteris's views, I think we can do no harm by waiting—say ten minutes or so" (1, 207).

Paralleling the separation between theatrical convention and realism in Cuthbertson, Shaw contrasts Craven's daughter Julia, a "womanly woman" who employs stagelike behavior, and Cuthbertson's daughter Grace, who is realistic even in a romantic situation.

> CHARTERIS. [. . .] Grace: is this your first love affair?
>
> GRACE Have you forgotten that I am a widow? Do you think I married Tranfield for money?
>
> CHARTERIS. How do I know? Besides, you might have married him not because you loved him, but because you didnt love anybody else. When one is young, one marries out of mere curiosity, just to see what it's like.
>
> GRACE Well, since you ask me, I never was in love with Tranfield, though I only found that out when I fell in love with you. But I used to like him for being in love with me. (1, 138–39)

Julia's interruption is theatrical: "*(A beautiful, dark, tragic looking woman, in mantle and toque, appears at the door, raging)*. Oh, this is charming. I have interrupted a pretty tete-à-tete. Oh, you villain!" (1, 144). Left alone with Charteris, she continues in a stagey vein: "*(She sinks on the piano stool, and adds, as she buries her face in her hands and turns away from him)* Better for me if I had never met you!" and "*(throwing herself at his feet)* Oh, Leonard, dont be cruel" (1, 148, 150).

Grace really is "an advanced woman" and a "New Woman" (1, 184–85). Julia's conventionality conforms to Cuthbertston's theatrified ideas, but Grace is a realist, a contrast that the women's scene together vivifies. Julia pleads, "*(suddenly throwing herself tragically on her knees at Grace's feet)* Dont take him from me. Oh dont—dont be so cruel." Grace refuses to play Julia's game: "Get up; and dont be a fool. [. . .] Do you suppose I am a man, to be imposed on by this sort of rubbish?" Soon:

> JULIA *(trying her theatrical method in a milder form: reasonable and impulsively goodnatured instead of tragic)* I know I was wrong to act as I did last night. I beg your pardon. I am sorry. I was mad.
> GRACE Not a bit mad. You calculated to an inch how far you could go. When he is present to stand between us and play out the scene with you, I count for nothing. When we are alone, you fall back on your natural way of getting anything you want: crying for it like a baby until it is given to you.

Although Grace loves Charteris, she rejects his marriage proposal since, she tells Julia, "I will not give myself to any man who has learnt how to treat women from you and your like. I can do without his love, but not without his respect; and it is your fault that I cannot have both" (1, 201–2).

Although, by contrast, Julia's agreement to marry Paramore provides a conventional happy close for a comedy, Grace undercuts it: "They think this is a happy ending, Julia, these men: our lords and masters" (1, 225). In further defiance of tradition, she gives the play's curtain line: "Never make a hero of a philanderer" (1, 227).

The Philanderer uses the theater to comment on the theater. A theater critic enunciates ideals of the stage, but when he is faced with difficult situations in real life, he does not act in accordance with them. Whereas his daughter embodies what he loathes in the theater, his friend's daughter exemplifies what he loves in it. The play's conclusion both reproduces and mocks the usual denouement of comedy, whose apparent happiness the realistic Grace denies.

Arms and the Man (1894)

Raina and Sergius, who are engaged to be married, perform for each other and her parents as if they were hero and heroine of a romantic melodrama or opera. "The theatrical concepts of the role, the disguise, [and] the pose are associated with both," as Marjorie Morgan observes.[8] They even look the roles. When we first see her, she is *"intensely conscious of the romantic beauty of the night, and of the fact that her own youth and beauty are part of it"* (1, 390). When we first meet him, we see *"a tall romantically hand- some man"* (1, 418).

Since they are aware that they are acting, they behave as their stage stereotypes would, yet she confesses that she once wondered, as he held her in his arms and looked into her eyes, whether they held their heroic ideas "because we are so fond of reading Byron and Pushkin, and because we were so delighted with the opera that season at Bucharest" (1, 392). When she hears the news that Sergius, disobeying his superiors, led a suc- cessful cavalry charge, her doubts are obliterated, especially when Blunt- schli says, "He did it like an operatic tenor." She is delighted—until she realizes that Bluntschli is not praising him. In fact, Bluntschli compares him to "Don Quixote at the windmills" (1, 404).

When Raina comes into a room or a garden, she does not merely walk in: she makes an entrance. For instance, Sergius asks, "How is Raina; and where is Raina?" At precisely this moment, a stage direction has her *"sud- denly coming round the corner of the house and standing at the top of the steps in the path,"* and she announces, "Raina is here."

> *She makes a charming picture as they turn to look at her. [. . .]*
> *Sergius goes impulsively to meet her. Posing regally, she presents her*
> *hand: he drops chivalrously on one knee and kisses it.*
> PETKOFF *(aside to Catherine, beaming with parental pride)* Pretty,
> isnt it? She always appears at the right moment.
> CATHERINE *(impatiently)* Yes: she listens for it. It is an abominable
> habit.

Sergius, too, performs: he *"leads Raina forward with splendid gallantry"* (1, 420–21). His manner is congruent with hers.

When they are alone together, they do not drop character. "My hero! My king!" she exclaims, *"placing her hands on his shoulders as she looks up at him with admiration and worship."* "My queen!" he exclaims, and kisses her forehead. "Be quick," he demands when she leaves to fetch her hat. "If you are away five minutes, it will seem five hours. *(Raina runs to the top of the steps, and turns there to exchange looks with him and wave him a kiss for a moment; then [he] turns slowly away, his face radiant with the loftiest exaltation.)"* (1, 424–25). Cuthbertson would recognize these two, who seem made for each other.

Their performance as if they were on a stage suggests they really know that life is different and that they are not what they pretend to be. Succinctly, Louka tells Sergius, "I know the difference between the sort of manner you and she put on before one another and the real manner." Recognizing the truth of her charge, he "*shivers as if she had stabbed him*" (I, 428). Indeed, his behavior a few minutes earlier provokes her assessment. The moment Raina is out of sight, he notices Louka, twirls his moustache, and swaggers toward her, asking if she is familiar with "the higher love." When she replies in the negative, he does not explain it but makes a bid for her affection: "Very fatiguing thing to keep up for any length of time, Louka. One feels the need of some relief after it." He takes her hand, which she "*pretend[s] to pull*." He refuses to let go. "Then stand back where we cant be seen," she demands. "Have you no common sense?" He then "*takes her into the stableyard gateway, where they are hidden from the house)*" (I, 425-26). In contrast to his technique with Raina, which is "put on," this is "the real manner."

Similarly, Bluntschli calls Raina's attention to the difference between her airs and authentic behavior: "When you strike that noble attitude and speak in that thrilling voice, I admire you; but I find it impossible to believe a single word you say." Since he is not cowed by her attempt to brazen out her posturing, she almost instantly drops the pose "*with a complete change of manner from the heroic to a babyish familiarity*" and asks, "How did you find me out?" Now at ease with him, she admits she has always attitudinized and orated that way. "I did it when I was a tiny child to my nurse. S h e believed in it. I do it before my parents. T h e y believe in it. I do it before Sergius. H e believes in it." "Yes," observes Bluntschli: "he's a little in that line himself, isnt he?" (I, 446-47).

At the end of the play, each of these young men and women pairs off with the one toward whom he or she behaves not affectedly but genuinely. Trite or conventional theatrical behavior, the sort Cuthbertson admires in the theater, is ridiculous in real life. In *Arms and the Man*, Shaw playfully spoofs playhouse-like romantic love and affectionately dramatizes realistic love.

The Man of Destiny (1895)

Whereas Raina and Sergius perform as if they were hero and heroine of a romantic melodrama, the Strange Lady acts as if she were both hero and heroine of a spy melodrama. The Lieutenant, who regards the world as

Cuthbertson does, acts as if he were a character in one. His views of reality, says Charles Berst, "are incapacitating and out of touch with realities." Furthermore, "In not playing but *being* a straight man," as Berst felicitously puts it, "he is an innocent, a dolt, a butt for trickery, scorn, and laughter on the stage of life."[9] Shaw calls the Lieutenant a *"credulous"* fool *"eminently qualified to rush in where angels fear to tread"* (1, 617). He has lost Napoleon's despatches by behaving as if life were a play. A youth in uniform swore eternal friendship, gave him his own pistols, horse, and despatches in order, he says, to show confidence in him. He was astonished when, after giving the boy his pistols, horse, and despatches to return the confidence, the boy never returned (1, 621).

Once the Strange Lady appears, he recognizes her as the knave who stole the despatches, concludes the lady is a man, or boy, now disguised as a woman, and demands, "Take off that skirt" (1, 623). She runs for protection behind Napoleon, whose arm she clasps to her breast as fortification. "Nonsense, sir," Napoleon admonishes him. "This is certainly a lady." In harmony with her conduct when she was in disguise, she improvises a response fit for a well-made play: "it must be my brother. [. . .] He is very like me." She presses her luck: *"(sweetly)* We are twins." The Lieutenant reacts true to form and dramatic formula: "That accounts for it" (1, 624–25).

Less obtuse or theatrified than his subordinate, Napoleon perceives what has happened and demands his despatches, which he knows to be hidden beneath the neckline of her dress. Continuing to act, she reproves him for speaking unkindly, touching her eyes with her fichu *"as if to wipe away a tear"* and *"producing an effect of smiling through her tears"* when she speaks. Not taken in, he adds that he will seize them by force if necessary. Histrionically, she *"throw[s] herself in tears on the chair,"* then *"throws herself on her knees,"* and uses the gambit, "I am only a weak woman, and you a brave man" (1, 626–28).

As these tactics are of no avail, she appeals to his male ego, praising his bravery, *"affecting a marked access of interest in him,"* at which he is so pleased, he postures theatrically, *"composing himself into a solemn attitude, modelled on the heroes of classical antiquity* [. . .]." Taking advantage of this lapse, she *"sink[s] on her knees before him"* in adoration and *"kisses his hand"* in allegiance; but she overplays her hand: *"(enraptured)* Your friend! You will let me be your friend! Oh! *(She offers him both her hands with a radiant smile).* You see: I shew my confidence in you." Her *"incautious echo of the Lieutenant undoes her."* Napoleon reminds her of the last time she used that stale, stagey trick and again demands the despatches. Refusing to concede defeat, she stagily dares him to take them by force.

> [S]he crosses her arms on her breasts in the attitude of a martyr. The gesture and pose instantly awaken his theatrical instinct: he forgets his rage in the desire to shew her that in acting, too, she has met her match. He keeps her a moment in suspense; then suddenly clears up his countenance; puts his hands behind him with provoking coolness; looks at her up and down a couple of times; takes a pinch of snuff; wipes his fingers carefully and puts up his handkerchief, her heroic pose becoming more and more ridiculous all the time.
>
> NAPOLEON (at last) Well?
>
> LADY (disconcerted, but with her arms still crossed devotedly) Well: what are you going to do?
>
> NAPOLEON. Spoil your attitude.

She then drops the attitude (1, 632–35).

Although she gives him the packet, she tries to persuade him to return one letter to her. She fails, but her truthful insinuations irritate him sufficiently that he hesitates to read it. Now he gets stagey and speaks like a playhouse hero:

> NAPOLEON. [. . .] I grant your request, madam. Your courage and resolution deserve to succeed. Take the letters for which you have fought so well; and remember henceforth that you found the vile vulgar Corsican adventurer as generous to the vanquished after the battle as he was resolute in the face of the enemy before it. (He offers her the packet).
>
> LADY (without taking it, looking hard at him) What are you at now, I wonder? (He dashes the packet furiously to the floor). Aha! Ive spoilt t h a t attitude, I think. (She makes a pretty mocking curtsey).

Moments later, she mimics him, saying she knows he forgives her because "(delicately reproducing his rhetorical cadence) you are as generous to the vanquished after the battle as you are resolute in the face of the enemy before it" (1, 642–43).

Determined to find a reason not to read the letter he knows will compromise him, he hides the packet in his breast pocket, then charges the Lieutenant with finding the culprit and retrieving the despatches from the Lady's brother, lest—using theatrified language—"the fate of the campaign, the destiny of France, of Europe, of humanity, perhaps," be lost (1, 644). To help the Lieutenant recover them, the Lady uses a theatrically trite method. She persuades him to make Napoleon promise that if he catches her brother, whom she will produce, the general will clear his character. His idiocy prompts Napoleon to promise.

Changing costume, she appears in uniform as her twin. Napoleon demands the despatches. She shifts from the well-made play to melodrama, a small change. Claiming that the sister is an enchantress who bewitched Napoleon, she says, echoing Napoleon's charge when she had the packet, that it is in the general's breast pocket. He did not grab them from her hiding place, but she takes them from his. Not outdone by cunning or melodrama, he orders the bewitched letters burnt. Fittingly, the two principals conclude the play stagily. Wondering if Caesar's wife would be above suspicion (a recurring phrase about the letter writer) if she saw them together, they watch the incriminating letter burn, then "*simultaneously turn their eyes and look at one another. The curtain steals down and hides them*" (I, 661).

With the Strange Lady and the Lieutenant behaving as if life were a well-made play, and Napoleon performing a role similar to that of *raisonneur*, a common feature of the well-made play, *The Man of Destiny* resembles such a play more than previous Shavian drama. Its action includes disguise and misunderstanding, a letter that gets into the wrong party's hands, a secret skillfully concealed then revealed, climactic ups and downs for the adversaries, and contrivances and coincidences. True, *Widowers' Houses* and *Arms and the Man* contain such crucial features as secrets (Sartorius's business, the identity of the chocolate cream soldier), coincidences (Lickcheese and Trench are in Sartorius's home at the same time, Petkoff sees Bluntschli when the Swiss returns the coat), misunderstanding (Blanche's of why Trench refuses her dowry), and a document getting into the wrong party's hands (Raina's photograph). Unlike these works, *The Man of Destiny* contains a prominent feature of the well-made play missing from Shaw's earlier pieces: a conclusion that restores the *status quo ante*. Unlike the endings of *Widowers' Houses* and *Arms and the Man*, wherein the characters learn so much of the truth about themselves and the world that they cannot conduct their lives as they did at the start of the plays, the happy end of *The Man of Destiny*, like that of the well-made play, essentially ratifies the world presented at the opening. Even though this play parodies the well-made play, it is, like the best of parodies, an example of what it spoofs.

You Never Can Tell (1896)

Whereas *The Man of Destiny* has a woman masquerading as her twin brother, *You Never Can Tell,* Shaw's next play, contains real male and female twins, Philip and Dolly Clandon. Unlike *The Man of Destiny,* which parodies the well-made play, *You Never Can Tell* parodies the harlequinade of English pantomime. The chief vehicles of the parody are the twins. Philip is harlequin; Dolly, columbine. By the late nineteenth century, the English pantomime had become an epilogue; Shaw's sprightly harlequinade occurs at the end of the play. Like a harlequinade, it contains music and satire, dancing and comic tumbling, a harlequin and a columbine, a pantaloon (Crampton) who tries to prevent a young woman (his daughter Gloria) from marrying a young man (Valentine, who accuses her of having "Thrown this enchantment [love] on me" [1, 737]), an exalted or angelic figure who takes the lovers under her wing and enables them to marry (Shaw's is a man, Bohun), a juxtaposition of a fanciful world and a comic real world, fantastic costumes, and a transformation.

In Shaw's harlequinade, music plays in the background. Immediately before Philip and Dolly enter, their father objects to their usual attire: "I think they ought to dress more quietly" (1, 778). Just after the Waiter reassures him that their clothing is "very choice and classy, very genteel and high toned indeed," a harlequin and a columbine waltz into the room. "*The harlequin's dress is made of lozenges, an inch square, of turquoise blue silk and gold alternately. His bat is gilt, and his mask turned up. The columbine's petticoats are the epitome of a harvest field, golden orange and poppy crimson, with a tiny velvet jacket for the poppy stamens. [. . .] [A]s the final chord of the waltz is struck, they make a tableau in the middle of the company, the harlequin down on his left knee and the columbine standing on his right knee, with her arm curved over her head*" (1, 780–81). The dancing duo, Philip and Dolly, wear the conventional costumes of their roles. Traditionally, a magic wand brings about a transformation scene in which the setting changes, but Shaw is interested in change of character, not of canvas and wood. The leap into a tableau is on the verge of farce:

> THE COLUMBINE *(screaming)* Lift me down, somebody: I'm going to fall. Papa: lift me down.
> CRAMPTON *(anxiously running to her and taking her hands)* My child!
> DOLLY. *(jumping down, with his help)* Thanks: so nice of you. [. . .] Oh, what fun! *(She seats herself with a vault on the front edge of the table, panting).* (1, 781)

While it is Harlequin who usually vaults, this variation is par for a harlequinade.

As befits her type, Dolly's columbine is witty and pert. When her mother introduces "Mr Bohun [pronounced *boon*], who has very kindly come to help us this evening," Dolly remarks that "he comes as a boon and a blessing." When her father, the pantaloon, comments derisively on her dress, she makes him back down:

> CRAMPTON *(propitiating her)* No, no. It's perhaps natural at your age.
> DOLLY. *(obstinately)* Never mind my age. Is it pretty?
> CRAMPTON. Yes, dear, yes. *(He sits down in token of submission)*.
> DOLLY. *(insistently)* Do you like it?
> CRAMPTON. My child: how can you expect me to like it or to approve of it?
> DOLLY *(determined not to let him off)* How can you think it pretty and not like it?

A type of angel, Bohun approves her method and dictates to the pantaloon—"You'd want this young lady here to give up dressing like a stage columbine in the evening and like a fashionable columbine in the morning. Well, she wont: never. She thinks she will but—" only to have this signature locution interrupted by the columbine, who is as saucy with him as with her father: "No I dont" (1, 781–82). She turns the tables on Bohun:

> DOLLY. [. . .] Youre going to bully us, Mr Bohun.
> BOHUN. I—
> DOLLY *(interrupting him)* Oh yes you are: you think youre not; but you are. I know by your eyebrows.
> BOHUN *(capitulating)* Mrs Clandon: these are clever children: clear headed well brought up children. (1, 783)

Upon Bohun's costuming himself as befits a harlequinade, the columbine and harlequin more clearly enact their roles. When Bohum dons a false nose, Dolly-columbine admiringly declares, "Oh, now you look quite like a human being" and asks him for dance. Philip, "*resuming his part of harlequin,*" performs one of the role's actions: he "*waves his bat as if casting a spell on them.*" As Bohun and Dolly dance off, Philip-harlequin aptly quotes Byron, "'On with the dance: let joy be unconfined'" (*Childe Harold's Pilgrimage*). His magic wand has helped transform Crampton-pantaloon.[10] "Dont let us be spoil-sports," says Crampton, agreeing to wear a false nose. True to the tradition of the harlequinade and of romantic comedy, the obstructive father joins the festivities and reunites with his family. He turns to his son *"with an attempt at genial father-liness"*; invites him, "Come along, my boy"; and leaves. True to his role, Philip *"cheerily"* follows: "Coming, dad, coming. *(On the window threshold he stops; looks after Crampton; then turns fantastically with his bat bent into a halo round his head, and says with lowered voice to Mrs Clandon and Gloria)* Did you feel the pathos of that? *(He vanishes)"* (1, 785–86).

As in traditional comedy, the young lovers of You Never Can Tell unite. Although Valentine does not kiss Gloria, *"she kisses him [. . .] and he reels back into a chair like a leaf before the wind"* (1, 790–91).

While Dolly waltzes in with the Waiter, Philip pirouettes alone. Gloria kisses her father and demands he bless them. When he objects to her marrying a penniless man, Dolly commands her twin brother to summon Bohun. Echoing Shakespeare and the harlequinade, he responds: "From the vasty deep. I go. *(He makes his bat quiver in the air and darts away through the window)*."[11] Half a minute later, he reappears: "He comes. *(He waves his bat over the window)"* (1, 791–92). As if by magic, the good angel Bohun returns, urging Crampton to approve the marriage and advising Valentine to insist on a settlement. Enchantingly, Bohun waltzes off with the bride-to-be, followed by Dolly with M'Comas and Philip with his mother. Crampton, transformed, follows them *"with senile glee"* and *"(goes into the garden chuckling)."* Valentine concedes with dismay that with his fiancée dancing off with another man, he might as well be married already. "Cheer up, sir, cheer up," the Waiter benignly tells him (1, 794). As in a harlequinade and romantic comedy, love wins and marriage reigns supreme.

In You Never Can Tell, Shaw uses harlequinade figures to make delectable by theatrical convention what is mandatory in romantic comedy: the union of young lovers and the reunion of father and children. He employs the theater to validate theatrical artifice.

The Devil's Disciple (1896)

The last act of You Never Can Tell has a harlequinade; the last act of The Devil's Disciple, written the same year, has a play-within-a-play, and the second act has another. This theatrical device illuminates differences between reading a play and seeing it performed, revealing why Shaw's ironies may misfire in productions of this work.

In his preface to Three Plays for Puritans, of which The Devil's Disciple is one, Shaw, referring to the first play-within-a-play, professes to grieve because his former colleagues, the London reviewers, mostly "shewed no sort of connoiseurship" when Murray Carson played Dick Dudgeon in 1899. "Why should a blackguard," they asked, "save another man's life, and that man no friend of his, at the risk of his own? Clearly, said the critics, because he is redeemed by love," and "his explicit denial of his passion was the splendid mendacity of a gentleman whose respect for a married woman, and duty to her absent husband, sealed his passion-palpitating lips." Once Carson read this "fatally plausible explanation," he changed his interpretation. Thereafter, he stole behind Judith Anderson and mutely confirmed his passion "by surreptitiously imprinting a heartbroken kiss on a stray lock of her hair whilst he uttered the barren denial" (2, 34, 36).

In the scene in question, Dick and Judith are alone. The stage business is in neither dialogue nor stage directions. She tells him that his death will break her heart, hints that she loves him, and twists from him a grudging admission that his saving her husband "must have been a little for your sake" (2, 110). When she misquotes him, changing "must have been" to "was" and omitting the words "a little," Dick *recoils with a gesture of denial.*" To her proposal that she go with him "to the end of the world," he holds her further from him and makes his denial of love explicit: "If I said—to please you—that I did what I did ever so little for your sake, I lied as men always lie to women" (2, 112–13). To romantic critics, actors, and audiences, his refutation of a love motive is a lie aimed at consoling her.

In the previous act, a sergeant and two privates find Dick and Judith at home, assume he is her husband, and arrest him. He stops her from blurting out the truth, pretends to be her husband, and joins them. "One gentleman to another, sir," says the sergeant. "Wouldnt you like to say a word to your missus, sir, before we go?" Speaking *"loudly, with ostentatious cheerfulness"* (that is, like an actor) for her benefit (as audience), he tells Dick, "No call for the lady to distress herself." Then: *"(in a lower voice, intended for Richard alone)"*—that is, in a stage whisper—"your last chance, sir." When the sergeant steps back to give them privacy, Dick urges her to get her husband out of harm's way. To dispel any doubts his onstage audience may have that he and she are a loving husband and wife, he acts a connubial farewell scene:

(He turns to go, and meets the eyes of the sergeant, who looks a little suspicious. He considers a moment, and then, turning roguishly to Judith with something of a smile breaking through his earnestness,

says) And now, my dear, I am afraid the sergeant will not believe that you love me like a wife unless you give one kiss before I go.

He approaches her and holds out his arms. She quits the table and almost falls into them.

JUDITH *(the words choking her)* I ought to—it's murder—

RICHARD. No: only a kiss *(softly to her)* for his sake.

JUDITH. I cant. You must—

RICHARD *(folding her in his arms with an impulse of compassion for her distress)* My poor girl!

Judith, with a sudden effort, throws her arms round him; kisses him; and swoons away, dropping from his arms to the ground as if the kiss had killed her. (2, 96–98)

Notwithstanding the sergeant's suspicious look and Dick's unambiguous statement why he wants to kiss her, critics, actors, and audiences often conclude that a leading man's request for a kiss from a leading woman is romantic, that a kiss (particularly when it is hers) is still a kiss, and a swoon is more than a sigh. Their conclusion conforms to the play-within-a-play tradition, in which the playhouse audience in the theater follows the cue of the onstage audience, which is convinced. Despite comic irony, the theatrical convention of the play-within-a-play subverts Shaw's intention. Perhaps what he says in his Epistle Dedicatory (1903) to *Man and Superman* applies here: "the lesson intended by an author is hardly ever the lesson the world chooses to learn from his book" (2, 498).

Another difficulty of Shaw's revolves around Judith and General Burgoyne in Act III. As Shaw wrote to Ellen Terry on 13 March 1897, the point of this act is that "Burgoyne is a gentleman [. . .]." Not only should Richard "be superior to religion and morality as typified by his mother and his home, or to love as typified by Judith. He must also be superior to gentility—that is, to the whole ideal of modern society." Burgoyne's plea for reciprocal politeness by both parties in the trial ignores "the villainy of his gallows, the unworthiness of his crime, and the murderousness of his profession."[12] The text bears out Shaw's interpretation.

Dick's trial becomes another play-within-a-play, with the roles and denouement scripted in advance. One onstage spectator is Judith, for whom Burgoyne pointedly orders a sergeant, "Give the lady a chair; and make her thoroughly comfortable" (2, 119).

During the trial, Burgoyne speaks wittily and *"with extreme suavity"*: "You will understand, sir, I hope, since you seem to be a gentleman and a man of some spirit in spite of your calling, that if we should have the misfortune to hang you, we shall do so as a mere matter of political necessity and military duty, without any personal ill-feeling." "Oh, quite so," says Dick. "That makes all the difference in the world, of course." The other men, who like Judith are spectators, *"all smile in spite of themselves; and some of the younger officers burst out laughing."* The reaction of Judith, the only spectator who is not a soldier, is largely mute: *"(her dread and horror deepening at every one of these jests and compliments)* How c a n you?" (2, 120). When Dick requests to be shot as a prisoner of war rather than be hanged, Burgoyne *"sympathetically"* asks: "Have you any idea of the average marksmanship of the army of His Majesty King George the Third?" Half of the firing squad would miss him and the rest would make a mess of the enterprise, leaving his execution to the provost-marshal's pistol, whereas they can hang him "in a perfectly workmanlike and agreeable way. *(Kindly)* Let me persuade you to be hanged, Mr Anderson?" Judith's reaction is again brief: *"sick with horror,"* she cries, "My God!" Burgoyne graciously tells her that the court is "greatly indebted to the admirable tact and gentlemanly feeling shewn by your husband." Her retort is neither tactful nor genteel: *"(throwing the words in his face)* Oh, you are mad. Is it nothing to you what wicked thing you do if only you do it like a gentleman? Is it nothing to you whether you are a murderer or not, if only you murder in a red coat?" (2, 122–23).

In reading the play, Judith's verbal responses and their accompanying stage directions heighten the scene's ironies. Her function as onstage audience of a play-within-a-play cues readers to share her reaction. However, in every production of the play that I have seen—in four countries on three continents—it was evident that Shaw gives her too few lines to convey what he intends the scene to convey; and in these productions, Burgoyne's wit, augmented by Dick's comic irony and the amused reaction of the soldier-spectators, so dominated the scene that the actor playing Burgoyne, if he had any charm, not only stole the show, he disarmed and captivated the playhouse spectators, who forgot he is a murderer. As the one female member of the onstage audience, who is supposed to cue the real audience into regarding him harshly, Judith receives too little opportunity to do so, and the male members of the onstage audience laugh at the verbal wit, which controverts Shaw's announced aim. However visually prominent her chair is, her outbursts, which differ from those of the soldier-spectators, are too few to bear the weight they need to overcome Burgoyne, who carries the play with him and overwhelms the author.

Whereas the first play-within-a-play works against Shaw's intentions, the second is insufficient to convey his theme, especially when it is subverted by an actor whose role, Burgoyne, has wit that endears him to audiences. The difficulties of a production of *The Devil's Disciple* in conveying the author's view are substantial.

Cæsar and Cleopatra (1898)[13]

Figuring prominently in *Cæsar and Cleopatra*, like *The Devil's Disciple* one of Shaw's *Three Plays for Puritans,* are appearances before audiences and coaching by director-like figures. Julius Caesar, of whose identity Cleopatra is initially unaware, arranges her costume and instructs her servants to clothe her with royal robes and crown, so that when Caesar arrives he will recognize her as Queen of Egypt. Since a slave might wear a queen's ornaments, costume alone is insufficient. Bearing, he tells Cleopatra, is crucial: Caesar will recognize her "by her pride, her courage, her majesty, and her beauty." Internal acting is also vital: "Cast out fear; and you will conquer Cæsar." Unable to do so, she is *"almost beside herself with apprehension"* (2, 192–93). When the Roman soldiers arrive and salute him, she recognizes the situation. In this scene, director Caesar has actress Cleopatra costumed and made up to play Queen. He succeeds only in arranging her external appearance.

In the last scene of Act I, Caesar's coaching helps Queen Cleopatra look good before an audience. In the first scene of Act II, Pothinus's coaching fails to help King Ptolemy speak well to an audience. Ptolemy has not completely memorized his lines, which he recites by rote.

> PTOLEMY *(without any vocal inflexions: he is evidently repeating a lesson)* Take notice of this all of you. I am the first-born son of Auletes the Flute Blower who was your King. My sister Berenice drove him from his throne and reigned in his stead but—but—*(he hesitates)*—
> POTHINUS *(stealthily prompting)*—but the gods would not suffer—
> PTOLEMY Yes—the gods would not suffer—not suffer—*(He stops; then crestfallen)* I forget what the gods would not suffer.

Prompted, Pothinus completes the speech that the gods would not suffer her impiety to go unpunished. When Ptolemy *"resumes his monotone"* about Mark Antony and his sister, his rote recitation still reveals he does not know the meaning of his words and he again forgets his lines, requiring another prompt to remind him of Cleopatra's sorcery over Caesar. He dries up once more: "Take notice that I will not suffer," and must ask what he will not suffer. His guardian *"(suddenly explod[es] with all the force and emphasis of a political passion)* The King will not suffer a foreigner to take from him the throne of our Egypt" (2, 196–97).

As the audience of Roman soldiers hails not Cleopatra but Rome, of which Caesar is the symbol, so the audience of this Egyptian faction applauds not Ptolemy but the political faction of which he is the symbol. In each case, a director coaches an actor, using theatrical elements (costume in one, delivery of a speech in the other), to make the actor seem impressive to an onstage audience. The ineffectuality of the director's work with Ptolemy does not contrast with the effectiveness of the director's work with Cleopatra but suggests that they parallel each other: as Ptolemy has the words but not their meaning, Cleopatra has the appearance but not what underlies it. Each director is aware of his limited accomplishment. Pothinus has to prompt Ptolemy; Caesar knows whom his soldiers salute. Ironically, Caesar tells Ptolemy's tutor Theodotus, "You teach men to be kings, Theodotus. That is very clever of you" (2, 199). The irony reverberates on himself.

How much Ptolemy learns later, we do not know, for he does not reappear after Act II. The next time an actor faces an onstage audience is in Act V.[14] Cleopatra is her own costumer; the audience is Caesar. "*Cleopatra, cold and tragic, cunningly dressed in black, without ornaments or decoration of any kind, and thus making a striking figure among the brilliantly dressed bevy of ladies [...], comes from the palace and stands on the steps*" (2, 288). Her behavior follows Caesar's advice to reveal her royalty by her pride, courage, majesty, and beauty, and his admonition that if she casts out fear she will conquer Caesar. She scorns his approval of Rufio's killing of Ftatateeta.

As before, the meaning behind appearances eludes her. Is "Cæsar's way," she scornfully asks, to rule without punishment, revenge, and judgment? He calls it "the right way, the great way, the only possible way in the end." When he approves Rufio's murder of Ftatateeta, which was committed for none of these reasons, but to save Caesar's life, Cleopatra shows she has not understood her director's most significant lesson, because all she concludes, petulantly, is that killing is justified "when a Roman slays an Egyptian" (2, 289–90). He has taught her only how to act like a queen. With striking attire and mien; with pride, courage, majesty, and beauty; and without fear, she looks impressively regal. Although she has not taken in the meaning of ruling Caesarianly, she has mastered how to look the role and create her own words, which unlike Ptolemy's are effective.

Contrary to Caesar's statement, casting out fear is insufficient to conquer him. Cleopatra fails, but Rufio, having learned the true meaning of

Caesarian rule, succeeds in doing so. Instead of conquering Caesar, which would result in his removing Rufio from office, she receives a consolation prize, Mark Antony. The end of Act V's echo of the end of Act I puts the theater spectators in the same position as that of the Roman soldiers: delighted by the attractive woman next to Caesar, but impressed by Caesar himself.

John Bull's Other Island (1904)

As Broadbent believes in the political, economic, romantic, and national-istic ideals of a stage Englishman and acts in accordance with his views, he does not consciously perform a role; rather, he naturally behaves as a stage Englishman would in real life. Unlike him, Tim Haffigan enacts the role of stage Irishman when he is in the presence of Englishmen like Broadbent. He "*gives a show of reckless geniality and high spirits, helped out by a rollicking stage brogue.*" He sprinkles his speech with such phrases as "The top o the mornin to you" (2, 896). His manner is as excessive and overdone as his consumption of Broadbent's whisky, which is consider-able. When his salary is at issue, he is cagey, "*trying to guess how far he may go*" (2, 901). He succeeds with Broadbent not because he is a con-vincing actor but because, as his countryman the expatriate Irishman Larry Doyle tells the Englishman, "you humbug yourself." Such suppos-edly Irish phrases as the one just quoted, says Larry, are "got up in En-gland to fool you," and in Ireland no Irishman uses them. When a worth-less Irishman finds England filled with "romantic duffers like you, who will let him loaf and drink and sponge and brag as long as he flatters your sense of moral superiority by playing the fool," he takes them in (2, 905).

When Larry is in the room with Tim, Tim's "*brogue decay[s] into a common would-be genteel accent with an unexpected strain of Glasgow in it,*" but once Larry leaves, he begins "*plunging again into his role of dare-devil Irishman,*" entreating Broadbent for money "*with all the brogue he can muster*" (2, 902–3). With a five-pound note in his hands, he dashes out the door before Larry returns. "Never was in Ireland in his life," Larry tells Broadbent of Tim, whose speech he picked up, with his other antics, "at the theatre or the music hall"; but Broadbent is "*still incredulous*" (2, 905–6).

After Broadbent arrives in Ireland, he hears no top-of-the-morning or broth-of-a-boy from the natives. If he does not perceive that Tim's theat-rical manner is assumed for the onstage audience of one Englishman, the audience does, and it knows too that Tim succeeds not because he is so skillful but because this English audience is accustomed to take such stagey speech and behavior as reality.

The mirror of the theater does not end when Broadbent and Doyle arrive in Ireland, it takes another form. Although *John Bull's Other Island* does not contain a play-within-a-play, it contains a story-within-a-play, which is comparable to this device, and—most importantly—reactions from two onstage audiences. The story, at the start of Act IV, is of Broadbent and the pig, and the storyteller is Barney Doran, whom Shaw places between the two groups of spectators: male villagers, some inside the house and others spilling beyond into the garden, and Aunt Judy, Nora, and Father Keegan at the table. The male villagers *"are screaming with laughter, doubled up,"* and cannot hear the tale often enough or chuckle and guffaw with more merriment at each telling. The other cluster of spectators disapproves of both the story and this response. "Ah now dont be tellin it all over and settin yourself off again, Barney," says Aunt Judy. "I dont know how you can laugh. Do you, Mr Keegan?" asks Nora. Keegan explains that the tale contains "danger, destruction, torment! What more do we need to make us merry?" and declares, *"(with intense emphasis)* It is hell: it is hell. Nowhere else could such a scene be a burst of happiness for the people." Shaw emphasizes the importance of Keegan's response partly by having made Keegan more intriguing and sympathetic than anyone else and partly by his directorial design, as he reveals in his stage directions: because Keegan is *"the central figure in a rather crowded apartment,"* his *"extraordinarily stern"* demeanor aims to cue the real audience's response to the story (2, 979–82).

Keegan's reaction to the story deftly foreshadows the play's conclusion, in which he predicts that the future of Rosscullen, which Broadbent's and Doyle's land development syndicate will snap up, will be diabolically "clean and orderly" and will be run by "an efficient devil" who will not do "the will of Heaven that is in himself" but will act "in the service of Mammon" (2, 1015–16). Just as the laughter of the male villagers is not stopped by the women or Keegan, so, he later admits to Broadbent and Doyle, "the gates of hell still prevail against me" (2, 1021).

Passion, Poison, and Petrifaction (1905)

Soon after Shaw began his next full-length play, *Major Barbara,* he was preoccupied by directing *You Never Can Tell, Candida,* and *Man and Superman* for the Court Theatre. His production responsibilities so consumed his time and drained his energies that he stopped work on the new play for almost three months.[15] During this period, perhaps taking a breather to recharge his writing batteries, he wrote *Passion, Poison, and Petrifaction*.[16]

Possibly because his time was so absorbed by the practical process of creating theatrical productions of his plays, the theater itself gushed from his pen, filling this one-act play, which makes the audience aware of the stage and its conventions, notably those of trite melodrama, from the outset, in which a cuckoo clock strikes sixteen times. In the opening dialogue between Lady Magnesia Fitztollemache and her maid, Phyllis, we learn that sixteen notes now indicate 11:00 P.M., but in the morning they mean 2:30 A.M. so that if they waken Lady Magnesia, she should not arise.[17] Exit the convention of realistic time, enter the world of theater, where the sound effect of a cuckoo clock has no relationship to time in the real world.

Before this dialogue, a stage direction cues the reader that the theater, not real life, dominates the play: "*A certain air of theatricality is produced by the fact that though the room is rectangular it has only three walls*" (3, 205). Since Shaw wrote his play to be performed, not merely read, he brings the stage direction into the dialogue and action, puncturing a convention on which much realism depends, the illusion that the audience is looking at a real room through an imaginary, invisible fourth wall that is framed by a proscenium arch and the stage floor. Phyllis asks whether her ladyship will undress for bed. "Not tonight, Phyllis," is the reply of Lady Magnesia, whom Shaw has acknowledge the audience's presence: "*Glancing through where the fourth wall is missing*," she sees the spectators and states, "Not under the circumstances" (3, 206).

With such an opening, an explicit indication that the characters are aware of the convention of an actor-audience divide, the imaginary partition is demolished. Few if any members of the audience would be aware that they are any place but in a theater and that what they witness is anywhere but a stage. Thunder (under such circumstances, a sound clearly produced by a backstage machine) roars. A choir of angels—here and later, when, as Ina Rae Hark happily puts it, "the traditional musical accompaniment that put the 'melo' in melodrama might be expected"[18]— sings a popular ditty, "Oh, wont you come home, Bill Baily?" which, if it could create any mood, her ladyship breaks by wondering, "Why should angels call me Bill Bailey? My name is Magnesia Fitztollemache." Emphasizing the theater by preventing any spectator from being affected by mood music, the angels soon "*sing out of tune*" (3, 210). When her husband surreptitiously enters the room, following the sound effect of "*A*

dull, heavy, rhythmic thumping—the beating of his heart," which he acknowledges, thus emphasizing the amplified sound as stage effect, "I can
no longer cower here listening to the agonized thumpings of my own
heart" (3, 206–7).[19] In the theater, stage lighting intensifies the mood.
Shaw parodies the lighting of melodrama, which was exaggerated enough,
when, for instance, "*All the colors of the rainbow chase one another*" up
the villainous husband's face, when it "*turns a dazzling green,*" and when
it "*is again strangely variegated,*" all in three pages, which prompts the
wife to remark, "Your complexion is really going to pieces" (3, 207–9).
Later in the play, husband, wife, and her lover, Adolphus Bastable, throw
shoes at the ceiling.[20] "*Flakes of plaster rain down which Adolphus de-
vours*" (3, 213) as a possible remedy for the poison Lord Fitztollemache
gave him, which, true to the play's title, is petrifying his body. This stage
business too cocks a snook at illusionistic realism and accents the theater
in the play, for it is obvious that a real ceiling is not broken but that food—
in a prefatory note, Shaw suggests the tops of wedding cakes—is dropped
from the flies by a property man. A moment before this action, Adolphus
reminds the audience of the theater: he exclaims, after Lord
Fitztollemache wonders whether an antidote might be too anticlimactic,
"Anti-climax be blowed! Do you think I am going to die to please the
critics?" (3, 213).

Such language as the husband's, which includes "you have but ten minutes to live—if so long" and "I must have your undivided love. I must have
your love: do you hear? LOVE! LOVE!! LOVE!!! LOVE!!!! LOVE!!!!!" —
the increasing number of exclamation marks indicating his increasing
passion, are redolent of the theater, not real life. Hark is correct when she
notes, of the word "Tragedy" in the subtitle, "Much of the dialogue parodies the overly rhetorical diction ('Horror on horror's head!' or 'My mind
misgives me') and inverted syntax ('What mean you?' or 'Finish that ceiling I cannot and will not') typical of 'serious' nineteenth-century drama,
especially when that drama attempted to appropriate to itself the language
and meter of Shakespearean tragedy."[21]

Like the beginning of this play, the end insists on the theater that is its
milieu. When the curtain falls, the band plays the National Anthem and
Attendants, "*in front*" of the curtain, tell the real audience, "All out for
the next performance. Pass along, please, ladies and gentlemen: pass
along" (3, 220).

Major Barbara (1905)

In *Major Barbara,* characters perform roles they want other characters to accept as real. The spectator-characters who are dazzled by idealistic attitudes do so; the realists do not. "[S]o transparent a humbug as Snobby Price," says Shaw in his 1906 preface to the play, in a statement that, *mutatis mutandis,* applies to Tim Haffigan and Broadbent, could not take in "any experienced Salvationist on a point on which the Salvationist did not wish to be taken in. But on the point of conversion all Salvationists wish to be taken in; for the more obvious the sinner the more obvious the miracle of his conversation." A converted burglar "can hardly have been too burglarious" (3, 42). In this respect, Salvationists resemble Henry Fielding's Partridge, in *Tom Jones,* who prefers the overacting of the performer of the king in *Hamlet* to the realistic portrayal of Garrick as the prince, since on a stage, conventionalized theatricality seems more real than simulated life. In *Major Barbara,* the recognition of humbuggery, or conventionalized theatricality, signals a realistic outlook.

Foreshadowing Salvationist acting and response in Act II is Lady Britomart's insistence in Act I that Cusins remain for her traditional prayer service rather than go to Barbara's informal one. Suavely quoting *The Book of Common Prayer* as he acts humble honesty, he claims that he could not bear to hear her recite such passages as "we have done things we ought not to have done, and left undone things we ought to have done, and that there is no health in us," for Lady Britomart would do herself an injustice. "As for myself, I flatly deny it: I have done my best." Therefore, "I must go to the drawing room." Not taken in, she tells him she suspects he joined the Salvation Army "to worship Barbara and nothing else. And I quite appreciate the very clever way in which you systematically humbug me" (3, 92–93). Though undeceived by his performance, she places it in a realistic perspective: he is a suitable husband for Barbara.

Whereas in Act I Cusins fails to humbug her on a point on which she does not want to be taken in, in Act II Snobby Price fools the Salvationists on a point on which they are gullible.[22] Acting with mock concern, he relieves Jenny Hill of her burden, the worn-out Peter Shirley, and sends her for food. After she leaves, Shirley protests that he is not old but only looks it, and is a hard worker. Price stops acting and "*cheerfully*" shuts him up. "Make the thievin swine give you a meal: theyve stole many a one from you. Get a bit o your own back." After Jenny returns with the food, Price pretends piety: "Awsk a blessin an tuck that into you." So does Rummy Mitchens: "God bless you, lovey! youve fed my body and saved my soul, havnt you?" When Jenny asks whether Price has eaten "a piece of bread," he replies, *"(with unction)* Yes, miss; but Ive got the piece that I value more; and thats the peace that passeth hall hannerstennin." "Glory Hallelujah!" exclaims Rummy (3, 99–100).

Barbara too is gullible:

> BARBARA. [. . .] Ive hardly ever seen them so much moved as they were by your confession, Mr Price.
> PRICE. I could almost be glad of my past wickedness if I could believe that it would elp to keep hathers straight.
> BARBARA. So it will, Snobby. (3, 123)

Undershaft and Cusins are audiences to Snobby's performance. When Barbara wishes she could devote her energies to conversion rather than begging for money, Undershaft, with *"profound irony,"* consoles her: "Genuine unselfishness is capable of anything, my dear." Cusins, who is undeceived, calls him "Mephistopheles! Machiavelli!" (3, 124). Barbara is taken in by the overplaying of Snobby and the underplaying of her father.

So is Mrs. Baines, who to remind Undershaft of when the poor broke the windows of rich men's clubs, asks Price if he remembers the incident. "My ole father thought it was the revolution, maam," says he. He would not break windows now, he asserts hypocritically, because "The windows of eaven av bin opened to me. I know now that the rich man is a sinner like myself." Convinced by such overacting, this female Partridge concludes, *"(with swimming eyes)* You see how we take the anger and the bitterness against you out of their hearts, Mr Undershaft." Wryly, Undershaft remarks that this is "most convenient and gratifying to all large employers of labor" (3, 129–30).

Cusins's sardonic commentary exposes Mrs. Baines's gullibility to Barbara. When Mrs. Baines calls Bodger's gift of money a design to make the poor "stop drinking—to take his own business from him," Cusins *"impishly"* exclaims, "Pure self-sacrifice on Bodger's part, clearly! Bless dear Bodger!" On cue, Undershaft claims "a little disinterestedness" for his donation and, *"remorselessly"* cataloguing the men killed and women widowed by his business, artfully proposes that since the Army preaches peace, "I give you this money to help you to hasten my own commercial ruin." Cusins, *"in an ecstasy of mischief,"* proclaims, "The millennium will be inaugurated by the unselfishness of Undershaft and Bodger." Mrs. Baines *"is affected to tears."* Cusins, *"in a convulsion of irony,"* commands, "Let us seize this"—and the actor might pause for a fraction of a second to find the appropriate term—"unspeakable moment" to march to the meeting. Barbara now understands the difference between performance and reality: "Dolly: you are breaking my heart." With a triple entendre that connects Dionysiac ecstasy, Undershaft's purchase of the Salvation Army, and his own performance, he states, "I am possessed" (3, 133–35). Visualizing Undershaft's purchase and Barbara's new perceptions, Shaw has her remove the Salvation Army brooch from her collar and pin it on his.

Act III confirms her understanding when she echoes her mother about Cusins. She asks if he were ever in earnest about the Army or would have joined were it not for her. When he "*disingenuously*" stammers, "Well—er—well, possibly, as a collector of religions—," he reveals the answer to be negative (3, 143).

In *Major Barbara,* Shaw employs acting to dramatize Barbara's blindness, then awakening to reality. Her recognition that Mrs. Baines is humbugged by the performances of Snobby and her father, and that Mrs. Baines misses the ironies of Cusins, heightens her insight that the Army, to quote Shaw's preface, "is even more dependent than the Church on rich people who would cut off supplies at once" if it truly threatened what Bodger and Undershaft represent (3, 40). Shaw uses the theater to support his theme.

The Doctor's Dilemma (1906)

Like *Passion, Poison, and Petrifaction,* Shaw subtitled *The Doctor's Dilemma* "A Tragedy."[23] As he stated in a press release, the later play is about death, which occurs with classical appropriateness in the fourth of its five acts; yet, referring to himself in the third person, he called it "the most amusing play he has ever written" (3, 437). Whereas in *Passion, Poison, and Petrifaction* he mentions theater critics, in *The Doctor's Dilemma* he is self-referential. "I dont believe in morality," says the amoral artist Louis Dubedat in the third act, which is set in his studio. "I'm a disciple of Bernard Shaw." To B.B., such a confession stops all conversation, for when a person "avows himself a follower of a notorious and avowed antivaccinationist, there is nothing more to be said." In contrast is Sir Patrick's reaction: "Bernard Shaw? I never heard of him. He's a Methodist preacher, I suppose" (3, 393–94). Making the audience aware of the stage by a dialogic reminder of the play's author, Shaw prepares spectators for a more daring use of theater later.[24]

In the next act, also set in Dubedat's studio, Shaw exploits the theater in a manner unlike his usage before or afterwards. Instead of contrasting staginess with reality, he dramatizes life using the theater to heighten itself. "*Cardinal Death,*" a figure wearing a cardinal's robe and hat, a scythe on its back and an hour glass in one hand, holds them "*like a sceptre and globe*" and, as it did not do in the previous act, sits on the studio throne, a chair on a dais (3, 408). The prop figure, which is justified by the setting, theatrically heightens the death scene that Dubedat both lives and enacts. Both: "*he is so weak physically that he can hardly move, lying on his cushions with complete languor; but his mind is active: it is making the most of his condition, finding voluptuousness in languor and drama in death*" (3, 413). He makes the most of what is, which differs from falsifying what is, and he finds, not imposes, drama in death. When the newspaperman asks what his plans are for the season, he quips, "My plans for the season are very simple. I'm going to die" (3, 414). He tells Jennifer not to cry since tears make her ugly, and to remarry, since it will demonstrate that she was happy in her marriage to him. Both admonitions are as true as his comment to the journalist.

Heightening his own death scene, he reminds her of one winter when they burned a bush, whose flames danced, and he asks to be cremated. "Whenever you see the flame, Jennifer, that will be me" (3, 416). He, or Shaw through him, alludes to the biblical burning bush, in which the angel of the Lord appeared to Moses and through which God spoke to Moses (Exodus 3:2–4). Dubedat's burning bush does not falsify reality theatrically but highlights it, and his enunciation of his creed as an artist is a poetic accentuation of his artistic conviction, not a stagey distortion of it.

Ridgeon responds to Sir Patrick's suggestion that he leave, "Would you deprive the dying actor of his audience?" Dubedat appreciates the gibe, but he ripostes that "it's not true. It's you who are still on the stage" —an accurate observation, for Ridgeon's response is simultaneously a performance for Jennifer (3, 418).

Although B.B.'s eulogy for Dubedat, which mixes quotations from *Macbeth* and *Hamlet*, is ludicrously funny, it is not a stagey falsification of reality but, like Dubedat's death scene, an attempt to find drama in death. As Shaw reminds us, and the actor, "*B.B.'s feeling, absurdly expressed as it is, is [. . .] sincere and humane*" (3, 423).

A play that differs in style from Shaw's other works, *The Doctor's Dilemma* utilizes the theater differently from his method elsewhere. Effectively and subtly, he dramatizes life heightening itself theatrically.

The Inauguration Speech: An Interlude (1907)[25]

As Shaw specifies, the theater program of the main play (as his subtitle says, this is an interlude) contains an insert indicating that before the play begins, the Manager will address the audience.[26] At its start, the interlude theatrically disorients spectators. Instead of the Manager addressing them, his wife, "*overcome with nervousness,*" enters in front of the curtain and addresses them to explain that "this speech—you know—this little slip in your programs—it says that Edwin—I mean Mr Goldsmith," then tears the paper into pieces. "I have to get this finished before he comes up from his dressing room," Angelina seems to confide to the spectators, supposedly in her own person, "because he doesnt know what I'm doing." She apologizes for how badly she is giving her speech, asks for applause to inspire her to continue, divulges how nervous her husband is, especially when he is building a theater, and begs them— "please, PLEASE" —not to make the slightest noise when he lectures (the very appearance of the comic actor Cyril Maude, the original, could prompt laughter) (7, 600–601). As the actress, playing a character who bears her real name, apparently addresses the spectators, as she receives their applause, and as the theater to which she refers is the one in which they are seated, Shaw obliterates the fourth wall and destroys the distinction between enactment and reality. The audience becomes part of the performance.

Continuing to remind the spectators that they are in a playhouse, not eavesdropping on real life, Shaw brings to the fore the manner in which theatrical devices enhance illusionism. The actress, on the forestage, has a dialogue with the Conductor of the orchestra, which is in the pit between her and the audience. When her husband "comes to the pathetic part," she asks the Conductor, "give him a little slow music. Something affecting," and she divulges his regret that no one will cast him in a melodrama. "Not that he likes melodrama; but he says that the slow music is such a support on the stage; and he needs all the support he can get tonight, poor fellow!" From one of the wings, the Carpenter warns of her husband's imminent arrival. "Not a word," she whispers to the audience before she hurries offstage. Wherever the fourth wall may have shifted, the members of the audience, who become her conspirators for the sake of the jest, are on the same side of it as she is (7, 602).

As the band plays "Auld Lang Syne," the curtain rises on a desk piled with unbound manuscript pages, a decanter of water, and a glass. This is a setting, now more obviously than it might have been before the actress's scene, for a lecture that will directly address the audience through the unwalled proscenium arch. The wife is seated, the husband standing and *"ghastly pale."* After comically abortive efforts to begin the oration, including the desk collapsing, at which she encouragingly tells him, "Never mind, dear, it was only the desk," he finally starts, "Dear friends—I wish I could call you ladies and gentlemen—" which triggers her prompt that it is the other way around. In what is designed to look like a departure from the prepared text, they bicker, and he apologizes to the audience for his wife's nervousness—gambits that deceive no one, for the spectators, in on the joke, know they are watching a scripted text (7, 602–3).

After more interruptions from his speech, such as starting to trace a history of the theater's site from the Domesday Book on, a line she tries to dissuade him from pursuing, he confesses, "If the true nature of my talent were understood I should be playing Hamlet. Ask the audience whether they would not like to see me play Hamlet." A stage direction indicates *"Enthusiastic assent"* from the audience, which would be forthcoming for any popular comic actor who made such a plea. The reason he does not act this part is that "anybody can play Hamlet," but only he can act his comic roles. "I leave Hamlet to those who can provide no livelier form of entertainment." When he returns to his historical subject, the Stage Manager (or an actor playing the role) enters, admonishing him, "You promised me you would be done in ten minutes. Ive got to set for the first act." Goldsmith blames his wife for his not having completed the speech, suggests that the spectators would be disappointed if he did not do so (at which, although Shaw does not specify, they might applaud), whereupon the Stage Manager gives up: "Only dont blame me if the audience loses its last train and comes back to sleep in the theatre: thats all. *(He goes off with the air of a man who is prepared for the worst)"* (7, 605).

During their conversation, Angelina steals all but the last two pages of the speech, which he reads as if he were resuming his oration. As he becomes emotional about his theatrical career, violins quiveringly play and a flute begins "Auld Lang Syne," which upsets him. "They are only supporting you, Edwin," says his wife, comfortingly, but he is not soothed: "They have emptied my soul of all its welling pathos. I never heard anything so ridiculous. Just as I was going to pile it on about you, too." At this, she urges him to continue, but he is too upset to do so. "Finish it yourself," he grumbles, and *"Exit in high dudgeon"* (7, 606–7).

She does so, in a more traditional speech to an audience at the opening of a theater, calling herself and her fellow actors servants of the public who are "most at our ease when we are doing our work" and who dread occasions when they step out of character and speak in their own persons, recitations that may put those on both sides of the footlights out of countenance, which she and her husband refuse to do.

> After all, you know how glad we are to see you; for you have the advantage of us: you can do without us: we cannot do without you. I will not say that
>
>> The drama's laws the drama's patrons give
>> And we who live to please must please to live,
>
> because that is not true and it never has been true. The drama's laws have a higher source than your caprice or ours; and in this [Playhouse] of ours we will not please you except on terms honorable to ourselves and to you.[27]

Following this come "*Assent & Applause*" from the audience, which concludes the interlude (7, 607–8).

Although the audience knows that the interruptions and altercations, which are performed as if they were improvised, are really part of the play, it accepts the convention that they are not and that the actors speak in their own, not in fictitious persons. Thus, the subject of *The Inauguration Speech* is the theater itself: actors, script, offstage associates, and even the audience.

Misalliance (1909)

Like *Arms and the Man*, *Misalliance* mocks the conception of how a stage hero behaves and speaks, which is in accordance with ideals of gentlemanly action and diction, by contrasting them with real-life behavior and speech. The method of *Misalliance* is partly to dramatize them as a fictitious version of real life and partly to reveal its basis as a theatrical convention.

When Hypatia rushes into the room, followed by Joey Percival, she claims that he "has been chasing me down the hill." However, Gunner, who, hiding in the Turkish bath, overheard her pursuit of the reluctant man, disputes her: "Who chased him up it?" (4, 221). Instantly, Percival assumes a role Cuthbertson would recognize as real: he defends Hypatia's virtue by playing the stage hero, that is, by acting like a gentleman, speaking "*sternly*" and with "*contained indignation*": "Am I to understand you as daring to put forward the monstrous and blackguardly lie that this lady behaved improperly in my presence?" In terms appropriate to a stage hero, he assures all present that "there is not one word of truth—not one grain of substance—in this rascally calumny, which no man with a spark of decent feeling would have uttered even if he had been ignorant enough to believe it" (4, 222). Unless Gunner retracts his accusation that Hypatia behaved improperly, he challenges Gunner to a fight. Although Gunner, who has not been trained to box and who has endured a life of malnourishment, disavows himself, Percival demands that—to clear Hypatia's reputation—he sign a formal refutation.

Hypatia is satisfied: "that will teach him to tell lies next time." Bentley, who recognizes that Percival's recasting of reality is false, quips, "You mean it will teach him to tell the truth next time" but goes along with the convention underlying the document (4, 225). When Mrs. Tarleton realizes that Gunner is Lucinda Titmus's son, she destroys the convention at a stroke. "Tear up that foolish paper, child," she tells him, adding, "I dont believe a word of it. If the poor lad was there in the Turkish bath, who has a better right to say what was going on here than he has?" Both her daughter and Percival, she insists, should be ashamed of themselves (4, 228–29).

Lord Summerhays concludes that "the correct thing depends for its success on everybody playing the game very strictly. As a single-handed game, it's impossible." Stagily posturing, Percival charges Mrs. Tarleton with "not playing the game" (4, 229–30). The game is the acceptance of convention, which is crucial to endorsing as appropriate in real life, behavior that is realistic in the theater or theatricalized life. If people acted in accordance with Cutherberton's notion of propriety, then his theatrified views of conduct would apply to life. But Charteris does not do so and Percival tries in vain to do so. *Misalliance* makes it clear to audiences that reality is different from stagey behavior.

The Shewing-up of Blanco Posnet (1909)

By contrast, *The Shewing-up of Blanco Posnet* shows reality to be highly theatrical. Before his trial, Blanco "*takes out a pocket comb and mirror, and retires towards the dais to arrange his hair*" (3, 780). At the end of the play he announces that he will preach a sermon on the moral of what has happened, which he does.

Elder Daniels, actually Blanco's brother Boozy, who makes a show of passionately upholding religion but whose income is from selling whisky, hypocritically reconciles the two: "what keeps America today the purest of the nations is that when she's not working she's too drunk to hear the voice of the tempter." "Dont deceive yourself, Boozy," says his brother. "You sell drink because you make a bigger profit out of it than you can by selling tea. And you gave up drink yourself because when you got that fit at Edwardstown the doctor told you youd die the next time; and that frightened you off it." Boozy refuses to drop character and admit the truth. Like Snobby Price, he maintains his theatrical posture: "*(fervently)* Oh thank God selling drink pays me! And thank God He sent me that fit as a warning that my drinking time was past and gone" (3, 773).

Exemplifying Shaw's employment of the theater in this play, in addition to Boozy's hypocrisy and Blanco's theatrical oratory, is a technique that Shaw uses more extensively the following year in *The Dark Lady of the Sonnets:* reference to the theater itself. While Blanco is being tried for his life, Shaw pointedly has him quote not only a play, but also a performance of a play: "As the actor says in the play, 'a Daniel come to judgment.' Rotten actor he was, too" (3, 782).[28] The drama is *The Merchant of Venice,* the speaker Shylock, the scene Antonio's trial. Whereas Shylock is the plaintiff, Blanco is the defendant. Whereas Shylock loses, Blanco wins. Perhaps Shaw implies that Blanco is a better actor than the unnamed thespian Blanco saw as Shylock.[29] Through the unsophisticated Blanco, Shaw gives another theatrical allusion, an ironic accusation that "the fair Euphemia," which echoes Hamlet's "the fair Ophelia," has had "immoral relations with every man in this town," including the sheriff (3, 783–84). Chiefly, it is the *Merchant of Venice* reference that is crucial, for Blanco's quotation of a performance of a Shakespearean drama reminds spectators that they are seeing a play of which he is the title character, and therefore that what they see is a theatrical event. If they recognize the quotation, their enjoyment is enhanced.

The Dark Lady of the Sonnets (1910)

The running joke that sparks *The Dark Lady of the Sonnets,* set at the turn of the sixteenth century, is that Shakespeare literally took his well-known phrases from real life. "Angels and ministers of grace defend us!" exclaims a Beefeater at the start, when a cloaked man (Shakespeare) claims that, as he is an actor, he is sometimes one person, sometimes another, and "anon" a Ghost (4, 309). According to tradition, Shakespeare played the Ghost in *Hamlet* (1601–2), the source of the Beefeater's line (I,iv), but not written in the dramatic present. Upon hearing the exclamation, which is so famous the audience probably recognizes it even if it does not know the source, the Bard jots it down. He is ecstatic when the Beefeater opines, "you may say of frailty that its name is woman" and writes it (*Hamlet,* I,ii). When the Beefeater, puzzled, asks if he is "a snapper-up of such unconsidered trifles," the thrilled dramatist records it for future use (*A Winter's Tale* [1611], IV,iii) and calls the man "greater than I" (4, 310–11). Shakespeare quotes his own writings. Upon learning that Lord Pembroke wrote sonnets to the same lady for whom he is waiting, he translates his recognizable phrase, "Thou, too, Brutus!" (*Julius Caesar* [1599], III,i) and adds, "Tis ever so. Twas ever so," for which he cites the source, "Two Gentleman of Verona!" ([1590–95], II,iii) (4, 311). What Shaw does in these instances is not buttress illusionism but, as audiences readily perceive, play with the theater.

Soon, a cloaked lady, talking as she sleepwalks, provides phrases that spectators know Shakespeare will use, minus the gags, of course: "*(rubbing her hands as if washing them)* Out, damned spot. [*Macbeth,* V,i] You will mar all with these cosmetics. God made you one face; and you will make yourself another. [*Hamlet,* III,i] Think of the grave, woman, not ever of being beautified. [*Hamlet,* II,ii] All the perfumes of Arabia will not whiten this Tudor hand" (*Macbeth,* V,i). The Bard is delighted: "'All the perfumes of Arabia'! 'Beautified'! 'Beautified'! a poem in a single word." In *Hamlet,* Polonius, with lack of connoisseurship, will call it "an ill phrase, a vile phrase." He wonders why the woman, who he believes is Mary Fitton, speaks poetically for the first time since he has known her, and calls, "Mary! Mary!" Thinking he alludes to another Mary (Stuart), the sleepwalker echoes him, "Mary! Mary! Who would have thought that woman to have had so much blood in her?"—which he will use for Duncan, "the old man" (*Macbeth,* V,i) (4, 312–13).

The sleepwalking woman is Queen Elizabeth I, who is not pleased when Shakespeare praises her voice: "Sir: you are overbold. Season your admiration for a while—" (*Hamlet,* I,ii), but the actor-writer interrupts her and repeats the phrase. Although she is aghast— "Fellow: do you dare mimic me to my face?"—she makes sure that he records her words right. He starts to write, "'Suspend your admiration for a space,'" but she corrects him: "I said 'Season your—'" and "You said 'for a space.' I said 'for a while.'" He revises his notes. Praising her as a "divine perfection of a woman," he stops, "no: I have said that before somewhere," which he did (*Richard III* [1592–3], I,ii) (4, 314–15).

Soon, she reveals who she is. Mary arrives and complains of Shakespeare's treatment of her, "I am of all ladies most deject and wretched," which he notes down (4, 320). This phrase will turn up in *Hamlet* (III,i), as will Elizabeth's admonition, "You lack advancement" (III,ii) (4, 322).

It is a truism that when a dramatist introduces Shakespeare as a character, the character reveals, intentionally and not, something of himself.

When one recognizes this to be the case, self-referentiality mixes with intertextuality. In *The Dark Lady of the Sonnets,* Shaw has Shakespeare echo his own view that Shakespeare wrote "two noble and excellent plays setting forth the advancement of women of high nature and fruitful industry even as your Majesty is: the one a skilful physician, the other a sister devoted to good works." Also echoing Shaw's view, which Shaw enunciates in his preface to the play, Shakespeare declares that he wrote "two of the most damnable foolishnesses in the world, in the one of which a woman goes in man's attire and maketh impudent love to her swain, who pleaseth the groundling by overthrowing a wrestler; whilst, in the other, one of the same kidney sheweth her wit by saying endless naughtinesses to a gentleman as lewd as herself." He showed his "scorn for such follies and for them that praise them by calling the one As You Like It [1599–1600], meaning that it is not as I like it, and the other Much Ado About Nothing [1598], as it truly is." Both hold the stage, "where indeed I cannot have my lady physician presented at all, she being too honest a woman for the taste of the town" (4, 322–23). The "noble and excellent plays" are *All's Well That Ends Well* (after 1599) and *Measure for Measure,* (1604, therefore an anachronism). The lady doctor is in the former, and as no evidence exists that it was performed in Shakespeare's lifetime, the humorous explanation of Shaw's Shakespeare is not as farfetched as it may appear.

Shaw's Shakespeare utters Shaw's belief—which many spectators would recognize, since unlike most of his other comedies this play is designed for special, not general audiences—that "this writing of plays is a great matter, forming as it does the minds and affections of men in such sort that whatsoever they see done in show on the stage, they will presently be doing in earnest in the world, which is but a larger stage." When Elizabeth I promises to speak to the Lord Treasurer about the matter, Shakespeare Shavianly despairs, "Then am I undone, madam; for there was never yet a Lord Treasurer that could find a penny for anything over and above the necessary expenses of your government, save for a war or a salary for his own nephew." The Queen agrees and, alluding to the Bible, tells him that it will be over three centuries until "my subjects learn that man cannot live by bread alone [Matthew, 4:4, paraphrasing Deuteronomy, 8:3], but by every word that cometh from the mouth of those whom God inspires." She recognizes that "until every other country in the Christian world, even to barbarian Muscovy"—a forecast of the Moscow Art Theatre—"and the hamlets of the boorish Germans, have its playhouse at the public charge, England will never adventure" (4, 323–24).

For years, Shaw strove publicly and privately for a national theater subsidized by the country and/or private donations. The year before he wrote this play, he drafted a letter urging millionaires to contribute a "nest egg" for use when appealing to the nation for subsidy, and arguing that "urban populations go to theatres instead of to places of worship" and that "the morality of the town is becoming more and more a sensational and romantic morality inculcated in the commercial theatres." The letter, whose ideas Shaw's Elizabeth I expresses, calls the theater "the most potent factor in the formation of our national conscience and character." No other European nation so neglects it, says Shaw, and like his virgin queen, he cites France and Germany, as well as Austria and Scandinavia.[30]

Shaw links himself to Shakespeare. "I care not for these new-fangled plays," says the Beefeater. "No man can understand a word of them. They are all talk" (4, 309–10), which points more to him than to Shakespeare, as does the Bard's regret, "the world for the most part will none of my thoughts" (4, 312). The Queen's charge against Shakespeare is often leveled against Shaw: "You have an overweening conceit of yourself" (4, 321). Such self-referentiality ensures that the fourth wall will not be reglazed.

Although these affinities between the fictive dramatist and his creator may be obvious, there is another, less obvious resemblance. If Shakespeare resembles Shaw in advocating a national subsidized theater, in his views of Shakespeare's plays, and in his belief that the theater serves a high moral purpose, it may follow that Shaw resembles Shakespeare in the chief premise of *The Dark Lady of the Sonnets:* he bases his plays on reality. In 1894, after the first production of *Arms and the Man,* he published "A Dramatic Realist to His Critics," claiming to put on stage what "is in real life" and to be so unoriginal that he takes all his "dramatic material either from real life at first hand, or from authentic documents" (1, 485). In 1892, in "Unconscious Villainy and Widowers' Houses," he defended his first play with a phrase from *Hamlet:* "it is only by holding [the mirror] up to nature that good work is produced."[31] By coupling himself with Shakespeare, who in *The Dark Lady of the Sonnets* copies phrases from real life, Shaw continues to position himself as "a dramatic realist."

Fanny's First Play (1911)

Unlike the single theater critic in *The Philanderer,* the four critics in *Fanny's First Play* exercise their profession onstage. Unlike the playwright in *The Dark Lady of the Sonnets,* the dramatist in *Fanny's First Play* is fledgling, fictitious, and female, although like Shakespeare, she draws on real life for her play, which unlike Shakespeare's scraps of dialogue, Shaw presents—as in *Shakes versus Shav* he says he presents—Shotover's daughters (playing on *Paradise Lost,* VIII) "all complete" (7, 475). Unlike the short plays-within-a-play in *The Devil's Disciple* and the acting sequences in *Arms and the Man,* which are more theatrical than what surrounds them, the inner play in *Fanny's First Play,* a play-within-a-play that occupies most of Shaw's play, is more realistic than the outer play that surrounds it, which consists of an Induction and Epilogue. Like *The Dark Lady of the Sonnets,* this frame play is permeated by intertextuality and self-referentiality that spoof the London theater scene and Shaw himself. As Peter Gahan says, this theatrically self-reflective comedy "is a drama about drama in which a playwright herself is one of the major characters" and in which "Shaw not only invokes the entire Western dramatic tradition of which *Fanny's First Play* is a product, but also places it in a critical context by parodying his contemporary London critics in the outer play."[32]

The first theater personage we see is the impresario Cecil Savoyard, whose surname means a producer (or performer or fan) of Gilbert and Sullivan's operettas, which were produced at the Savoy Theatre.[33] He typifies Shaw's view of theater people: he is an idiot, or less pejoratively, an uneducated Englishman whose knowledge and understanding are limited by and to the world of the theater. Shocked that Count O'Dowda considers all critics to be intellectuals, he exclaims, "Lord! no: heaven forbid! You must be careful what you say about that: I shouldnt like anyone to call me an Intellectual: I dont think any Englishman would!" (4, 360). When the Count approvingly quotes an anti-English sentiment by Byron (a letter to John Murray, 7 June 1819)—"'I am sure my bones would not rest in an English grave, or my clay mix with the earth of that country. I believe the thought would drive me mad on my deathbed could I suppose that any of my friends would be base enough to convey my carcase back to her soil. I would not even feed her worms if I could help it'"—Savoyard is flabbergasted that Byron would make such a statement.

> SAVOYARD. It dont sound like him. I saw a good deal of him at one
> time.
> THE COUNT. You! But how is that possible? You are too young.
> SAVOYARD. I was quite a lad, of course. But I had a job in the original
> production of Our Boys.
> THE COUNT. My dear sir, not t h a t Byron, Lord Byron, the poet.
> SAVOYARD. Oh, I beg your pardon. I thought you were talking of
> t h e Byron. (4, 353)

To Savoyard, *the* Byron is not the great English poet but the popular, now virtually forgotten playwright H. J. Byron, whose most successful, often revived work, *Our Boys*, opened in 1875 to an initial record run of 1,362 performances.

Savoyard does not blink when O'Dowda confides that in early rehearsals his daughter had difficulties with "the gentleman you call the producer, because he hadnt read the play; but the moment he found out what it was all about everything went smoothly" (4, 355). This practice was common for stage directors of the day.

Toward critics, Savoyard is disdainful. He speaks of them as he would of actors: "they get long engagements: forty years sometimes," and so they should be less expensive to engage than actors. He hires them for a pittance or for nothing. Since "Out of a hundred notices you wont find more than four at the outside that say anything different," he selected four to obtain representative opinions (4, 357).

As their names show, three of the four critics are such thinly disguised satires of real reviewers that audiences of the first production would recognize the personae on their side of the fourth wall: Trotter is Arthur Bingham Walkley (dedicatee of the prefatory epistle to *Man and Superman*); Vaughan, E. A. Baughan; and Gilbert Gunn, Gilbert Cannan.[34] The fourth, Flawner Bannal, is a composite critic "representing the lower echelons of criticism—the hacks who echoed the opinions of their superiors in the trade and pandered to public taste" (Hugo, p. 77). A fifth critic is Fanny's father, whose reaction to the play suggests, for reasons indicated below, Clement Scott.

Far from taking offense, Walkley, says Shaw's preface, "assisted the make-up by which [the actor] so successfully simulated his personal appearance," which for those in the know further chipped away the fourth wall (4, 346). Cannan was no longer reviewing plays, but the rest, in their reviews, joined the fun. "'We rather like Mr Trotter,'" said Walkley, "'probably for the usual reason that we are all apt to admire our opposites.'" The other critics "'have obvious originals,'" but Trotter is "'a pure figment of the imagination, wholly unlike any actual person.'"[35] Baughan called all the critics except Trotter "'very dull dogs.'"[36] "The critics whom I did not introduce were somewhat hurt," says Shaw, "as I should have been myself under the same circumstances; but I had not room for them all; so I can only apologize; and assure them that I meant no disrespect" (4, 346). In other words, he meant no disrespect in not publicly disrespecting them. Disrespect them he surely did, most ironically when Count O'Dowda, Fanny's father, addresses them as "the choice and master spirits of this age" (4, 434–35), which is what Shakespeare's Mark Antony calls Caesar's murderers in *Julius Caesar* (III,i), an allusion they do not catch; nor have others caught it.[37]

The tastes of the first reviewer to appear, Flawner Bannal, conform more than those of any other, says Savoyard, to the public's. He "represents the British playgoer. When he likes a thing, you may take your oath there are a hundred thousand people in London thatll like it [. . .]. He's the man in the street" (4, 360). Their approbation is what Shaw had not yet received in London. *Fanny's First Play* was his first box-office success there, running for 622 performances.

The second to appear is Trotter, author of *Playful Impressions* (a lampoon of *Playhouse Impressions*, a collection of Walkley's reviews). Like Walkley, Trotter is a member of the Academic Committee, which the Royal Society of Literature established the year before *Fanny's First Play*. Like Walkley, he speaks French, admires French actors, upholds Aristotle as arbiter of the drama, and "turn[s] up his nose at the theatre and says people make too much fuss about art" (4, 359). "Ive supported the Censorship in the face of ridicule and insult," he boasts (4, 368). Two years before *Fanny's First Play*, Walkley told the Joint Select Committee of the House of Lords and the House of Commons on the [Censorship of] Stage Plays that the importance of the drama was "overrated," and he refused to denounce censorship, since "it probably matters very little either to the art of drama or to the public welfare whether a Censor exists or not."[38]

Trotter's view of Shavian drama burlesques Walkley's. *John Bull's Other Island*, said Walkley, "delights by its policy of pin-pricks. Mr. Shaw takes up the empty bladders of life, the current commonplaces, the cant phrases, the windbags of rodomontade, the hollow conventions, and the sham sentiments; quietly inserts his pin; and the thing collapses with a pop." It also delights by "its able dialectic. Its interlocutors never shirk a point or swerve from it; every side gets a fair hearing [. . .]." After the build-up comes the put-down. The play disappoints "because of its wilful, perverse disregard of anything like construction. It is written [. . .] without beginning, middle, or end. People wander in and out quite casually and say whatever happens to come into Mr. Shaw's head at the moment." The only reason the play ends when it does is that "Shaw has had enough of it."[39] The year before *Fanny's First Play*, summarizes Leon Hugo, Walkley objected that Shaw's plays "were loose and rambling, lacked cohesion and organic unity; his plays were not plays but conversation pieces tossed pell mell on to the stage."[40]

As Walkley might, Trotter reacts to Fanny's reference to a modern type of drama whose "style and construction, and so forth, are considered the very highest art nowadays," by asserting that "these productions, whatever else they may be, are certainly not plays." He adds a reference to Shaw: "I am aware that one author, who is, I blush to say, a personal friend of mine, resorts freely to the dastardly subterfuge of calling them conversations, discussions, and so forth, with the express object of evading criticism." So Shaw did. He called *Major Barbara* "an ethical discussion in three long acts" (3, 186). He subtitled *Getting Married* "A Disquisitory Play" with "nothing but talk, talk, talk, talk, talk—Shaw talk," and with "no plot" (3, 665, 667). Like his model, Trotter insists that Shaw's pieces "are not plays. Dialogues, if you will. Exhibitions of character, perhaps: especially the character of the author. [. . .] But plays, no." When Fanny asks if he enjoys them, he disarmingly replies, "Of course I do. Do you take me for a fool? Do you suppose I prefer popular melodramas? Have I not written most appreciative notices of them? But I say theyre not plays" (4, 365–66).

The third reviewer is Vaughan, who like Baughan "does music as well as the drama." According to Savoyard, he "has no sense of humor; and if you joke with him he'll think youre insulting him on purpose" (4, 358–59). To Baughan, *Cæsar and Cleopatra* shows that Shaw "'is not really a humorous man at all'" and "he had not been amused" by *Getting Married*.[41] Through Vaughan, Shaw mocks Baughan's humorlessness.

Gilbert Gunn, the fourth critic, is one of "the chaps that go for the newest things and swear theyre oldfashioned" (4, 358). Unlike the others, he "is one of the young Intellectuals: he writes plays himself," and "he pitches into the older Intellectuals who are standing in his way" (4, 360). In 1905, Gunn's original, Cannan, belittled *Man and Superman* for "the narrowness and, I am bold enough to say, the shallowness of [Shaw's] outlook on life." In 1910, he derided *Misalliance* because rhetoric is "'a poor substitute for wit' [. . .]."[42] Shaw told Arthur Wing Pinero that he had superseded Pinero "as the whipping boy of the youthful educator of the public in the higher drama." Playing on a phrase in *The Master Builder,* he ranked Cannan as one of "the still younger generation knocking at the door [who] knocks on my nose."[43]

Representing a fifth view is Count O'Dowda, whose name suggests *dowd,* that is, a dowdy person. Among its meanings are "old-fashioned" and "out of date in style of dress or taste," characteristics that apply to him but not to his daughter, whose tastes and values are in the vanguard of her time.[44] Attired elegantly but in eighteenth-century clothes and living in an "old-fashioned house," this "Count of the Holy Roman Empire"—which began over a millennium earlier and by 1756 was, in Voltaire's phrase, "neither holy, Roman, nor an Empire" (*Essais sur les Moeurs*) — is determined to "shut out the nineteenth century." To do so, he rejects present reality and creates his own enclave in Venice. While some of his utterances resemble Shaw's — "I find England ugly and Philistine" and "My ears are offended by the Cockney twang" — his solutions to these aversions do not: "I dont live in it" and "I keep out of hearing of it [. . .]." Shaw does not retreat from and hermetically seal off the world around him; he tries to change it. A tip-off that O'Dowda is not Shaw's raisonneur is the Count's view of music: "I find Beethoven's music coarse and restless, and Wagner's senseless and detestable" (4, 352–54).

How do the critics respond to Fanny's play? The last is the first to speak. At the start of the Epilogue, the Count, "*dazed and agitated*," approaches the "*bored and weary*" critics.

Is this a play? Is this, in any sense of the word, Art? Is it agreeable? Can it conceivably do good to any human being? Is it delicate? Do such people really exist? Excuse me, gentlemen: I speak from a wounded heart. There are private reasons for my discomposure. This play implies obscure, unjust, unkind reproaches to all of us who are parents. [. . .] But there are reticences which everybody should respect. [. . .] People could not talk to one another as those people talk. No child could speak to its parent: no girl could speak to a youth: no human creature could tear down the veils [. . .]. (4, 433–34)

His reaction recalls Shaw's description of Clement Scott's response to Ibsen's plays, which expressed "the warmest personal feeling" and whose "resentment is angry and genuine." When the new ideas of *Ghosts* challenged the old, Scott "gave utterance to his horror like a man wounded to the quick in his religion, his affections, his enthusiasms: in the deepest part of him."[45]

Gunn reacts "*(with studied weariness)* It seems to me the most ordinary sort of old-fashioned Ibsenite drivel" (4, 434). He is close to the mark. Margaret's adventures, which are at the core of the inner play, are a sort of sequel to *A Doll's House,* and its third act echoes that of Ibsen's play. Margaret says to her fiancé, recalling what Nora says to her husband, "Ive something to tell you. Sit down and lets be comfortable" (4, 402). Gunn calls the play "an old-fashioned domestic melodrama" whose hero, like all melodramatic heroes, says he, is a naval lieutenant. "The heroine gets into trouble by defying the law (if she didnt get into trouble, thered be no drama)," and her "good old pious mother turns on her cruel father when he's going to put her out of the house, and says she'll go too." The comic relief includes a shopkeeper, a "footman who turns out to be a duke," and a young scapegrace who gives the author an excuse to drag in a fast woman. "All as old and stale as a fried fish shop on a winter morning" (4, 436). True: the play derives from domestic melodrama. Although the Count might consider it "new and unusual and original" because the "naval lieutenant is a Frenchman who cracks up the English and runs down the French," such a reversal betrays "the hackneyed old Shaw touch." Other traces of staleness include characters who are "second-rate middle class, instead of being dukes and millionaires," a heroine who "gets kicked through the mud: real mud," "no plot," "old stage conventions and puppets without the old ingenuity and the old enjoyment," and "a feeble air of intellectual pretentiousness kept up all through to persuade you that if the author hasnt written a good play it's because he's too clever to stoop to anything so commonplace." The author, says Gunn, is Granville Barker, and "old Gilbey is straight out of The Madras House" (4, 436–37). The characteristics he fires off are critical clichés about Barker's plays. He might have added, as Peter Gahan does, that the setting of *Fanny's First Play* is Denmark Hill, which is the scene of Act I of *The Madras House*.[46] Furthermore, whereas the Gilbeys have a son to be married off, the Huxtables of Barker's play have six daughters in this situation. Naming Barker is consistent with citing Shaw, since Gunn would consider Barker a lower-keyed, less theatrical Shaw.

"Utter nonsense!" explodes Vaughan. The play is "intensely disagreeable. Therefore it's not by Barrie, in spite of the footman, whos cribbed from The Admirable Crichton." The author's "saying silly things that have no real sense in them [. . .] just to set all the fools in the house giggling," the "attempt to expose the supposed hypocrisy of the Puritan middle class in England," and "the inevitable improper female" carry the imprint of Pinero, author of *The Second Mrs. Tanqueray* and *Iris* (4, 437). When Bannal argues that the Frenchman's long speech points to Shaw, Vaughan explodes again:

> VAUGHAN. Rot! You may put that idea out of your head, Bannal. Poor as this play is, theres the note of passion in it. You feel somehow that beneath all the assumed levity of that poor waif and stray, she really loves Bobby and will be a good wife to him. Now Ive repeatedly proved that Shaw is physiologically incapable of the note of passion.

BANNAL. Yes, I know. Intellect without emotion. Thats right, I always say that myself. A giant brain, if you ask me; but no heart. [. . .]

VAUGHAN. Well, at all events, you cant deny that the characters in this play are quite distinguishable from one another. That proves it's not by Shaw, because all Shaw's characters are himself: mere puppets stuck up to spout Shaw. (4, 438)

Baughan chastised Shaw for these reasons. His 1907 review of *Cæsar and Cleopatra* singles out the murder of Pothinus for applause because, uncharacteristically of Shaw, "There is passion at least in this scene [. . .]."[47]

Bannal, who initially declines to utter an opinion of the play until he knows who the author is—"If it's by a good author, it's a good play" (4, 435)—waits until Gunn has named Shaw before he does so, whereupon he utters such clichés as "Shaw doesnt write his plays as plays. All he wants to do is to insult everybody all round and set us talking about him" (4, 438). Shaw mocks Bannal through his encouragement of Fanny when she is revealed as the author: "A jolly good little play, Miss O'Dowda. Mind: I dont say it's like one of Shakespear's—Hamlet or The Lady of Lyons, you know—but still, a firstrate little bit of work" (4, 440). When *Fanny's First Play* was first produced, the joke was funnier: *The Lady of Lyons,* a popular melodrama, was considered high class because of its high-class author, the poet and novelist Edward Bulwer-Lytton.

Trotter is the one critic who correctly deduces that Fanny is the author. As Hugo says, this may be Shaw's "back-handed compliment" to his friend Walkley.[48]

The other theater personage in *Fanny's First Play* is the dramatist, a member of the Cambridge Fabian Society, who wrote the play on the basis of her experience and viewpoint.[49] The artificiality of social classes—the lower-class Dora becomes engaged to Bobby and the upwardly risen Juggins to Margaret—stems partly from her socialism. Among her play's subjects are police harassment of and brutality to women:

TROTTER. [. . .] That bit about the police was real. Youre a Suffraget, Miss O'Dowda. You were on that Deputation.
THE COUNT. Fanny: is this true?
FANNY. It is. I did a month with Lady Constance Lytton; and I'm prouder of it than I ever was of anything or ever shall be again.
TROTTER. Is that any reason why you should stuff naughty plays down my throat?
FANNY. Yes: itll teach you what it feels like to be forcibly fed. (4, 440)

Forced feeding was one of the shocking methods police used when jailed suffragettes went on hunger strikes. Katherine E. Kelly cites other characteristics of Fanny's play that reflect "suffrage culture." The "description of women being attacked by the police would have reminded contemporary audiences of 'Black Friday,' 18 November 1910 [less than four months before the play opened], when suffragettes set out for the House of Commons and tried to rush the police who held them back." Duvallet's admiration of Margaret's "mastery of 'jujitsu'" mirrors "standard additions to suffrage theatrical programs, where spectators would both see plays promoting suffrage and take brief lessons in how to defend themselves against police attacks." Only in England, says Duvallet, "are women trained to box and knock out the teeth of policemen as a protest against injustice and violence" (4, 427).[50]

Fanny's First Play's employment of the theater is not simplistic. Its theatrical impresario reflects the limited knowledge of such people. Three of its critics draw upon real figures. The fourth mirrors others as well as audiences, for whom he speaks. A fifth voice (O'Dowda) suggests a real reviewer. The reasons for the authors they guess inhere in Fanny's play, which draws on features of works by Ibsen, Barker, Pinero, and of course Shaw. Typical of an inner play, her drama reflects themes of the frame play, including the generation gap between parents and children. Inner play and outer play provide alternatives to each other. Paradoxically, the inner play, wherein the center of emotional gravity lies, ends happily, whereas the frame play, which is a comic spoof, does not—thus ironically stressing the difference between the world behind and before the footlights. The titular play derives from its author's socialist and feminist values, which suggests that Shaw, like his fictive Shakespeare, draws plays from real life.[51]

The play's ending, which breaks the fourth wall, climaxes Shaw's calling attention to theater. When the impresario asks the Count to congratulate the actors, who are upset because they have had no curtain call, *Fanny's First Play* comes full circle, for it begins with his entrance. O'Dowda admits he has been remiss and has the curtains drawn, revealing the actors of the play-within-the-play on its last set. The characters of the Epilogue congratulate and shake hands with them. "Whatever we may think of the play, gentlemen," says the Count, "I'm sure you will agree with me that there can be only one opinion about the acting." "Hear hear!" exclaim the critics, who "*start the applause*" (4, 441), which ends Shaw's play and begins the applause of the audience in the real theater, as the onstage audience turns and, with the actors of the inner play, acknowledges it.[52] That is, after actors who pretend to be real for us acclaim actors who pretend to be real for them, we acclaim both. Reality mirrors reality, theatricality embraces theatricality.

Androcles and the Lion (1912)

After dramatizing a performance onstage in *Fanny's First Play*, Shaw moves backstage in this, his next play, where performers prepare to go onstage, behind-the-scenes workers ready animal and other acts, and a Call Boy announces the next skit. One of the bases of the comedy in Act II, the first part of which is set *"where the performers assemble before entering the arena"* (4, 611), is that Shaw treats backstage in Rome's Coliseum, with gladiators preparing to battle and Christians about to be cast to a lion, as if it were backstage in London's Coliseum.

The first words in the act are the Call Boy's, "Number six. Retiarus versus Secutor," which suggest the next skit in a music-hall show or a musical review. Although these entertainers are gladiators, they behave like actors, *"the net thrower taking out a little brush and arranging his hair as he goes,"* the helmeted man *"shaking his shoulders loose,"* which actors do to relax their muscles. *"Both look at themselves in the mirrors before they enter the passage"* (4, 611–12).

The Editor informs the Christians that gladiators as well as Christians can be killed. Androcles's queries befit the theater: "But dont they ever just only pretend to kill one another? Why shouldnt you pretend to die, and get dragged out as if you were dead; and then get up and go home, like an actor?" The Editor stops this line of questioning: "See here: you want to know too much" (4, 612). By underscoring that the potentially deadly show is theatrical, Shaw keeps the play comic. By reminding us that the climax is throwing the Christians to a lion, he cranks up the suspense.

When Spintho, trying to save himself, inadvertently enters the cage of the lion, who eats him, the Christians are agitated, but the gladiators are amused. Shaw maintains a comic tension. The lion's not pouncing on Androcles later is realistically justified (he is no longer hungry) and is funny. "Perhaps the lion wont eat me now," suggests Androcles. "Yes: thats just like a Christian: think only of yourself!" exclaims the Keeper (4, 616).

Theatrical references abound. "Number eleven! Gladiators and Christian," announces the Call Boy (4, 619). Because Ferrovius delays, the Boy returns, reminding him, and us, "The stage is waiting" (4, 622). When

Ferrovius kills the gladiators, he makes a happy ending possible: Caesar ends the persecution of Christians, decrees that if this is how Christians fight only they will fight for him, and orders the other gladiators to convert to Christianity. The impresario-Emperor graciously returns the subject to the theater. Setting the Christians free, he invites them to "go into the front of the house and enjoy the spectacle," and asks the Captain to conduct them to seats reserved for his personal friends (4, 628).

The transition to the climax between the title characters is a transformation scene in the tradition of English pantomime. Instantaneously, the scenery changes from backstage to the amphitheater, where Caesar enters his box and Androcles marches into the arena. So does a pantomime lion—an actor obviously costumed as a lion, who sniffs Androcles; "*purrs like a motor car; finally rubs himself against Androcles, knocking him over.*" Limping on three paws, he mimes a wounded fourth paw. Recognizing him, Androcles "*flaps his hand as if it had a thorn in it, and pretends to pull the thorn out and to hurt himself. The lion nods repeatedly.*" They shake hand and paw, then embrace and waltz around the arena—a reprise of their waltz in the prologue—"*amid a sudden burst of deafening applause*" from the onstage audience (4, 630).

The play's theatricality is thematically apt. In *Androcles and the Lion,* the conflict is between orthodoxy and heterodoxy—the Romans orthodox, the Christians heterodox. As Shaw says in an afterword, he dramatizes Rome's persecution of Christians "not as the conflict of a false theology with a true," but as "an attempt to suppress a propaganda that seemed to threaten the interests involved in the established law and order, organized and maintained in the name of religion and justice by politicians" (4, 635). Like the audience in the Coliseum, the audience of Shaw's play has the values of the Establishment, and the Christians are rebels, perhaps like the socialist iconoclasts of which Shaw was one. By paralleling the Roman Coliseum and the London Coliseum, and then by making his onstage Roman audience face its own audience in the theater, Shaw has the spectators onstage theatrically mirror the spectators in the playhouse.

Pygmalion (1912)

In *The Dark Lady of the Sonnets,* a dramatist gathers material for his plays; in *Fanny's First Play,* completed the next year, a character's play is performed and critics comment on it; in *Androcles and the Lion,* finished a year later, backstage operations are in view. *Pygmalion,* written the same year as *Androcles,* shows a woman auditioning for lessons in diction and speech, which are requirements for acting, by a man who directs her to act a role—that is, to make her audience believe she is someone else. It also shows a speech lesson, his coaching her at a preview performance, after which a spectator criticizes it, and her performance to favorable responses on the Night.[53]

When Liza visits Higgins to arrange for speech lessons, he bullies her so much that she becomes terrified, and he threatens to hit her with a broomstick if she does not stop crying. He gives her his handkerchief. "What's this for?" she asks. "To wipe your eyes. To wipe any part of your face that feels moist. Remember: thats your handkerchief; and thats your sleeve. Dont mistake the one for the other if you wish to become a lady in a shop" (4, 690). This sequence is his first lesson—in social deportment, not speech. His method of teaching (bullying) prompts Pickering to ask whether it has occurred to Higgins that Liza has feelings:

> HIGGINS *(looking critically at her)* Oh no, I dont think so. Not any feelings that we need bother about. *(Cheerily)* Have you, Eliza?
> LIZA. I got my feelings same as anyone else.
> HIGGINS *(to Pickering, reflectively)* You see the difficulty?
> PICKERING. Eh? What difficulty?
> HIGGINS. To get her to talk grammar. The mere pronunciation is easy enough. (4, 694–95)

Higgins's sole concern is his job.

The coaching scene in the printed play shows Higgins's teaching of diction to be mechanical—as diction lessons usually are and as Shaw's were when Shaw the director and acting coach gave them. *Bernard Shaw, Director* quotes such Shavian exercises in diction as "try, first eer, ér, èr &c, and ree, ré, rè &c," and it quotes the coaching scene in this play in which Higgins, belittling and bullying Liza, teaches her how to say "a cup of tea" correctly (see above, p. 50).

Liza's performance at the home of Higgins's mother is a preview at which he unobtrusively coaches her while she partly recites, partly improvises dialogue. When Mrs. Higgins's guests, the Eynsford Hills, arrive—a larger audience—he exclaims with unintentional rudeness, "Yes, by George! We want two or three people. Youll do as well as anybody else" (4, 725).

At Liza's entry, he is like a nervous director watching a novice, and he coaches her. "*He stands on tiptoe and makes signs over his mother's head to Eliza to indicate to her which lady is her hostess. [. . .] Guided by Higgins's signals, she comes to Mrs Higgins with studied grace.*" "How do you do, Mrs Higgins?" she asks, "*speaking with pedantic correctness of pronunciation and great beauty of tone*," and repeats her How-do-you-do's to Pickering and the Eynsford Hills, impressing Clara and making Freddy instantly "*infatuated*." Cued by Higgins to talk of the weather, she enunciates from memory: "The shallow depression in the west of these islands is likely to move slowly in an easterly direction. There are no indications of any great change in the barometrical situation." When the subject turns to health, Liza ad libs in a "*tragic tone*" — cutting each word with a knife, as diction coaches used to advise — that "it's my belief they done the old woman in" (speaking of her aunt, who had survived diphtheria, and so surely could have come through influenza), and "them as pinched [her new straw hat] done her in." She adds such details as "Gin was mother's milk to her" (4, 727–29). The climax of her improvised speech contains Shaw's most famous phrase. To Freddy's proposal of walking across the park with her, she replies, "*(with perfectly elegant diction)* Walk! Not bloody likely. *(Sensation)*" (4, 730). Although she impresses the Eynsford Hills, Mrs. Higgins recognizes that her acting is mechanical.

The real performance occurs at the ambassadorial reception, where she arrives elegantly costumed. She experiences no stage fright. She speaks "with a beautiful gravity that awes her hostess," and when she passes through the rooms, "She is so intent on her ordeal that she walks like a somnambulist in a desert instead of a débutante in a fashionable crowd." So successful is her acting, and so perfect is her diction, that a former pupil of Higgins declares her a fraud. The only people who speak English well, says he, are foreigners who have been taught to do so. He calls Liza "Hungarian. And of royal blood" (4, 741–43).

In *Pygmalion,* a woman auditions for classes in diction and speech. Her teacher coaches her and later unobtrusively directs her at a preview performance whose dialogue she partly improvises. After more rehearsals, her performance wins the intended audience. Is this description of the play in theatrical terms farfetched? Recall Shaw's preface: "the change wrought by Professor Higgins in the flower-girl is neither impossible nor uncommon. The modern concierge's daughter who fulfils her ambition by playing the Queen of Spain in Ruy Blas at the Théâtre Français is only one of many thousands of men and women who have sloughed off their native dialects and acquired a new tongue" (4, 664). Shaw's use of the theater fits a play that takes as a major theme the transformation of a person from one social class to another. Liza accomplishes this change theatrically, by learning speech and behavior.

Cæsar and Cleopatra: The Ra Prologue (1912)

Behind Shaw were such works as *Passion, Poison, and Petrifaction,* with an acknowledgment of the audience; *The Inauguration Speech,* with direct address to the audience and references to drama and theater; *Fanny's First Play,* with metatheatrical references to audience tastes and to real authors, including Shaw; and *Androcles and the Lion,* with a mirroring of onstage and playhouse audiences. In the latter part of 1912, to try to ensure that Act III of *Cæsar and Cleopatra* would not be cut in performance, Shaw wrote a new prologue, shorter than the original one. Forbes Robertson first performed it on 25 October 1912 in Liverpool, then in London.

The new prologue consists of a single character, the Egyptian god Ra, who directly addresses audiences and acknowledges the theater in which they sit. His first word is striking, an injunction for the spectators to stop talking so that the performance might begin: "Peace!" Ra links the realities of time present and fictively recreated time past. "Be silent and hearken unto me, ye quaint little islanders," says this ancient god to twentieth-century Britons, whose males have "white paper on your breasts and nothing written thereon (to signify the innocency of your minds)," and whose females (at a time when feminist agitation was high) "adorn yourselves alluringly and conceal your thoughts from your men, leading them to believe that ye deem them wondrous strong and masterful whilst in truth ye hold them in your hearts as children without judgment." Although he boasts he was "once in Egypt a mighty god," a phrase that alludes to theatrical time past, he observes, calling attention to real time present, that the spectators "cannot kneel or prostrate" themselves before him, since they "are packed in rows without freedom to move, obstructing one another's vision" (2, 161).

Yet he recognizes, reflecting the theme that anachronisms are only apparent, that modern Britons do not essentially differ from ancient Egyptians, compared to both of whom Caesar is an advanced personage. Satirically, Ra tells the "compulsorily educated ones" in the auditorium that "even as there is an old England and a new, and ye stand perplexed between the twain; so in the days when I was worshipped was there an old Rome and a new, and men standing perplexed between them." Then as now, he points out, nailing down the similarities, the rulers "robbed their own poor until they became great masters of that art, and knew by what laws it could be made to appear seemly and honest." He stresses the play's theme with such observations as "This Cæsar was a great talker and a politician: he bought men with words and with gold, even as ye are bought" (2, 162–63).

As Shaw tinkers with his audience's expectations in his play, so he toys with them in this god, who might speak in the godlike author's name: "Are ye impatient with me? Do ye crave for a story of an unchaste woman? Hath the name of Cleopatra tempted ye hither?" He admonishes these "foolish ones" that Cleopatra is still a child, and that the play is what he (Ra, but also Shaw) is "about to shew you for the good of your souls" (2, 166).

With theatrical oratory, Ra recapitulates the theme that "men twenty centuries ago were already just such as you, and spoke and lived as ye speak and live, no worse and no better, no wiser and no sillier." But Ra (or Shaw) amuses them as he hectors them. He calls them "a dull folk, and instruction is wasted on you"; he promises not to speak to them again; and he admonishes them, "do not presume to applaud me" (2, 166–67). Such playfulness between a character (or author) and an audience takes the sting out of his rebukes and, like one of the key tactics in the play, it entertainingly makes them feel superior (to a fiction) while it enlightens them (to inner truths).

The Music-Cure (1914)

Whereas *Pygmalion* hinges on a verbal performance, *The Music-Cure* centers on a musical one. A piano recital, which is the titular remedy for Reginald's despondency, is a variation of the play-within-a-play. Shaw disclaims seriousness and calls his work "a Variety Turn for two musicians. It is written for two pianists, but can be adapted to any instruments on which the performers happen to be proficient." Mock-modestly, he adds, "There is, however, no pressing reason why the thing should be played at all" (4, 878). The play is hilarious, but as Father Keegan says in *John Bull's Other Island*, "My way of joking is to tell the truth. It's the funniest joke in the world" (2, 930).

At the start, much of the comedy derives from character, Reginald's "fatuous self-satisfaction" and "impenetrable inability to see any reason" why he should not have used his inside knowledge, as a government official, to make a fortune by buying shares on the stock exchange. He calls his action "simple common sense. I'm not a financier; but you cant persuade me that if you happen to know that certain shares are going to rise you shouldnt buy them." When the Doctor argues that public officials must not gamble, he responds, "I wasnt gambling. I k n e w" (4, 880–81). Comedy also derives from attitudes toward prescriptions. To soothe Reginald's nerves, the Doctor gives "the old-fashioned remedy: opium."[54] When he prescribes no more than one opium pill, since "opium is a poison," Reginald brainlessly insists, "Yes, opium. But not pills" (4, 883).

The humor turns farcical when Reginald, awakened by Strega Thundridge's piano playing, rolls off the sofa. Pleading with her to stop playing, he runs to her on his knees and snatches at her hands. When he "*exclaims ecstatically*" how lovely they are, "*She hurls him to the carpet*" (4, 887). A barrage of double entendre, sarcasm, and farce follows his announcement that he too is a pianist and her question about what he plays. "I wish you belonged to me," he answers. She is "*outraged.*" He explains it is the title of a tune, plays it, and asks whether she likes it.

STREGA. What is it? Is it intended for music?

REGINALD. Oh, you beautiful doll.

STREGA. Take that (*she knocks him sprawling over the keyboard*)! Beautiful doll indeed!

REGINALD. Oh, I say! Look here: thats the name of the tune too. (4, 889)

Strega plays with immense virtuosity. In fact, her first appearance is as a recitalist preparing a concert performance: "*[S]he goes to the piano and tantalizes the expectant audience for about two minutes by putting down her flowers on the candle-stand; taking off her gloves and putting them with the flowers; taking off half a dozen diamond rings in the same way; sitting down to the keyboard and finding it too near to the piano, then too far, then too high, then too low: in short, exhausting all the tricks of the professional pianist before she at last strikes the keys and preludes brilliantly*" (4, 885). Later, she plays Liszt's version of Schubert's *Erl König*, a Liebeslieder waltz, and "*a violent Chopin study. He goes into convulsions.*" She prepares "to make a man" of him by playing Chopin's Polonaise in A-flat (also known as the "Polonaise Militaire"). "Imagine that you have just been in a battle," she commands; "and that you have saved your country by deeds of splendid bravery; and that you are going to dance with beautiful women who are proud of you." He reacts pantomimically to her performance. "*She plays the first section of the Polonaise. Reginald flinches at first, but gradually braces himself; stiffens; struts; throws up his head and slaps his chest.*" When she plays the chords in the middle section, he joins her in a comically sexual duet.

REGINALD. [. . .] *(She plays the chords again. He plays the octave passages; and they play the middle section as a duet. At the repeat he cries)* Again! again!

STREGA. It's meant to be played again. Now.

They repeat it. At the end of the section she pushes him off the bench to the floor, and goes on with the Polonaise alone. (4, 890–91)

True to his given name but appropriate to his surname, Fitzambey (*Fitz* indicates illegitimate sons of royalty and *ambey,* a variant of the prefix ambi, means "both"), this young man surrenders his kingly powers to her and, as described below, accepts the traditional role of a woman. True to her name, she bewitches him (Strega means "witch") by the strength and force (Thundridge) of her piano playing. At the end, he tells her he adores her, she fiercely embraces him, they agree to marry, and "*He plays a wedding march. She plays the bass*" (4, 893–94).

Reginald reiterates "I never meant any harm" so often, the Doctor demands, "Dont go on saying that over and over or you will drive us all as distracted as you are yourself" (4, 879–80). The phrase echoes Nora in *A Doll's House,* who protests she meant no harm in forging her father's signature on a promissory note. The reverberation is hardly accidental. Shaw began *The Music-Cure* on 27 April 1913 and completed it on 21 January 1914. The year 1913 saw numerous demonstrations for woman suffrage in London, and Mrs. Emmeline Pankhurst, a leader in the movement, was sentenced for inciting people to place explosives in the house of Chancellor of the Exchequer. In 1913, newspapers and periodicals contained ten Shavian items on woman suffrage, including excerpts of speeches and a review of Sir Almroth Wright's book *The Unexpurgated Case against Woman Suffrage,*[55] in which Shaw calls it "impossible [. . .] to deny that Man as he exists at present is what Sir Almroth Wright calls Woman" and that "there is no evidence that the qualities of intellect and character needed for political organization are any more specifically sexual than digestion or blood circulation or cell structure."[56] Also, as Shaw partly spent 1912 revising *The Quintessence of Ibsenism* for publication in 1913, he reread such passages as "If we have come to think that the nursery and the kitchen are the natural sphere of a woman, we have done so exactly as English children come to think that a cage is the natural sphere of a parrot: because they have never seen one anywhere else."[57]

Shaw comically expresses his views in *The Music-Cure,* which satirizes traditional gender roles. Reginald confesses his unfitness "for public affairs" and bemoans living "at home with five coarse and brutal sisters who care for nothing but Alpine climbing and looping the loop on aeroplanes, and going on deputations, and fighting the police" (4, 891). He proposes marriage to Strega:

> I want a strong arm to lean on, a dauntless heart to be gathered to and cherished, a breadwinner on whose income I can live without the sordid horrors of having to make money for myself. I am a poor little thing, I know, Strega; but I could make a home for you. I have great taste in carpets and pictures. I can cook like anything. [. . .] I get on splendidly with children: they never talk over my head as grown-up people do. I have a real genius for home life. And I shouldnt at all mind being tyrannized over a little: in fact, I like it. It saves me the trouble of having to think what to do. Oh, Strega, dont you want a dear little domesticated husband who would have no concern but to please you, no thought outside our home, who would be unspotted and unsoiled by the rude cold world, who would never meddle in politics or annoy you by interfering with your profession? (4, 892)

She is, she says, "a hard, strong, independent, muscular woman" who dreams "of a timid little heart fluttering against mine, of a gentle voice to welcome me home, of a silky moustache to kiss my weary fingers when I return from a Titanic struggle with Tchaikovsky's Concerto in G major, of somebody utterly dependent on me, utterly devoted to me, utterly my own, living only to be cherished and worshipped by me" (4, 892–93). The concluding wedding march suits the union of this man and woman, each comfortable in the gender role that is traditionally the other's.

What the knockabout farce, reversals of stereotyped gender roles, and dazzling piano recital have in common is their hilarious unexpectedness. Each bolsters the others. As acted, the farce makes the reversal of roles funny and sensible. The bravura piano playing, unexpected in a "straight play," is of a piece with the other surprising features. It enhances Strega's stature, and it makes comprehensible Reginald's adoration of her and his willingness to function in a wifely role.

The Inca of Perusalem (1915)

As in *The Inauguration Speech,* the prologue to *The Inca of Perusalem* cocks a snook at illusionistic realism and the convention of the fourth wall, and it candidly acknowledges the theater itself, but such metatheatricality is central only to the prologue, which occupies less than five minutes. In it, an English Archdeacon enters the forestage through the curtains, speaks to someone behind them, and parks himself on the top step of a flight of stairs from the stage to the orchestra (stalls). From this position, he persuades his daughter Ermyntrude, the recent widow of a millionaire, who enters through the front curtain, that as her inheritance has collapsed to zero, yet her habits of luxury make any house whose maintenance costs less than a hundred thousand dollars a year seem squalid,[58] to become a lady's maid to a princess until she finds another millionaire to marry her. He then "*descends the steps into the auditorium and makes for the door*" at the rear of the orchestra; she barks and shrieks at him until he is "*out of hearing in the corridor*" (4, 955). The single-scene play that follows contains no more frisky mixing of the world before and behind the edge of the stage. While delightful in itself, the sparkling promise that begins *The Inca of Perusalem* is unfulfilled.

The play proper consists of Ermyntrude's first obtaining a position as lady's maid to a Princess whom the Inca of Perusalem, incognito, visits to decide which of his sons she is suitable to marry, and then acts as the maid. Although the plot's pivot is characters acting roles—Ermyntrude a haughty maid, and the arrogant Inca, Captain Duval—role-playing is a gimmick. Shaw only superficially contrasts performed personae with real selves, and he fails to make their dissimilarities resonate a dramatized theme. The Inca merely states, anticipating *The Apple Cart,* that a constitutional monarch is a mere "india-rubber stamp," a puppet with fewer powers than a democratically elected American president, and that once he is deposed, his genius will be revealed and he will be invited to become "Super-president of all the republics" of which he is now emperor (4, 977).

Still, Shaw gets a bit of fun from Ermyntrude's arrogance as a maid and her change to the demeanor and attire of a Princess, whom she pretends to be, and from the Inca, who calculatedly "*advances with a marked and imposing stage walk*" (4, 967). He also generates some humor from the Inca's forgetfulness that he is in disguise when Ermyntrude treats him in a way befitting the disguise, for example:

> THE INCA. I beg you, madam, to be quite at your ease, and to speak to me without ceremony.
> ERMYNTRUDE (*moving haughtily and carelessly to the table*) I hadnt the slightest intention of treating you with ceremony. (*She sits down: a liberty which gives him a perceptible shock*). I am quite at a loss to imagine why I should treat a perfect stranger named Duval: a captain! almost a subaltern! with the smallest ceremony.

THE INCA. That is true. I had for the moment forgotten my position. (4, 967)

Shaw elicits comedy in the contrast of the Inca intentionally laughing *"harshly and mirthlessly"* as Duval, then inadvertently doing so *"genially and sincerely"* as himself, thereby becoming *"much more agreeable"* (4, 968). The theater reenters when, after describing street hawkers who, "at the pulling of a simple string," make their imitation moustaches turn up and down (which lets the audience know how the trick is done), *"he makes his moustache turn up and down several times"* (4, 971), and when, as he prepares to begin a speech and she starts to rise, he stops her, "No: I prefer a seated audience *(she falls back into her seat at the imperious wave of his hand)"* (4, 980). The "Comedietta," as Shaw subtitles the piece, ends with her declaring that while he is not rich enough to marry, she will drive round the town with him and join him in tea at the zoo.

One should not denigrate the frolicsome fun of the major part of *The Inca of Perusalem*. Still, because it is not at the imaginative level of the theater as a dramatic device in the prologue, the play that follows the prologue is a let-down.

Back to Methuselah (1920)

In each of the last three parts of this dramatic pentateuch, all set in the future, Shaw uses the theater differently.

Part III ("The Thing Happens"), which takes place in the year 2170, employs an imaginative, stunning multimedia effect that demolishes any notion that what happens on stage is illusionistic realism: a television-telephone, with a video of the party at the other end of the line projected on a screen *"nearly as large as a pair of folding doors"* on the rear wall (5, 439). This device, which was not invented at the time, is therefore unrealistic and clearly reinforces the spectators' awareness that what it sees occurs on a stage. The impact of the videophone calls, which is strikingly theatrical even today, also heralds the stage time as 250 years later (than 1920).

After the Archbishop and Mrs. Lutestring, to whom "The Thing [great longevity] Happens," leave, the President of the British Islands meditates. *"He is positively glaring into the future"* (5, 488) when the Minister of Health, a Negress with whom the President flirts from afar, calls on the videophone, inviting him to fly, then parachute to her on her yacht. With the possibility of three centuries of existence, and of contracting lifelong rheumatism in the cold sea, he decides that the tryst is not worth the gamble. Shaw's use of the theater enforces his theme. After characters discuss the consequences of immense longevity, the theatrically multimedia futuristic device reappears, dramatizing a possible consequence of such longevity.

Until the recent possibility of closed circuit television, one might imagine that this sequence would be done with a film, with prerecorded voices substituting for the various parties on the other end of the videophone.[59] However, when Shaw completed the play, *The Jazz Singer*—the first talkie—was seven years in the future. He knew it was only a matter of time before movies became talkies, but the time had not come. For this multimedia effect, he may have imagined silent movies of the offstage speakers while offstage actors (possibly but not necessarily the same as those on screen) voice-synched dialogue through a microphone. Considering these dates, the multimedia sequence he envisioned is even more striking and daringly avant-garde.[60]

Long-livers and short-livers coexist in Part IV ("Tragedy of an Elderly Gentleman"). Shaw employs the theater to demonstrate the folly and short-sightedness of the latter, who, unable to see life without illusions, are impressed by stagey artifice. Beyond a brightly lit gallery in the oracle's temple is a void, which awes the short-livers. "*Organ music of the kind called sacred in the nineteenth century begins. Their awe deepens*" (5, 553). The indifference of a long-liver to this hokum irritates the short-livers, who kneel. "*The vapour of the abyss thickens; and a distant roll of thunder seems to come from its depths.*" The oracle rises from her tripod, terrifying the short-livers, who fall on their faces, affected "*with a dreadful sense of her supernaturalness*" (5, 554–55). When the short-lived Envoy resorts to stale political rhetoric as prelude to his question, a long-liver impatiently tells him to stop raving and speak. Because they continue to cackle, the oracle, whose appearance she later calls "*a foolish picture of me thrown on a cloud by a lantern*" (5, 562), uses a theatrical effect to silence them: "*Terrific lightning and thunder. The Elderly Gentleman is knocked flat [. . .]. The ladies cover in terror. The Envoy's hat is blown off, but he seizes it just as it quits past his temples, and holds it on with both hands.*" After more chatter, "*The oracle raises her hands to command silence. [. . .] Invisible trombones utter three solemn blasts in the manner of Die Zauberflöte.*" She speaks: "Go home, poor fool!" (5, 558–60). As audiences are not taken in by the oracle's stagey effects, they recognize, with thematic pertinence, the folly and inadequacy of the short-livers, who are like children compared to the long-livers.

In Part V ("As Far As Thought Can Reach"), set at the end of the thirty-second century, a sculptor named Pygmalion exhibits two creations. Unlike Shaw's other plays-within-plays, the characters of this one do not play roles but are artificial human beings who behave in a way that today we would call programmed, that is, as stereotypical men and women of the early twentieth century, for an audience of the sculptor's contemporaries, whose behavior, we recognize, is similarly programmed. In this inner play, a tableau vivant and mouvant that begins and ends with music, the automata dance.

Like *The Dark Lady of the Sonnets* and *Fanny's First Play*, this inner play is theatrically self-referential. Pygmalion, a sculptor, who is analogous to a dramatist, introduces his creations with a paradox that befits drama: "I have succeeded in making artificial human beings. Real life ones, I mean." Characters complain that he, as critics complain that Shaw, "is constitutionally incapable of exhibiting anything without first giving a lecture about it to explain it" (5, 590). Onstage spectators interrupt his explanation with "Cut it short, Pyg!" and "No more talking" (5, 591, 600).

His creations are "a pair of human creatures who are all reflexes and nothing else." Onstage and real audiences are told, "Take warning by them." He is uncertain if they are truly alive or if they seem human because they respond to outside stimuli. They are conscious, can talk and read, and tell lies, which is "very lifelike." To one onstage spectator, lying is not lifelike: "Give them a clip below the knee, and they will jerk their foot forward. Give them a clip on their appetites or vanities or any of their lusts and greeds, and they will boast and lie, and [. . .] hate and love" (5, 598–99).

A performance follows the discussion. Flutists play. A "*man and woman of noble appearance, beautifully modelled and splendidly attired, emerge,*" smile at their audience "*with gratified vanity,*" and posture. Pygmalion asks them to perform—"You dance so beautifully, you know"—and tells a spectator "how sensitive they are to the stimulus of flattery." They "*dance pompously*" and, at the end, "*acknowledge the applause in an obvious condition of swelled head*" (5, 600).

The female figure is jealous when Pygmalion suggests the male might put his arm around a woman in the audience. Asked what he thinks of the spectators, the male replies, "I have not seen the newspaper today." To the onstage audience, "He is a mere automaton." "Free will is an illusion," he declares. "We are the children of Cause and Effect." Ironically, Shaw has him quote Shelley's "Ozymandias": "My name is Ozymandias, king of kings: / Look on my works, ye mighty, and despair." Referring to The Revelation of Saint John the Divine, he calls the female figure "Cleopatra-Semiramis, consort of the king of kings, and therefore queen of queens." He commands, "worship us twain as one: two in one and one in two, lest by error ye fall into irretrievable damnation" (5, 601–2). His injunction—different from Father Keegan's description of heaven, with a trinity of three in one and one in three, including a priest who is both worshipper and worshipped—suggests that the two in one may be damnation. When the figures argue whether woman or man is better than the other, Cleopatra-Semiramis starts to throw a stone at Ozymandias. Pygmalion wrests it from her. She bites his hand, killing him—a major variation of the Pygmalion myth.

To the onstage audience, these twentieth-century stereotypes are "a pair of horrors!" and "dangerous" (5, 604). Ironically, Shaw has the man declaim a passage from Sir Walter Scott's "The Lady of the Lake": "Come one: come all: this rock shall fly / From its firm base as soon as I." The woman declares herself proud of him. Rather than destroy them, as one spectator wants, another calls for an Ancient to adjudicate the issue. A He-Ancient appears and laments, "A child lost! A life wasted!" Each of the automata blames the other. A She-Ancient arrives, confirming that these "dolls" are "dangerous." "Do you blame us for our human flesh and blood?" asks Ozymandias. Although each wants the other killed, at the touch of the Ancients on them, he demands, "Spare her; and kill me" and she, more sensibly, "Kill us both. How could either of us live without the other?" (5, 605–8). As both die, the musicians, symmetrically, play.

After the performance comes the moral: "be content with lifeless toys, and not attempt to make living ones," says the She-Ancient, who points out that when the youths play with each other they play with their bodies, which makes them supple and strong, "but if we played with you we should play with your minds, and perhaps deform them" (5, 610). One spectator is appalled that the earth was once inhabited by people like the figures they have observed.

True to the play-within-a-play tradition, the onstage audience cues the auditorium audience's response to the play. Unfortunately, the inner play and its characters are so stale and the ironies so rusty, no prompting is necessary. While this play-within-a-play is successful, which was not so in The Devil's Disciple, its success is academic, not theatrical. Although some of Shaw's self-mockery is amusing, he pokes fun at himself more successfully in other works, notably Fanny's First Play.

As I have argued elsewhere,[61] character and plot are less important in

Back to Methuselah than ideas are. Here, ideas are not fully imbedded in them, which is one reason so much of this play is dull. In *The Perfect Wagnerite,* Shaw asserts, "There is only one way of dramatizing an idea; and that is by putting on the stage a human being possessed by that idea, yet none the less a human being with all the human impulses which make him akin and therefore interesting to us."[62] With similar overstatement, *The Quintessence of Ibsenism* maintains that "an interesting play cannot in the nature of things mean anything but a play in which problems of conduct and character of personal importance to the audience are raised and suggestively discussed."[63] Shaw mostly ignores such precepts in *Back to Methuselah,* where situations provide an excuse for characters to talk. He attempts to show that there is more than one way to dramatize an idea and that an interesting play may mean something other than character and conduct. Although both notions are true, it is questionable that the ways he dramatizes ideas in *Back to Methuselah* are effective and that it is interesting as a play.

Saint Joan (1923)

After composing plays that contain plays, a piano recital, and a sculpture exhibit with a dance, Shaw presents an apparent miracle as a theatrical event: a magic show. In Scene 2 of *Saint Joan,* the assemblage at the Dauphin's castle hears that Joan has "struck Foul Mouthed Frank dead for swearing." "A miracle!" exclaims the Dauphin, who thinks Joan an angel. To the Archbishop, coincidence explains what happened. Bluebeard proposes a test: "Let us arrange when she comes that I shall be the Dauphin, and see whether she will find me out." Charles agrees: "If she cannot find the blood royal I will have nothing to do with her." Although the Archbishop reminds them not to usurp the Church's job in conferring sainthood, he agrees to the test (6, 103).

As Bluebeard prepares to stage the event, the Archbishop explains that the magic show or miracle will succeed because Joan knows what everyone else knows, that the Dauphin is the worst-dresssed person at court and that the blue-bearded man is Gilles de Rais. Calmly, the Archbishop defines miracles: "if [events] confirm or create faith they are true miracles" (6, 105).

Bluebeard's performance begins with the drawing of curtains that separate the antechamber from the throne area. He stands *theatrically on the dais, playing the king, and, like the courtiers, enjoying the joke rather obviously.* Shaw cannily makes him an amateur actor. Enter Joan, dressed as a soldier. "Where be Dauphin?" she asks. *"[C]ondescendingly,"* Bluebeard replies, "You are in the presence of the Dauphin." Joan examines him skeptically. *"Fun dawns in her face."* She cries, "Coom, Bluebeard! Thou canst not fool me. Where be Dauphin?" As the group roars with laughter, Bluebeard, dropping character, gives a gesture of surrender. Grinning, Joan searches among the audience of courtiers and grabs Charles. She releases him, curtseys, and announces she has been sent to drive away the English and crown him king. Triumphantly, he declares that "she knew the blood royal" (6, 107–9). Joan's magic or miracle is successful.

This incident typifies Shaw's use of miracles in *Saint Joan*. Although Joan denies that what happened to Foul Mouthed Frank was her doing, and although she does not use the term "miracle" to describe anything she accomplishes, others consider this (finding the Dauphin) and at least two other events to be miraculous: the hens laying eggs and the wind on the Loire River changing direction.[64] In Scene 1, the term is used before the hens resume laying. "Oh! You think the girl can work miracles, do you?" asks Baudricourt. "I think the girl herself is a bit of a miracle," replies Poulengey (6, 90). Shaw's dramatic stratagem is not to establish what Joan does as miraculous but to refute skepticism characters have about Joan. Like the selection of the Dauphin, all of her alleged miracles have realistic explanations. All are treated, the Dauphin incident most obviously, with its drawn curtain and main actor on a dais, like stage tricks. Partly for these reasons, Shaw enhances Joan's stature: one need not believe in miracles to believe her capable of doing what she does. The magic or miracle show in *Saint Joan* is a vital part of the dramatic process.

The Epilogue, which recapitulates the play's dramatic movements (affiliation with Joan, then rejection of her) and major theme (the difficulty between distinguishing an advanced individual from a social menace), also recapitulates the use of the theater. This scene announces Joan's canonization, which takes place four centuries later, as a theatrical event. In addition to using theatrical devices (costume and projected images) that remind spectators that they are in a theater, it employs a play-within-a-play, but with a difference: after clearly dividing performer and audience, the former joins the latter.

Warwick jokingly predicts that when Joan is made a saint, "you will owe your halo to me," and Joan laughs. Then, *"A clerical-looking gentleman in black frockcoat and trousers, and tall hat, in the fashion of the year 1920* [three years before Shaw wrote the play], *suddenly appears,"* whereupon the characters *"stare at him"* and *"burst into uncontrollable laugh-*

ter" at what Warwick calls "a most extraordinarily comic dress." That is, the characters on stage mock the style of clothing worn by some members of the audience—a disruption of theatrical illusion. Next, Shaw breaches the play-within-a-play convention by having the object of the onstage spectators discuss attire with them. The gentleman recites for them an announcement that in 1920 the Vatican has canonized Joan. Dunois emphasizes Shaw's theatrical use of theatrical time, in which 1920 enters 1456 (the year of the Epilogue): "Half an hour to burn you, dear Saint: and four centuries [closer to five, actually] to find out the truth about you!" Further disrupting illusionism, a slice projector casts an image: "*A vision of the statue in Winchester Cathedral is seen through the window,*" then fades, whereupon Shaw has the twentieth-century man quip that the French secular authorities have asked him "to mention that the multiplication of public statues to The Maid threatens to become an obstruction to traffic," but in a display of even-handedness he adds that the statue of Joan's horse "is no greater obstruction to traffic than any other horse." A slide projector casts another image, her statue in front of Rheims Cathedral, which Joan comically criticizes as a "funny little thing." It then fades (6, 203–5). Both jokes, commentaries on the theatrical device, further disrupt illusionistic realism and reinforce the sense of the theater in this drama.

Fifteenth-century characters kneel before Joan, in homage to the twentieth-century saint. After she proposes that, since a saint can execute miracles, she return from the dead, Shaw employs another theatrical effect: sudden darkness, followed by dim light that makes only the figures and the bed visible. The twentieth-century visitor, who has performed for a fifteenth-century audience, joins that audience: he and they reject Joan and, one by one, exit what Shaw has distinctly depicted as a stage—except for Charles, who goes back to bed.

Too True To Be Good (1931)

At the end of Act I, a microbe breaks the fourth wall by directly addressing the audience: "The play is now virtually over; but the characters will discuss it at great length for two acts more. The exit doors are all in order" (6, 455–56). Although the play is not virtually over and, as Eric Bentley points out, the characters do not spend the next two acts lengthily discussing what has happened,[65] the comedy's self-referential theatricality at this moment saturates the talk and action that follow, imbuing them with a sense of the theater. Indeed, some consider Aubrey's claims that he possesses "a gift of lucidity as well as of eloquence," that he "can explain anything to anybody; and I love doing it," and that he "must preach and preach and preach no matter how late the hour and how short the day, no matter whether I have nothing to say" (6, 470–71, 527–28) to be Shaw revealing himself,[66] thereby reminding audiences of the theater by reminding them of the play's author. At the end of Act III, Aubrey gives a sermon, during the early moments of which all of his onstage audience leave, as the microbe proposed that the real spectators do. Although Aubrey continues to preach for about three pages, Shaw does not say that he addresses the audience. Neither, for that matter, do stage directions indicate that the microbe does, but unlike Aubrey's speech, the content of the microbe's remarks implies it. Aubrey seems to preach to no one in particular and for no reason other than sheer enjoyment of speechifying, but after the theater-evoking climax of the first act, an actor may suggest, or spectators may feel, that he is talking to them.

Foreshadowing dramatic self-references are a theatrical costume for the microbe, which strikingly contrasts with realistic attire for the other characters, calling attention to itself as a theater costume, and this character's asides that, because other characters do not hear them and because they break the fourth wall of illusionistic realism, remind audiences of the theater. Another anticipation of Shaw's use of the theater in terms that this study has defined and illustrated is Sweetie playing the role of a nurse in dealing with Mrs. Mopply, but dropping her act, revealing it to be a pretense that intentionally deceives a character, when she is alone with the patient, Mops, whom she alternately ignores and bullies.

In harmony with the reference to theater at the end of Act I, Act II begins with sound effects that, willy-nilly, call attention to the stage. In the theater, it is a truism that the sound of hooves immediately preceding a character's arrival by horse is (usually unintentionally) laughable because it signifies staginess rather than realism (a horse, spectators recognize, is not in the wings). The same is true of the sound of mechanical vehicles. With Act I ending as it does, it is likely that Shaw intentionally elicits the stage rather than the illusion of reality when he opens Act II with Colonel Tallboys, seated in a deck chair reading *The Times*, "*disturbed by a shattering series of explosions announcing the approach of a powerful and very imperfectly silenced motor bicycle from the side*" (one of the wings, that is, which is especially obvious since the setting is an exterior). The unseen rider "*races his engine with a hideous clatter*" and Tallboys commands him to stop, which he does (6, 457). Despite the change of setting, Shaw reassures his audience that they are still in a theater.

Following the duologue between Tallboys and Meek, who arrives on the motorcycle, are impersonations by the young women of Act I. Sweetie plays a countess, wearing "*a variegated silk wrap*" and speaking in a dialect that "*is a spirited amalgamation of the foreign accents of all the waiters she has known.*" Mops, costumed with "*headdress, wig, ornaments, and girdle proper to no locality on earth except perhaps the Russian ballet,*" plays "*the character of a native servant*" to the countess (6, 464). While "*trying to look as indigenous as possible,*" Mops coughs to tip off Sweetie that her diction is less upper class than it should be, surreptitiously "*pokes the chair with the sun umbrella*" in revenge for Sweetie's spiteful remark to Mops as onstage audience. When Tallboys discloses plans that might thwart their and Aubrey's ransom scheme, "*The two conspirators exchange dismayed glances,*" and after the countess slaps her servant, Mops "*obeys humbly until the Colonel delicately turns his head away, when she shakes her fist threateningly at the smiter*" (6, 466–67). In short, the disguised extortionists theatrically break character with each other when they think no one will notice.

Tallboys and Meek reappear to find Mops threateningly rushing at Aubrey; but "*unable to stop herself in time,*" she "*crashes into [Tallboys's] arms.*" He demands she cease her noise and unclench her fists. Obsequiously, she states, "*(salaaming and chanting)* Bmal elttil a dah yram, Tuan," and explains, "no Engliss." Meek, recognizing that she has been speaking "English back slang," discloses that she said "'Mary had a little lamb'" backwards (6, 484–85). Disingenuously, she stops acting, drops character, and congratulates him.

Near the conclusion of the act, the onstage characters respond to offstage noises that, like those that open it, confirm to the audience that the locale is a stage. After a klaxon blares, announcing an offstage battle, the sounds of exploding maroons come from both wings. The klaxon and explosions are obviously sound effects.

The final act begins with Sweetie dropping the character of countess when she locates the sergeant at whom she intends to make a pass, which she does. When he addresses her as her ladyship, she instantly cuts him short—"Can all that stuff, Sergeant. [. . .] Garn, I'm no countess; and I'm fed up with pretending to be one"—and swings into action: "you're my fancy. I love you" (6, 493–94). Once Aubrey hears his father preaching, he too drops his pretence. Although the appearance of Mrs. Mopply prompts Mops to stop role-playing and reveal her identity to her mother, Mrs. Mopply finds her so changed that she does not believe her and commands, "Dont you call me mother" (6, 521).

Ignorance about disease and medicine, which the doctor and the patient's mother display in the first act, foreshadow ignorance about other people's identity. Both are analogous to ignorance about reality, which the final act confirms. Aubrey's father recites the disillusionment that World War I revealed to him: "Determinism is gone, shattered, buried with a thousand dead religions, evaporated with the clouds of a million forgotten winters. The science I pinned my faith to is bankrupt [. . .]. Its spread of enlightenment has been a spread of cancer: its counsels that were to have established the millennium have led straight to European suicide" (6, 505–6). Mrs. Mopply is shaken to discover that what she thought were verities are lies: "How am I to behave in a world thats just the opposite of everything I was told about it?" (6, 521). The war has revealed to Aubrey that what previously had been considered divine order is random and absurd: "I have no Bible, no creed: the war has shot both out of my hands" (6, 527). To the recognition that what seemed to be real is unreal, Shaw uses theatricality as a parallel, painstakingly introducing the theater and theatrical effects as staginess that prevents spectators from becoming deceived by illusionistic realism.

The Simpleton of the Unexpected Isles (1934)

Usually, characters in Shaw's plays-within-plays perform human beings. In *The Simpleton of the Unexpected Isles,* they enact gods. A garden of a stately home on a Pacific island contains four shrines, on which are two beautiful goddesses and two handsome gods. Their ages range from seventeen to twenty.

To Iddy, a clergyman of the Church of England, they suggest a Christian icon: "St Peter in Rome is only a bronze image; but his feet have been worn away by the kisses of Christian pilgrims. You make me feel as I have never felt before. I must kiss you." He kisses one of the goddesses. "*She smiles as her eyes turn bewitchingly towards him.*" "Beware" and "On guard," warn the gods. "His lips are sweet and pure," says the other goddess. "'For he on honey dew hath fed—'" says the one he kissed, and the other completes the line, "'and drunk the milk of paradise.'" The quotation, from Coleridge's *Kubla Khan,* whose verse the poet remembered after an opium-induced dream, hints that the four figures are as unreal as Khan's pleasure dome. As the youths, Janga and Kanchin, counsel suspicion, the women, Vashti and Maya, entice Iddy with mesmerizing biblical phrases: "We are the way," "We are the life," "I am the light" (John 14:6 and 8:12). Vashti twists the meaning of another biblical phrase: "Perfect love casteth out choice" ("fear" in the First Epistle General of John 4:18) (6, 789–91). When Prola, one of their mothers, arrives, she tells them to stop their nonsense and leave the bewildered young man alone. They whirl away, ending this play-acting in the play.

Iddy, which is short for Idiot, is unable to explain his religion. "Well, it is—well, I suppose it is the Christian religion," he stumbles. To him, it means "everything that is good and lovely and kind and holy. I dont profess to go any further than that" (6, 789). Like the catchwords of those Iddy mistakes for gods, his slogans are meaningless, therefore without value. He is an appropriate mate for the goddesses. His efforts to protect himself against their allure demonstrate that his Anglicanism also consists of empty or fossilized phrases: "I will think of England and tighten myself up and pull myself together. England! The Malverns! the Severn plains! the Welsh border! the three cathedrals! England that is me: I that am England! Damn and blast all these tropical paradises: I am an English clergyman; and my place is in England. Floreat Etona! Back to England and all that England means to an Englishman! In this sign I shall conquer." Instead, he is conquered. Maya, an arm around his neck, sinks beside him, demanding, "Speak to me from your soul, and not with words that you have picked up in the street." When he pleads with her to respect his cloth, she calls herself "the veil of the temple" and commands, "Rend me in twain." She charges him to love Vashti too, for he cannot love one unless he loves the other. Vashti throws an arm around his shoulders, asking, "Do you not love me?" He replies, "I would die for either, for both: for one, for the other." She concludes, "Your lives and ours are one life" (6, 801–3).

With the arrival of Judgment Day, on which the criterion for survival is a useful life, it becomes clearer that the children have "splendid words" and "beauty," but "no minds" (6, 818–19). As Iddy's name indicates, neither has he a mind. "I am a futile creature," he admits (6, 810). So are they. "Heaven and earth shall pass away; but I shall not pass away [Mark 31:12]. That is what she said. And then there was nothing in my arms." He realizes, "There never had been anything." The others also disappear. "They said 'Our names shall live forever.' What were their names?" Their true names, (the meaningless ideals they personify), he perceives, are "Love, Pride, Heroism and Empire. Love's pet name was Maya. I loved Maya. I loved them all; but it was through love of Maya that I loved them." Not only did love seduce him to a worship of the other ideals, but what he loved was illusory (Maya means "illusion"). Focusing on "my little treasure of words spoken by my Lord Jesus," he insists, "I shall not forget [the name of the Lord] as I shall forget Maya's" (6, 832–33). As he has said, however, his life and their lives were one life.

The mini-play, in which the children enact gods and goddesses, has an audience of Iddy, who is drawn into their pretense. The sequence encapsulates the entire play. Enchanted by them, Iddy weds two and unites with all four. Their unreality highlights that of his nationalism and religion, which consist of attractive phrases whose meaning he fails to understand. To employ a phrase in *Heartbreak House,* the heavens may not be empty (an Angel drops from and ascends to them), but the earth that is represented by Iddy (platitudes that go by the name of religion) and the four children (the ideals they represent) is useless. Only responsible adults are able to give it worth and therefore to inherit it.

Shakes versus Shav (1949)

Shaw's last play to be performed in his lifetime, *Shakes versus Shav* differs from his other plays in that he wrote it for puppets. It contains two plays-within-a-play based on works by each of the title characters, Shakespeare and Shaw, and a prizefight-within-a-play between them. Although Shaw had one more play to write (*Why She Would Not*) before his death a year later, his preface calls *Shakes versus Shav* "in all actuarial probability [. . .] my last play and the climax of my eminence, such as it is" (7, 469). Sally Peters is correct in calling it "all the more valuable because Shaw is orchestrating the 'climax' of his career [. . .]."[67]

First to enter is Shakespeare, who quotes the opening lines of, thereby identifying himself with, the eponymous villain, Richard III. Shaw changes the final phrase to the site of the puppet play's first performance, the Malvern Festival: "Now is the winter of our discontent / Made glorious summer by the Malvern sun." Shakes slightly misquotes Ben Jonson's tribute to him, that he is "not for [of] an age / But for all time," and he charges the "fiend of Ireland" with having pretended, by having a drama festival devoted to him, "to reincarnate my very self" (7, 473). No dramatist but himself, implies Shakes, is worthy of such a festival.

Shav reviles Shakes for not recognizing him, though G.B.S.'s features are known throughout the world. Shakes challenges him to fight. A boxing-match-within-the-play begins. *"They spar. Shakes knocks Shav down with a straight left and begins counting him out, stooping over him and beating the seconds with his finger."* Up pops Shav at the count of nine *"and knocks Shakes down with a right to the chin."* Although Shav is "Younger [. . .] / By full three hundred years," Shakes is as resilient as he and bounces back (7, 473–74). The match ends in a draw.

Since the battle is really about drama, the playwrights contend with plays. Plaintiff Shakes puts his case first: "Couldst write Macbeth?" "No need," replies Shav. "He has been bettered / By Walter Scott's Rob Roy" (7, 474). Shaw's defense stratagem relies on his long-held contention that later times demand different fictive creations. Recall that the well-known subtitle in his preface to *Three Plays for Puritans,* "Better Than Shakespear?" ends with a question mark, and that his answer is, "I do not profess to write better plays" (2, 37, 41).

Although the first puppet play-within-a-play parodies *Macbeth,* Macbeth's opening lines, like Shakes's, are from *Richard III* (V,ii): "Thus far into the bowels of the land / Have we marched on without impediment." Shaw links the superiority or inferiority of the dramatic creation with that of the dramatic creator. Wittily paraphrasing one of Macbeth's most famous lines (V,vii), Shaw's Shakespearean Macbeth challenges, "Lay on, Rob Roy; / And damned be he that proves the smaller boy." "Ma fet is on ma native heath," Roy declares metatheatrically, for Malvern is Shaw's turf. Like Shakespeare's Macduff, Scott's hero draws his sword and cuts off Macbeth's head. "Whaur's your Wullie Shaxper the noo?" he asks, continuing to link character and author. As Rob Roy dances off to bagpipe and drum music, the decapitated Macbeth puppet picks up his head; states, referring to the world of the playwright, not of the inner play, that he will "return to Stratford: the hotels / Are cheaper there"; and leaves, carrying it *under his arm to the tune of British Grenadiers"* (7, 474–75).

Like his counterpart, Macduff, Rob Roy wins in the play-within-a-play, but his triumph does not signal Shav's defeat of Shakes, who refuses to be drawn from the central challenge, himself versus Shav, not versus Scott. One line of *Macbeth,* he boasts, "Is worth a thousand of your piffling plays." Shav challenges him to quote one. He quotes, "'The shardborne beetle with his drowsy hum'" (III,ii). Whether Shaw intends this quotation to demonstrate Shakespeare's enchanting word music or twaddle, I do not know. Shav evades the issue by reciting none of his own lines, but doggerel by a minor nineteenth-century Australian poet, Adam Lindsay Gordon: "'The beetle booms adown the glooms / And bumps among the clumps.'" The couplet sets Shakes roaring with laughter (7, 475).

Suspicious, Shakes asks, "Pullst thou my leg?" Shav responds with a quip derived from *Hamlet* (I,v): "There is more fun in heaven and earth, sweet William, / Than is dreamt of in your philosophy." Shakes demands that Shaw produce his *Hamlet* and asks if he could write *King Lear.*

"Aye," says Shav, "with his daughters all complete." The defendant's play-within-a-play is *Heartbreak House,* which Shav calls "my Lear" (7, 475). In a tableau, Shotover and Ellie Dunne recite speeches from it. Unlike *Macbeth,* no challenger undercuts this work.

After the image disappears, Shakes seizes upon Shotover's "Let the heart break in silence," charging that Shav "stole that word from me" and misquotes himself: "did I not write / 'The heartache and the thousand natural woes / That flesh is heir to'?" (*Hamlet,* III,i, has "shocks," not "woes"). Although, notes Shav, Shakes was not the first to write of broken hearts, the second inner play ends in a draw (7, 475–76).

Shakes starts to quote from *The Tempest* (IV,i), "The great globe itself, / Yea, all which it inherit, shall dissolve," but Shav interrupts and changes the line, "and like this foolish little show of ours ["insubstantial pageant" in the original] / Leave not a wrack behind." Although he calls Shakes "Immortal William," acknowledging the Bard's eminence, he also says, "We both are mortal. For a moment suffer / My glimmering light to shine," and a momentary glimmer is less than immortal. On cue, "*A light appears between them.*" Shakes has the last words, which are Macbeth's (V,v), "Out, out, brief candle!" (7, 476–77). Framing *Shakes versus Shav* are Shakespearean quotations, but while the play moves from summer to darkness, it also goes from litigation to accommodation between the disputants.

The play's conflict concludes without a victor. Theatrically, Shaw has Shakes blow out the candle, after which comes "*Darkness. The play ends*" (7, 477). Immortal or glimmering, the illumination of both fades. Neither a fight nor a play-within-a-play resolves the challenge. If, as Peters says, *Shakes versus Shav* orchestrates the climax of Shaw's career, it reveals him placing himself in Shakespeare's company, but not surpassing him.

Shaw's Use of the Theater as Dramatic Device

From Opus 1, in 1892, to Opus 51 (or 52, if one counts *The Inauguration Speech*), in 1949—that is, from his first play to the last performed in his lifetime—Bernard Shaw makes extensive use of the theater in his drama, and he does so with dazzling variety. Characters act for other characters; a theater critic views life in terms of his playhouse predilections; a character directs another during a preview performance; a dramatist has her work performed before and criticized by professional reviewers. Some characters directly address the audience, breaking the fourth wall that characterizes illusionistic realism; one of them reticently refuses to undress because she sees spectators on the other side of the fourth wall. Shaw utilizes plays-within-plays and such other entertainments as a harlequinade, a piano recital, a sculpture exhibit, and a prizefight. One play has a back-stage scene, and another has a character exit by way of the auditorium.

For the most part, Shaw's employment of the theater is traditional (the exception is the unique multimedia effect in *Back to Methuselah*). His usage reflects themes, and cues the audience to respond to the play of which it is a part. Mainly, he is successful. Where he is not, his use of theater helps to explain why. In *The Devil's Disciple,* one play-within-a-play shows why his intention is subverted, and another reveals his depic-tion of the onstage audience as inadequate. In *Back to Methuselah,* the deficiencies of the inner play reflect those of the outer play.

Of his slightly more than fifty plays, twenty-five—about half—employ the theater as a dramatic device. Although they range from his first play to his last work performed in his lifetime, they are not spread evenly among his six decades as a dramatist but come chiefly in three clusters. The first is his initial experience as a dramatist, six plays in five years (1892–96), using the theater as he tries to carve a path for himself in it. The technique appears five times when he is actively engaged in it as director-playwright during the Vedrenne-Barker seasons at the Court Theatre (1904–1907), when for the first time in his career he is certain that his new play will be produced; but two of these works, *Passion, Poison, and Petrifaction* and *The Inauguration Speech,* were not done at the Court. The third period occurs when he is involved in promoting a theater not for himself but for the nation: seven plays in four years (1909–12). In this period, his works employ the theater more extensively and with greater virtuosity than at any other time.

Fittingly, Shaw's last play performed while he lived brings him onstage with Shakespeare, the latter's second appearance in a Shavian play, Shaw's titular rival and the standard by which he would be measured (why not the best?). They challenge the audience as well as each other to evaluate Shaw as a dramatist. Although neither wins, audiences and readers are left to assess their relative eminence. What is incontestable is the sense of right-ness that if any dramatists in the English language may share a stage, it is these two.

Notes

I. Bernard Shaw, Director

[Bracketed notes are 1999 additions to the 1971 edition of "Bernard Shaw, Director."]

1. Letter to Ellen Terry, 16 April 1897, *Ellen Terry and Bernard Shaw: A Correspondence*, ed. Christopher St. John (New York: The Fountain Press, 1931), p. 150 (hereafter cited as *Terry-Shaw*).

2. 4 December 1897, Bernard Shaw, *The Drama Observed*, ed. Bernard F. Dukore (University Park: Pennsylvania State University Press, 1993), vol. 3, p. 960.

3. Letter to Ellen Terry, 14 September 1897, *Terry-Shaw*, p. 207.

4. Raymond Mander and Joe Mitchenson, *Theatrical Companion to Shaw* (London: Rockliff, 1954), pp. 21, 36. [Stanley Weintraub's edition of Bernard Shaw, *The Diaries 1885–1897*, 2 vols. (University Park: Pennsylvania State University Press, 1986), makes clear that Shaw's work on *Widowers' Houses* involved far more directing than was clear in 1971; see entries from 14 November to 9 December 1892.]

5. Mander and Mitchenson, *Theatrical Companion to Shaw*, pp. 11–18; Archibald Henderson, *George Bernard Shaw: Man of the Century* (New York: Appleton-Century-Crofts, 1956), pp. 669–88; Eric Bentley, *Bernard Shaw 1856–1950* (New York: New Directions, 1957), pp. 220–32; William A. Armstrong, "George Bernard Shaw: The Playwright as Producer," *Modern Drama 8* (February 1966), 347–61. During Shaw's lifetime, several actors received titles. I shall refer to them by their titles only if they had these titles at the time of reference. Thus, the actress is Sybil Thorndike when she played the title role in *Saint Joan*, but Dame Sybil Thorndike when she wrote the article in Mander and Mitchenson.

6. [Thereafter, there has been one, Vincent Wall's *Bernard Shaw: Pygmalion to Many Players* (Ann Arbor: University of Michigan Press, 1973).]

1. Theater Background and Experience

1. Henderson, *Shaw: Century,* pp. 30–31, 39.

2. Shaw, *The Drama Observed,* vol. 2, p. 478.

3. Henderson, *Shaw: Century,* pp. 40–41; Shaw, *The Drama Observed,* vol. 4, pp. 1388, 1430–31; Martin Meisel, *Shaw and the Nineteenth-Century Theater* (Princeton, N.J.: Princeton University Press, 1963), p. 14.

4. Shaw, *The Drama Observed,* vol. 4, pp. 1510–11; for confirming opinions, written when Shaw was much younger, see vol. 2, pp. 394–95, 471–73; and his introduction to *Terry-Shaw,* vol. 4, pp. 1422–23. Although one would ordinarily question the accuracy of a nonagenarian's account of a production he saw when he was a teenager, Shaw's 1947 description of Sullivan is in no way incompatible with those he gave in 1895 and 1929.

5. B. C. Rosset, *Shaw of Dublin: The Formative Years* (University Park: Pennsylvania State University Press, 1964), pp. 198–99.

6. Letter to Archibald Henderson, 3 January (completed 17 January) 1905, Bernard Shaw, *Collected Letters 1898–1910,* ed. Dan H. Laurence (London: Max Reinhardt, 1972), p. 499 (hereafter cited as *Collected Letters,* vol. 2); Rosset, *Shaw of Dublin,* pp. 228–36.

7. Rosset, *Shaw of Dublin,* pp. 329–33.

8. Bernard Shaw, *Collected Letters 1874–1897,* ed. Dan H. Laurence (New York: Dodd, Mead, 1965), p. 115 and plate facing p. 115 (hereafter cited as *Collected Letters,* vol. 1).

9. Henderson, *Shaw: Century,* p. 669. [Dan H. Laurence, *Shaw: An Exhibit,* a catalogue (Austin: Humanities Research Center, University of Texas, 11 September 1977–28 February 1978), p. 17; Weintraub, *The Unexpected Shaw,* pp. 48–51; Shaw, *Diaries,* vol. 2, p. 686.]

10. [See *The Bodley Head Bernard Shaw: Shaw's Music,* ed. Dan H. Laurence (London: Max Reinhardt, 1981), 3 vols. (hereafter cited as *Shaw's Music*); *Bernard Shaw on the London Art Scene,* ed. Stanley Weintraub (University Park: Pennsylvania State University Press, 1989); and Shaw, *The Drama Observed,* vol. 1.]

11. [True, but throughout August 1891 he coached Florence Farr (Florence Farr Emery), with whom he also had a love affair, on Ibsen's *Rosmersholm,* reading the play with her for a possible revival (she had produced it on 23 February 1891) and using it as a vehicle to give her elocution and voice lessons. See Shaw, *Collected Letters,* vol. 1, and *Diaries* for August 1891.]

12. Letter to Charrington, 14 December 1892, Shaw, *Collected Letters,* vol. 1, p. 372.

13. [See introduction, n. 4.]

14. Mander and Mitchenson, *Theatrical Companion to Shaw,* p. 10.

15. Rehearsal notes: *Arms and the Man:* 1911, Harry Ransom Humanities Research Center, University of Texas, Austin (hereafter cited as HRHRC), and British Library, Add. MS 50644; 1919, the Bernard F. Burgunder Collection of

George Bernard Shaw, Division of Rare and Manuscript Collectons, Cornell University Library, Ithaca, N.Y. (hereafter cited as Burgunder). [These notes, as well as other sources of advice and injunctions to actors in these productions and in those of 1894 and 1907, have been collated with the text of the play in *Bernard Shaw's Arms and the Man: A Composite Production Book,* ed. Bernard F. Dukore (Carbondale: Southern Illinois University Press, 1982.]

16. "Granville-Barker: Some Particulars," Shaw, *The Drama Observed,* vol. 4, p. 1503; Barker's admission was made in a testimonial speech, quoted in *Desmond MacCarthy's The Court Theatre 1904–1907: A Commentary and Criticism,* ed. Stanley Weintraub (Coral Gables, Fla.: University of Miami Press, 1966), p. 164.

17. *Desmond MacCarthy's The Court Theatre,* pp. 12–14.

18. Ibid., p. 103.

19. Shaw, *The Drama Observed,* vol. 4, pp. 1384–85.

20. Letter to Louis Wilkinson, 6 December 1909, in Frank Harris, *Bernard Shaw* (Garden City, N.Y.: Garden City Publishing Co., 1931), p. 254.

21. Shaw, *The Drama Observed,* vol. 4, pp. 1507, 1516. Italics in original.

2. The Director: Goals and Groundwork

1. Shaw, *The Drama Observed,* vol. 4, pp. 1516, 1519–20.

2. Ibid., p. 1381.

3. *Shaw's Music,* vol. 1, pp. 608–9.

4. Shaw, *The Drama Observed,* vol. 3, pp. 842–43.

5. *Shaw's Music,* vol. 2, p. 414.

6. Letter to Joseph Harker, no date, in Harker, *Studio and Stage* (London: Nisbet, 1924), p. 189.

7. Shaw, *The Drama Observed,* vol. 4, pp. 1507–8.

8. *Terry-Shaw,* pp. xxix, 238.

9. Letter to Golding Bright, 26 September 1896, in Shaw, *Collected Letters,* vol. 1, p. 670.

10. Letter to Trebitsch, 18 December 1902, in *Bernard Shaw's Letters to Siegfried Trebitsch,* ed. Samuel A. Weiss (Stanford, Calif.: Stanford University Press, 1986), p. 29 (hereafter cited as *Shaw-Trebitsch*).

11. Shaw, *The Drama Observed,* vol. 4, p. 1522.

12. *Shaw's Music,* vol. 1, p. 180.

13. Shaw, *The Drama Observed,* vol. 2, p. 753.

14. Letter to R. E. Golding Bright, 2 December 1894, in Shaw, *Collected Letters,* vol. 1, p. 464.

15. [Quotations from Shaw's plays and prefaces to them are from *The Bodley Head Bernard Shaw: Collected Plays with Their Prefaces,* ed. Dan H. Laurence, 7 vols. (London: Max Reinhardt, 1970–74). They will be cited, as here, parenthetically by volume and page numbers.]

16. Harris, *Bernard Shaw,* pp. 253–54; Shaw, preface to *Plays Unpleasant* (1, 30–32).

17. Lee Simonson, *Part of a Lifetime* (New York: Duell, Sloan and Pearce, 1943), p. 51. [British scene designer Jocelyn Herbert concurred: "A lot of people think they don't have to take too much notice of Shaw's strict directions, but when you do the play, you realize that every move and every relationship is thought out in his head, with reference to where the doors are and so on. It's also closely integrated with the words; and if you alter it too much, it gets very difficult. When John [Dexter] and I did *Pygmalion*, we started off by thinking this wasn't so, but we gradually discovered that if you didn't have the fireplace on the opposite side, when Higgins gets up and falls over the coal-scuttles it doesn't work if he's got to go over the other side of the room." Unsigned interview, "Only Connect," *Plays and Players* (March 1983): 12.]

18. Sir Cedric Hardwicke (as told to James Brough), *A Victorian in Orbit* (Garden City, N.Y.: Doubleday, 1961), p. 126.

19. Letter to Jones, 8 January 1899, Shaw, *Collected Letters*, vol. 2, pp. 72–73.

20. Shaw, *The Drama Observed*, vol. 3, p. 1086.

21. "Arms and the Man," 1894 typescript, Beinecke Rare Book and Manuscript Library, Yale University. All further references to the 1894 version are to this typescript.

22. Letter to Siegfried Trebitsch, 10 December 1902, *Shaw-Trebitsch*, p. 27.

23. Shaw, *The Drama Observed*, vol. 3, p. 1517.

24. British Library, 50597. The paperback edition used as a prompt book (London: Constable, 1906) contains no indication of a date of production, though the play was produced at the Court Theatre in 1907. The description of the set in this edition, quoted here, differs little from the description in *The Bodley Head Bernard Shaw* (1, 166). Unless otherwise indicated, sketches from Shaw's blocking notes and rehearsal notes are mine, copied from Shaw's. The specially numbered illustrations, however (Figures 1–10), are reproductions of Shaw's own drawings.

25. British Library, 50600. The copy used was *Plays: Unpleasant* (London: Grant Richards, 1900). The prompt book contains no indication of a date of production, though the play was presented in London by the Stage Society at the New Lyric Club in 1902. In revising the play for the 1931 Standard Edition, Shaw rewrote this scene.

26. British Library, 50611. For the prompt script, a paperback edition was used (London: Grant Richards, 1904). [The dialogue quoted here is the same as that in *The Bodley Head Bernard Shaw* (2, 191)].

27. *Shaw's Music*, vol. 2, p. 454; vol. 3, pp. 229–30.

28. MS in HRHRC. In my quotations from the text, I use the same edition that Shaw used in blocking the action (see n. 26). [He later revised the text quoted in this paragraph.]

29. Letter to Siegfried Trebitsch, 18 June 1906, *Shaw-Trebitsch*, p. 104.

30. MS in the Hanley Collection, in HRHRC (hereafter cited as Hanley, HRHRC).

31. Ibid.

32. Letter to Granville Barker, 26 May 1903, in *Bernard Shaw's Letters to Granville Barker,* ed. C. B. Purdom (London: Phoenix House, 1956), pp. 13–14 (hereafter cited as *Shaw-Barker*).

3. GENERAL DIRECTING PRACTICES

1. "Bernard Shaw to Gilbert Murray," *Drama,* n.s. 42 (Autumn 1956): 27.

2. Letters: to Barker, 29 July 1906, in *Shaw-Barker,* p. 66; to Vedrenne, 6 April 1908 (Hanley, HRHRC).

3. Letter to Welsh, 30 January 1899, in Shaw, *Collected Letters,* vol. 2, p. 74. Welsh did play the Waiter, as Shaw suggested. Valentine was not played by any of the actors Shaw proposed but by Yorke Stephens.

4. Letter to Langner, 29 July 1921, in Shaw, *Collected Letters 1911–1925* (London: Max Reinhardt, 1985), p. 727 (hereafter cited as *Collected Letters,* vol. 3).

5. Letter to Murray, 30 March 1894, in Shaw, *Collected Letters,* vol. 1, p. 422.

6. Letter to Calvert, 23 July 1905, in Shaw, *Collected Letters,* vol. 2, pp. 542–43.

7. Shaw, *The Drama Observed,* vol. 4, pp. 1516–17.

8. Letters to Lillah McCarthy, 24 June 1918, in Shaw, *Collected Letters,* vol. 3, p. 553; and 12 August 1918, in Bernard Shaw, *Theatrics,* ed. Dan H. Laurence (Toronto: University of Toronto Press, 1995), p. 144.

9. Shaw, *The Drama Observed,* vol. 3, p. 845.

10. Letters: to Janet Achurch, 21 April 1892, in Shaw, *Collected Letters,* vol. 1, p. 337; to Barker, 28 September 1905, in *Shaw-Barker,* p. 53. Arthur Laceby played Snobby.

11. Shaw, *The Drama Observed,* vol. 1, p. 185.

12. Letters: to William Faversham, 19 April 1917, and Theresa Helburn, 10 November 1928, in Shaw, *Theatrics,* pp. 135, 181.

13. Shaw, *The Drama Observed,* vol. 4, p. 1517.

14. Letter to Cecil Lewis, 18 April 1932, in Shaw, *Collected Letters 1926–1950* (London: Max Reinhardt, 1985), p. 287 (hereafter cited as *Collected Letters,* vol. 4).

15. Letter to Yorke Stephens, 21 May 1900, in Shaw, *Collected Letters,* vol. 2, p. 166.

16. Shaw, *The Drama Observed,* vol. 4, p. 1517.

17. Cedric Hardwicke, *Let's Pretend: Recollections and Reflections of a Lucky Actor* (London: Grayson and Grayson, 1932), pp. 201–2; Hardwicke, *A Victorian in Orbit,* p. 155.

18. Patrick Campbell, 29 January 1920, in *Bernard Shaw and Mrs. Patrick Campbell: Their Correspondence,* ed. Alan Dent (New York: Knopf, 1952), pp. 232–33 (hereafter cited as *Shaw-Campbell*).

19. Letter to Trebitsch, 18 December 1902, in *Shaw-Trebitsch,* p. 29.

20. Shaw, *The Drama Observed,* vol. 4, pp. 1383, 1517.

21. Ibid., pp. 1383–84, 1517–19; letter to Siegfried Trebitsch, 18 December 1902, in *Shaw-Trebitsch*, p. 29.

22. Shaw, *The Drama Observed*, vol. 4, pp. 1385–86.

23. Hardwicke, *A Victorian in Orbit*, p. 159.

24. Shaw, *The Drama Observed*, vol. 4, p. 1520.

25. Ibid., pp. 1384, 1519; letter to Siegfried Trebitsch, 18 December 1902, in *Shaw-Trebitsch*, p. 29.

26. Shaw, *The Drama Observed*, vol. 4, pp. 1519, 1522.

27. *Shaw's Music*, vol. 1, pp. 791, 793–94.

28. Letter to Louis Wilkinson, 6 December 1909, in Harris, *Bernard Shaw*, p. 254; Shaw, *The Drama Observed*, vol. 4, p. 1358.

29. Letters to Annie Russell, 20 and 27 November 1905, in Shaw, *Collected Letters*, vol. 2, pp. 581, 583.

30. Letter to Tompkins, 5 April 1923, in *To a Young Actress: The Letters of Bernard Shaw to Molly Tompkins*, ed. Peter Tompkins (New York: Potter, 1960), p. 41 (hereafter cited as *Shaw-Tompkins*).

31. Shaw, *The Drama Observed*, vol. 4, p. 1384.

32. G. W. Bishop, *Barry Jackson and the London Theatre* (London: Barker, 1933), p. 27.

33. For example: Forbes Robertson (Sir Johnston Forbes-Robertson, *A Player under Three Reigns* [Boston: Little, Brown, 1925], p. 129); Lillah McCarthy (McCarthy, *Myself and My Friends* [New York: Dutton, 1933], p. 59); Sir Cedric Hardwicke (Hardwicke, *Let's Pretend*, p. 203); Dame Sybil Thorndike and Sir Lewis Casson (Mander and Mitchenson, *Theatrical Companion to Shaw*, pp. 13–14, 17).

34. Harris, *Bernard Shaw*, p. 19. Shaw is quoted as having called the book "My autobiography by Frank Harris" (Hesketh Pearson, *G.B.S.: A Postscript* [New York: Harper, 1950], p. 7) and having said, "I wrote the book" (Allan Chappelow, ed., *Shaw the Villager and Human Being* [London: Skilton, 1961], pp. 150–51). The passage quoted in the text is in Harris, *Bernard Shaw*, p. 247.

35. Letter to Edith Craig, 17 July 1940, in Shaw, *Collected Letters*, vol. 4, p. 571.

36. Shaw, *The Drama Observed*, vol. 4, p. 1520.

37. Letters: to Lillah McCarthy, 6 February 1908, in Shaw, *Collected Letters*, vol. 2, p. 756; to Mrs. Patrick Campbell, 12 April 1914, in Shaw, *Collected Letters*, vol. 3, p. 224.

38. Letter to Louis Calvert, 29 November 1905, in Shaw, *Collected Letters*, vol. 2, pp. 584–85. Calvert's mother, Mrs. Charles Calvert, was a famous actress. Fred Cremlin played Peter Shirley in the 1905 production and apparently understudied Undershaft; Granville Barker acted Cusins; the Bill who annihilated Calvert was the character Bill Walker, played by Oswald Yorke; Clare Greet played Rummy Mitchens. The statement that Greet took all eyes from Calvert may refer to the end of the second act, wherein Undershaft "buys" the Salvation Army. Rummy is at that point sitting in the loft, doing and saying very little.

39. Letters to Alma Murray, 11 May and 1 June 1894, in Shaw, *Collected Letters*, vol. 1, pp. 435, 437–38.

40. Letter, Hiller to Dukore, 12 July 1964.

41. Letters to Lillah McCarthy, 6 February 1908 and 7 June 1905, in Shaw, *Collected Letters*, vol. 2, pp. 755, 528.

42. Letters: to Lillah McCarthy, 30 December 1907, in Shaw, *Theatrics*, p. 87; to J. L. Shine, 29 October 1904, in Shaw, *Collected Letters*, vol. 2, pp. 461–62; to Mrs. Patrick Campbell, 11 April 1914, in Shaw, *Collected Letters*, vol. 3, pp. 224–25.

43. Shaw, *The Drama Observed*, vol. 4, pp. 1518–19.

44. Ibid., p. 1519.

45. Letter to Mrs. Patrick Campbell, 29 January 1920, in *Shaw-Campbell*, pp. 232–33.

46. Shaw, *The Drama Observed*, vol. 2, p. 662.

47. Ibid., vol. 3, p. 1102. The statement is from "The Dying Tongue of Great Elizabeth," 11 February 1905. Irving died on 14 October 1905.

48. Letter to John Barrymore, 22 February 1925, in Shaw, *Collected Letters*, vol. 3, p. 903; Shaw, *The Drama Observed*, vol. 2, p. 384.

49. *Shaw's Music*, vol. 1, p. 497; Shaw, *The Drama Observed*, vol. 4, pp. 1337–38, 1340–41.

50. *The Drama Observed*, vol. 3, pp. 905, 910; Shaw, *The Black Girl in Search of God and Some Lesser Tales* (London: Constable, 1934), p. 151.

51. Letters to Ellen Terry, 6 and 8 September 1896, in Shaw, *Collected Letters*, vol. 1, pp. 646–53.

52. Mander and Mitchenson, *Theatrical Companion to Shaw*, p. 6.

53. Letters: to Trebitsch, 26 December 1902, in *Shaw-Trebitsch*, p. 17; to Mansfield, 16 March 1895, in Shaw, *Collected Letters*, vol. 1, p. 499; to Faversham, 9 December 1917, in Shaw, *Collected Letters*, vol. 3, p. 518.

54. Hardwicke, *A Victorian in Orbit*, p. 253.

55. *The Drama Observed*, vol. 4, p. 1520.

56. Letter to J. B. Fagan, 20 October 1921, in Shaw, *Collected Letters*, vol. 3, p. 738.

57. *The Drama Observed*, vol. 4, p. 1520.

58. *Shaw's Music*, vol. 3, p. 583; letter to Barker, 17 May 1906, in Shaw, *Collected Letters*, vol. 2, p. 621.

59. Letter to Siegfried Trebitsch, in Shaw, *Collected Letters*, vol. 2, p. 619.

60. For instance, he cut Mrs. Higgins's speech about the Eynsford Hills from the third act of *Pygmalion:* "What a horrible thing poverty is! That poor woman was brought up in a rich country house; and she cant understand why her children, without any education or any chances, dont get asked anywhere. Why w i l l people living in a grove off the Fulham Road with a general servant and a hundred and fifty pounds a year call themselves the Eynsford Hills and go on as if they had five thousand." Although Shaw gave no reason for removing this passage, he may have felt that it was too explicit. The passage appears in Shaw's "rehearsal edition" of

the play: *Pygmalion: A Play in Five Acts: By a Fellow of the Royal Society of Literature* (London: Constable, 1913), British Library, 50639. All later references to the rehearsal edition of *Pygmalion* are to this one. For information on Shaw's use of special rehearsal editions, see F. E. Loewenstein, *The Rehearsal Copies of Bernard Shaw's Plays* (London: Reinhardt and Evans, 1950).

61. Typed prompt script, "Major Barbara," Houghton Library, Harvard College.

62. Letter to James B. Fagan, 20 October 1921, in Shaw, *Collected Letters*, vol. 3, p. 738.

63. [*Plays: Pleasant and Unpleasant* (London: Grant Richards, 1898).]

64. Letter to Craig, 20 August 1897, in Shaw, *Collected Letters*, vol. 1, p. 797.

65. Rehearsal notes, *Arms and the Man*, 1919, Burgunder.

66. Rehearsal notes, *Pygmalion*, 1914 (Hanley, HRHRC).

67. [For more on Shaw's rehearsal notes influencing future editions of this play, see Part II of this volume, "The Director as Interpreter: Shaw's *Pygmalion*."]

4. The Actor

1. Shaw, *The Drama Observed*, vol. 4, p. 1350.

2. Undated inscription in *The Tragedie of Hamlet Prince of Denmark*, ed. J. Dover Wilson, illustrated by Edward Gordon Craig (Weimar: Cranach Press, 1930), in Bernard Shaw, *Flyleaves*, ed. Dan H. Laurence and Daniel J. Leary (Austin: W. Thomas Taylor, 1977), p. 16.

3. Shaw, *The Drama Observed*, vol. 3, p. 846.

4. Letter, Shaw to Tompkins, 16 July 1922, in *Shaw-Tompkins*, pp. 23–24.

5. Bernard Shaw, *Cashel Byron's Profession* (London: Constable, 1950), pp. 91–92.

6. *Shaw on Theatre*, ed. E. J. West (New York: Hill and Wang, 1958), p. 185.

7. Shaw, *The Drama Observed*, vol. 2, pp. 596, 648.

8. Letter to Charles Charrington, 1 March 1895, in Shaw, *Collected Letters*, vol. 1, p. 492.

9. Shaw, *The Drama Observed*, vol. 2, p. 418.

10. Ibid., vol. 1, p. 39.

11. Ibid., vol. 4, p. 1356.

12. Ibid., vol. 1, p. 40.

13. Quoted in Henderson, *Shaw: Century*, p. 748.

14. Handwritten notes on back of printed ticket to British Library Reading Room, HRHRC; "Notes to The Devil's Disciple" (2, 142–50).

15. Letter to Ellen Terry, 21 September 1896, in Shaw, *Collected Letters*, vol. 1, p. 659.

16. Letter to Florence Farr, 1 May 1891, ibid., pp. 296–97.

17. *Shaw's Music*, vol. 3, p. 537; Shaw, *The Drama Observed*, vol. 1, p. 40.

18. Lillah McCarthy, *Myself and My Friends*, p. 68.

19. *Shaw's Music*, vol. 1, p. 45; Rosset, *Shaw of Dublin*, pp. 116–21, 203–4. A

typed manuscript, dated 1882 and entitled "The Voice," is in the Berg Collection of English and American Literature, New York Public Library, Astor, Lenox, and Tilden Foundations.

20. *Shaw's Music*, vol. 1, p. 695; vol. 2, p. 700.

21. "The Voice," p. 26.

22. Letter to Molly Tompkins, 10 December 1922, in Shaw, *Collected Letters*, vol. 3, p. 792; *Shaw's Music*, vol. 2, p. 811.

23. Letter to Charles Charrington, 15 April 1900, in Shaw, *Collected Letters*, vol. 2, p. 159; *Bernard Shaw's Book Reviews Originally Published in the Pall Mall Gazette from 1885 to 1888*, ed. Brian Tyson (University Park: Pennsylvania State University Press, 1991), p. 209.

24. *Shaw's Music*, vol. 2, pp. 955–56, 979; vol. 3, p. 540.

25. Letter to Florence Farr, 6 June 1902, in Shaw, *Collected Letters*, vol. 2, pp. 274–75; Shaw, *The Drama Observed*, vol. 2, p. 377.

26. Shaw, *The Drama Observed*, vol. 4, p. 1440.

27. Letters: to Florence Farr, 6 June 1902, and to Mrs. Patrick Campbell, 6 February 1928, in Shaw, *Collected Letters*, vol. 2, p. 274; vol. 4, p. 91.

28. Bernard Shaw, *Sixteen Self Sketches* (London: Constable, 1949), p. 64.

29. Letter to Janet Achurch, 29 January 1896, in Shaw, *Collected Letters*, vol. 1, p. 592.

30. "The Voice," p. 9.

31. Letter to Molly Tompkins, 10 December 1922, in Shaw, *Collected Letters*, vol. 3, p. 792. The obscure vowel, also called the "schwa vowel," is symbolized phonetically by an upside-down e, which the quotation from *Pygmalion* employs.

32. Letter to Molly Tompkins, 10 December 1922, in Shaw *Collected Letters*, vol. 3, p. 793.

33. Shaw, *The Drama Observed*, vol. 2, p. 418; *Shaw's Music*, vol. 1, p. 702.

34. "Proposed Diploma in Dramatic Art," carbon copy, dated 25 June 1922, Hanley, HRHRC.

35. Bernard Shaw, *Love among the Artists* (London: Constable, 1932), pp. 101–2, 113–25.

36. Bernard Shaw, *The Matter with Ireland*, ed. David H. Grene and Dan H. Laurence (London: Hart-Davis, 1962), p. 12; Shaw, *The Drama Observed*, vol. 4, pp. 1431–32, 1521.

37. *Shaw's Music*, vol. 1, pp. 432–33, 437.

38. Ibid., p. 780; Shaw, *The Drama Observed*, vol. 3, pp. 965–66.

39. Letter to Ellen Terry, 4 July 1897, in Shaw, *Collected Letters*, vol. 1, p. 779.

40. Shaw, *The Drama Observed*, vol. 3, p. 967.

41. Ibid., p. 1090.

42. Letter to Charrington, 4 March 1900, in Shaw, *Collected Letters*, vol. 2, p. 150.

43. Rehearsal notes: *Arms and the Man*, 1919, Burgunder; *Pygmalion*, 1914, Hanley, HRHRC.

44. Rehearsal notes: *Misalliance,* 1910, Hanley, HRHRC; *Arms and the Man,* 1911, HRHRC.

45. Letters: to Alan S. Downer, 12 November 1947, in Meisel, *Shaw and the Nineteenth-Century Theater,* pp. 107–8; to Granville Barker, 15 June 1907 and 19 January 1908, in *Shaw-Barker,* pp. 93, 115.

46. Shaw, *The Drama Observed,* vol. 4, p. 1460.

47. Rehearsal notes: *Major Barbara,* 1935, British Library, 50644; *Arms and the Man,* 1911, HRHRC; *Macbeth,* 1926, British Library, 50644.

48. Letters: to Henry Arthur Jones, 20 February 1902, in Doris Arthur Jones, *Taking the Curtain Call: The Life and Letters of Henry Arthur Jones* (New York: Macmillan, 1930), p. 178; to Granville Barker, 24 May 1907, in Shaw, *Collected Letters,* vol. 2, p. 690.

49. Letter to William Faversham, 19 April 1917, in Shaw, *Theatrics,* pp. 135–36.

50. Letter to Ellen Terry, undated but assigned to 2 July 1897, in Shaw, *Collected Letters,* vol. 1, p. 776.

51. Shaw, *The Drama Observed,* vol. 2, pp. 538, 631; vol. 3, p. 963.

52. Ibid., vol. 1, p. 283.

53. Letter to Charles Charrington, 30 March 1891, in Shaw, *Collected Letters,* vol. 1, p. 289.

54. Shaw, *The Drama Observed,* vol. 1, p. 91; vol. 2, pp. 349, 420; vol. 3, pp. 901–2.

55. Letter to Trebitsch, 10 January 1903, in Shaw, *Collected Letters,* vol. 2, pp. 299–300.

56. Shaw, *The Drama Observed,* vol. 2, pp. 367, 528, 727.

57. Letter to Mrs. Patrick Campbell, 29 January 1920, in *Shaw-Campbell,* p. 231.

58. Shaw, *The Drama Observed,* vol. 2, p. 718; rehearsal notes, *Pygmalion,* 1914, Hanley, HRHRC.

59. Shaw, *The Drama Observed,* vol. 2, p. 368; vol. 3, pp. 1117, 1121.

60. Ibid., vol. 4, p. 1357.

61. Letter to Laurence Irving, 26 December 1900, in Shaw, *Collected Letters,* vol. 2, p. 209.

62. Shaw, *The Drama Observed,* vol. 1, p. 99.

63. Ibid., vol. 2, pp. 364–65, 382.

64. Letter to Ellen Terry, 8 September 1896, in Shaw, *Collected Letters,* vol. 1, p. 651.

65. Interview with Dame Sybil Thorndike, 29 June 1964.

66. Letter to Hiller, 17 August 1936, in Shaw, *Collected Letters,* vol. 4, p. 438.

67. Letter to Annie Russell, 20 November 1905, in Shaw, *Collected Letters,* vol. 2, p. 580.

68. Letter to Vanbrugh, 26 March 1930, ibid., vol. 4, pp. 180–81.

69. Letter to Janet Achurch, 25 December 1900, in Shaw, *Collected Letters,* vol. 2, pp. 207–9, and in *Shaw on Theatre,* pp. 81–83.

70. Shaw, *The Drama Observed,* vol. 1, pp. 183–85; vol. 2, pp. 488–89.

71. *Shaw's Music,* vol. 3, pp. 710–11.

72. Letter to Janet Achurch, 20 March 1895, in Shaw, *Collected Letters,* vol. 1, p. 502.

73. Rehearsal notes: *Man and Superman,* 1907, British Library, 50735; *Major Barbara,* 1905, British Library, 50733; *Arms and the Man,* 1911, HRHRC.

74. "John Bull's Other Island: The Author's Instructions to the Producer," 25 December 1904, in Shaw, *The Drama Observed,* vol. 3, p. 1094.

75. Letter to Robert Loraine, 14 December 1919, in Shaw, *Collected Letters,* vol. 3, p. 646.

76. Rehearsal notes, *Pygmalion,* 1914, Hanley, HRHRC.

77. Letter to George Tyler, 6 October 1914, in Shaw, *Collected Letters,* vol. 3, p. 255.

78. Rehearsal notes: *Getting Married,* 1908, Enthoven Collection, Victoria & Albert Library; *Pygmalion,* 1914, Hanley, HRHRC.

79. Rehearsal notes: *Getting Married,* 1908, Enthoven.

80. Letter to Louis Calvert, 27 November 1915, in "George Bernard Shaw as a Man of Letters," *New York Times,* 5 December 1915, sec. VI, p. 6.

81. Letter to Matthew Boulton, 1 September 1929, the Philbrick Library, Los Altos Hills, Calif.

82. Shaw, *The Drama Observed,* vol. 3, pp. 614–15.

83. Interview with Dame Sybil Thorndike, 29 June 1964.

84. Letters: to Helburn, 1928 (no month or day given [but the Theatre Guild opened *Major Barbara* in New York on 20 November]), in Lawrence Langner, *G.B.S. and the Lunatic* (New York: Atheneum, 1963), p. 110; to Barker, 3 August 1905, in *Shaw-Barker,* p. 50; to Pascal, 9 July 1944, in *Bernard Shaw and Gabriel Pascal,* ed. Bernard F. Dukore (Toronto: University of Toronto Press, 1996), pp. 171–72 (hereafter cited as *Shaw-Pascal*).

85. Rehearsal notes: *Pygmalion,* 1914, Hanley, HRHRC.

86. Rehearsal notes: *John Bull's Other Island,* undated; *Cæsar and Cleopatra,* 1912; and *Arms and the Man,* 1911, HRHRC.

87. Letter to Ellen Terry, 8 September 1896, in Shaw, *Collected Letters,* vol. 1, pp. 651–52.

88. Rehearsal notes: *Macbeth,* 1926, and *Pygmalion,* 1920, British Library, 50644.

89. Shaw, *The Drama Observed,* vol. 4, p. 1384.

90. Ibid., vol. 3, pp. 452, 783.

91. Rehearsal notes: *Candida,* 1920, and *Macbeth,* 1926, British Library, 50644.

92. Rehearsal notes: *Macbeth,* 1926, and *Arms and the Man,* 1911, British Library, 50644; *Misalliance,* 1910, Hanley, HRHRC.

93. Letter to the B.B.C., 1 September 1941, Burgunder.

94. *Shaw's Music,* vol. 2, p. 661.

95. Letter to Granville Barker, 19 July 1906, in *Shaw-Barker,* p. 65.

96. Rehearsal notes: *The Doctor's Dilemma,* 1913, HRHRC; *Macbeth,* 1926, British Library, 50644.

97. Letter to Shine, 29 October 1904, in Shaw, *Collected Letters,* vol. 2, pp. 460–61.

98. Rehearsal notes, *Macbeth,* 1926, British Library, 50644; *Pygmalion,* 1914, Hanley, HRHRC.

99. Letter to Mrs. Patrick Campbell, 22 December 1920, in *Shaw-Campbell,* pp. 245–46.

100. Rehearsal notes: *Pygmalion,* 1914, Hanley, HRHRC; *Arms and the Man,* 1911, British Library, 50644.

101. Rehearsal notes: *Misalliance,* 1910, Hanley, HRHRC.

102. Letter to Ellen Terry, 31 January 1897, in Shaw, *Theatrics,* p. 23.

103. Rehearsal notes: *Heartbreak House* [1921?], Burgunder; *Major Barbara,* 1935, and *Candida,* 1920, British Library, 50644; *Arms and the Man,* 1911, HRHRC; *Pygmalion,* 1920, British Library, 50644.

104. Rehearsal notes: *Man and Superman,* undated, British Library, 50732; *Arms and the Man,* 1919, Burgunder.

105. Rehearsal notes: *Man and Superman,* 1907, British Library, 50735; *Macbeth,* 1926, British Library, 50644.

106. Rehearsal notes: *Misalliance,* 1910, Hanley, HRHRC; note in margin of Shaw's rehearsal copy of *Pygmalion* (London: Constable, 1913), p. 17, used for 1914 London production, British Library, 50639.

107. Rehearsal notes: *Getting Married,* 1908, Enthoven; *Pygmalion,* 1920, and *Macbeth,* 1926, British Library, 50644.

108. Letter to Shine, 29 October 1904, in Shaw, *Collected Letters,* vol. 2, p. 461.

109. Rehearsal notes: *Pygmalion,* 1914, Hanley, HRHRC; *Major Barbara,* 1905, British Library, 50733; *The Doctor's Dilemma,* 1913, HRHRC; *Saint Joan,* 1924, British Library, 50644.

110. Rehearsal notes: *John Bull's Other Island,* undated, Hanley, HRHRC; postcards to Ellen Terry, 14 March 1906, in Shaw, *Collected Letters,* vol. 2, p. 609. [Shaw's uncharacteristic apostrophe in "That's" is on the published postcard.]

111. Rehearsal notes: *Misalliance,* 1910, Hanley, HRHRC; *Major Barbara,* 1905, British Library, 50733; *The Doctor's Dilemma,* 1913, HRHRC; *Saint Joan,* 1924, British Library, 50644.

112. Interview with Dame Sybil Thorndike, 29 June 1964.

113. Rehearsal notes: *Pygmalion,* 1914, and *Misalliance,* 1910, Hanley, HRHRC; *Arms and the Man,* undated, Enthoven.

114. Letter to Russell, 27 November 1905, in Shaw, *Collected Letters,* vol. 2, p. 582; rehearsal notes: *Heartbreak House,* 1921, Burgunder; *Man and Superman,*

1907, British Library, 50735; note in margin of Shaw's rehearsal copy of *Pygmalion*, p. 31, used for 1914 London production, British Library, 50639.

115. Rehearsal notes: *Arms and the Man*, 1919, Burgunder; *Misalliance*, 1910, Hanley, HRHRC.

116. Rehearsal notes: *Cæsar and Cleopatra*, 1912, and *Arms and the Man*, 1911, HRHRC.

117. Letter to Barker, 14 March 1906, in Shaw, *Collected Letters*, vol. 2, p. 608.

118. Rehearsal notes: *Candida*, 1920, British Library, 50644; *Man and Superman*, 1907, British Library, 50735.

119. Rehearsal notes: *Major Barbara*, 1935, and *Candida*, 1920, British Library, 50644.

120. Letter to Mrs. Patrick Campbell, 13 January 1921, in Shaw, *Collected Letters*, vol. 3, p. 706.

121. Shaw, *The Drama Observed*, vol. 3, p. 803.

122. Ibid., vol. 4, p. 1459; Winifred Loraine, *Head Wind: The Story of Robert Loraine* (New York: William Morrow, n.d.), p. 90.

123. G. W. Bishop, *Barry Jackson and the London Theatre* (London: Barker, 1933), pp. 28–29.

124. Interview with Dame Sybil Thorndike, 29 June 1964.

125. Rehearsal notes: *Man and Superman*, 1907, British Library, 50735; *Pygmalion*, 1914, Hanley, HRHRC.

126. For example, Langner, *G.B.S. and the Lunatic*, p. 12; Hardwicke, *A Victorian in Orbit*, p. 155.

127. Interview with Dame Sybil Thorndike, 29 June 1964.

128. Sir Lewis Casson, "A Remembrance," in *Setting the Stage: A Guidebook to Season '66: The Minnesota Theatre Company, Fourth Season* (Minneapolis: Tyrone Guthrie Theatre, 1966), p. 21.

129. Shaw, *The Drama Observed*, vol. 4, pp. 1460, 1462–63.

130. Letter to Archer, 11 June 1889, in Shaw, *Collected Letters*, vol. 1, p. 214.

131. Shaw, *The Drama Observed*, vol. 2, p. 518; vol. 3, p. 1050.

132. Rehearsal notes: *Macbeth*, 1926, British Library, 50644.

133. Letter to Cedric Hardwicke, 20 August 1929, in Hardwicke, *Let's Pretend*, pp. 205–6.

134. Rehearsal notes: *Man and Superman*, 1907, British Library, 50735; *Misalliance*, 1910, and *Arms and the Man*, 1911, Hanley, HRHRC; *Heartbreak House*, 1921, and *Major Barbara*, 1929, British Library, 50644.

135. Letter, Shaw to Gabriel Pascal, no date given in source [July 1944], in *Shaw-Pascal*, p. 173.

136. Shaw, *The Drama Observed*, vol. 3, pp. 1093–95.

137. *The Shaw Alphabet Edition of Androcles and the Lion* (Harmondsworth: Penguin, 1962).

5. STAGE EFFECTS AND STAGE EFFECTIVENESS

1. Letter to William Faversham, undated [c. 1 August 1917], in Shaw, *Collected Letters,* vol. 3, p. 496.

2. Undated reply in margin of letter-questionnaire dated 15 March 1930, sent by Sobieniowski, Hanley, HRHRC.

3. Rehearsal notes, *Heartbreak House,* 1921, British Library, 50644.

4. Note in margin of prompt copy of *Arms and the Man* (London: Constable, 1905), British Library, 50602. Although the date of the production is not indicated, the play was produced at the Savoy Theatre in 1907.

5. Letter to Granville Barker, 20 July 1907, in *Shaw-Barker,* pp. 96–97.

6. Letters: to Forbes Robertson, 21 and 22 December 1903, in Shaw, *Collected Letters,* vol. 2, pp. 383–84; to Robert Loraine, 19 April 1919, in Loraine, *Head Wind,* pp. 260–61.

7. Rehearsal notes, *Pygmalion,* 1914, Hanley, HRHRC.

8. Letter to Wendy Hiller, 17 August 1936, in Shaw, *Collected Letters,* vol. 4, p. 438.

9. Rehearsal notes, *Arms and the Man,* 1911, HRHRC.

10. Rehearsal notes, *Arms and the Man,* 1919, Burgunder.

11. Rehearsal notes, *Arms and the Man,* 1911, HRHRC.

12. For example, *Shaw's Music,* vol. 3, p. 538; Shaw, *The Drama Observed,* vol. 2, p. 392.

13. Letter to Mrs. Patrick Campbell, 7 November 1901, in Shaw, *Collected Letters,* vol. 2, pp. 239–40. In the British theater, "P" ("Prompt Side") is the side of the stage off which the prompter sits—usually, stage left. "O. P." is "Opposite Prompt," stage right. These stage directions are from the viewpoint of the actor as he faces the audience.

14. Rehearsal notes: *Pygmalion,* 1914, Hanley, HRHRC; *Arms and the Man,* undated, Enthoven.

15. Letter to Lawrence Langner, 1 February 1924, in Shaw, *Collected Letters,* vol. 3, p. 863.

16. Letter to Granville Barker, 24 May 1907, in ibid., vol. 2, p. 690.

17. Rehearsal notes: *Misalliance,* 1910, Hanley, HRHRC; *Arms and the Man* [1921?], Burgunder; *Pygmalion,* 1914, Hanley, HRHRC; *Macbeth,* British Library, 50644.

18. Shaw, *The Drama Observed,* vol. 3, pp. 1096–97.

19. Letter to William Archer, 11 June 1889, in Shaw, *Collected Letters,* vol. 1, p. 214.

20. Shaw, *The Drama Observed,* vol. 3, pp. 854–55.

21. Rehearsal notes: *Misalliance,* 1910, Hanley, HRHRC; *Cæsar and Cleopatra,* 1912, HRHRC.

22. Rehearsal notes: *The Doctor's Dilemma,* 1913, HRHRC; *Pygmalion,* 1914, Hanley, HRHRC.

23. Rehearsal notes: *The Doctor's Dilemma*, 1913, and *Arms and the Man*, 1911, HRHRC; *Pygmalion*, 1914, Hanley, HRHRC.

24. Shaw, *The Drama Observed*, vol. 3, p. 1385.

25. Rehearsal notes: *Getting Married*, 1908, Enthoven; *Macbeth*, 1926, British Library, 50644.

26. Shaw, *The Drama Observed*, vol. 3, p. 1385.

27. Letter to Ellen Terry, 23 September 1896, in Shaw, *Collected Letters*, vol. 1, p. 666.

28. Rehearsal notes: *Pygmalion*, 1920, British Library, 50644.

29. Shaw, *The Drama Observed*, vol. 4, p. 1385; letter to Elizabeth Robins, 3 March 1893, in Shaw, *Collected Letters*, vol. 1, p. 385.

30. Shaw, *The Drama Observed*, vol. 3, p. 965; *Shaw's Music*, vol. 2, p. 34.

31. Rehearsal notes: *Misalliance*, 1910, Hanley, HRHRC; *The Doctor's Dilemma*, 1913, HRHRC.

32. Letter to Lillah McCarthy, 7 June 1905, in Shaw, *Collected Letters*, vol. 2, p. 528.

33. Letter to B.B.C., 27 May 1941, Burgunder. In this letter, Shaw observes that this principle is true for the stage as well as for radio.

34. Shaw, *The Drama Observed*, vol. 4, pp. 1384, 1518.

35. Rehearsal notes: *Saint Joan*, 1924, British Library, 50644; *The Doctor's Dilemma*, 1913, HRHRC; *Getting Married*, 1908, Enthoven.

36. Rehearsal notes: *Arms and the Man*, 1911, HRHRC; *Heartbreak House*, 1921, British Library, 50644; *Getting Married*, 1908, Enthoven.

37. Rehearsal notes: *Pygmalion*, 1914, and *Arms and the Man*, 1911, HRHRC.

38. Rehearsal notes: *Major Barbara*, 1905, British Library, 50733; *John Bull's Other Island*, undated, Hanley, HRHRC; *The Doctor's Dilemma*, 1913, HRHRC.

39. Letter to Laurence Irving, 26 December 1900, in Shaw, *Collected Letters*, vol. 2, p. 209.

40. Rehearsal notes: *Misalliance*, 1910, Hanley, HRHRC; *Candida*, 1920, British Library, 50644; *Arms and the Man*, 1911, HRHRC.

41. Rehearsal notes: *Major Barbara*, 1929, British Library, 50644; *The Doctor's Dilemma*, 1913, HRHRC; *Macbeth*, 1926, British Library, 50644.

42. Rehearsal notes: *Pygmalion*, 1920, British Library, 50644.

43. Rehearsal notes: *Major Barbara*, 1929, British Library, 50644; *Arms and the Man*, 1911, HRHRC; *Man and Superman*, 1907, British Library, 50735; *Getting Married*, 1908, Enthoven.

44. Rehearsal notes: *Arms and the Man*, 1911, and *Misalliance*, 1910, Hanley, HRHRC.

45. Rehearsal notes: *Major Barbara*, 1935, British Library, 50644; *Getting Married*, 1908, Enthoven.

46. Letter to Matthew Boulton, 1 September 1929, the Philbrick Library, Los Altos Hills, Calif.

6. The Technical Elements of Production

1. Mander and Mitchenson, *Theatrical Companion to Shaw,* p. 16.

2. *Shaw's Music,* vol. 2, p. 229.

3. Letters to Ellen Terry, 25 September 1896 and 27 July 1897, in Shaw, *Collected Letters,* vol. 1, pp. 668, 789.

4. *Shaw's Music,* vol. 3, pp. 251, 271–72; Shaw, *The Drama Observed,* vol. 1, p. 296; vol. 2, p. 539; vol. 3, p. 841.

5. Shaw, *The Drama Observed,* vol. 2, pp. 386, 742.

6. Ibid., p. 476.

7. See, for example: ibid., vol. 3, p. 1123; vol. 4, pp. 1447–48; *Terry-Shaw,* p. 342; *Shaw on Theatre,* pp. 208–9.

8. Shaw, *The Drama Observed,* vol. 1, pp. 256–57; vol. 2, pp. 391–92, 399–400, 642; vol. 3, p. 938.

9. Ibid., vol. 3, p. 939.

10. Ibid., vol. 2, p. 476; vol. 4, pp. 1278, 1395; letter to Granville Barker, 13 February 1912, in Shaw, *Theatrics,* pp. 113–14.

11. McCarthy, *Myself and My Friends,* p. 108.

12. I am grateful to Sidney P. Albert, Professor [Emeritus] of California State University at Los Angeles, for having called my attention to the relevance of the *Man and Superman* passage to the different settings of *Major Barbara.*

13. Shaw, *The Drama Observed,* vol. 2, p. 674.

14. Letter to Lawrence Langner, no date given, in Langner, *G.B.S. and the Lunatic,* p. 58.

15. Sketch and working drawing of *Pygmalion,* Act 1, Hanley, HRHRC; letter to J. E. Vedrenne, 10 January 1906, Enthoven.

16. Letter to Granville Barker, 25 December 1912, in *Shaw-Barker,* p. 185.

17. Rehearsal notes: *Man and Superman,* 1907, British Library, 50735; *The Doctor's Dilemma,* 1913, HRHRC; *Major Barbara,* 1929, and *Fanny's First Play,* 1915, British Library, 50644.

18. Letter to Trebitsch, 10 August 1903, in Shaw, *Collected Letters,* vol. 2, p. 343.

19. "Notes to Act I [of *Cæsar and Cleopatra*]," undated typed manuscript, Berg; Shaw, *The Drama Observed,* vol. 3, pp. 1093–94.

20. Letter to Faversham, 3 August 1916, Hanley, HRHRC.

21. Letter to Simonson, 23 August 1920, in Shaw, *Collected Letters,* vol. 3, p. 686; Simonson, *Part of a Lifetime,* pp. 51–53.

22. Shaw, *The Drama Observed,* vol. 2, pp. 385–86, 494; *Shaw's Music,* vol. 3, p. 252.

23. Shaw, *The Drama Observed,* vol. 3, p. 1123; vol. 4, p. 1394; letters: to Florence Farr, 27 December 1905, in Shaw, *Collected Letters,* vol. 2, p. 590, and to William Faversham, 19 April 1917, in Shaw, *Theatrics,* p. 135.

24. Rehearsal notes: *Heartbreak House,* British Library, 50644; *You Never Can*

Tell, undated, British Library, 50732; *Misalliance,* 1910, Hanley, HRHRC; *Arms and the Man,* 1911, British Library, 50644.

25. Letter to Lee Simonson, 23 August 1920, in Shaw, *Collected Letters,* vol. 3, p. 686.

26. Shaw, *The Drama Observed,* vol. 2, pp. 407, 520, 529.

27. *Shaw's Music,* vol. 3, pp. 364, 538.

28. Ibid., vol. 2, p. 229; Shaw, *The Drama Observed,* vol. 1, p. 256.

29. *Shaw's Music,* vol. 3, p. 371; Shaw, *The Drama Observed,* vol. 1, p. 297; vol. 3, pp. 849–50.

30. Shaw, *The Drama Observed,* vol. 2, pp. 642–43; vol. 3, p. 1041.

31. Letter to Charles Ricketts, 10 April 1911, in Ricketts, *Self-Portrait,* ed. Cecil Lewis (London: Peter Davies, 1939), pp. 162–63.

32. Postal card, 15 February 1922, in *Shaw-Tompkins,* p. 19. *You Never Can Tell* takes place in 1896.

33. Letters: to Janet Achurch, 25 December 1900; to Granville Barker, 26 May 1903; to J. E. Vedrenne, 26 April 1908, to Lawrence Langner, 1 February 1924, in Shaw, *Collected Letters,* vol. 2, pp. 207, 327, 773; vol. 3, p. 862; Barker to Lytton, 12 October 1906, Berg.

34. Rehearsal notes: *You Never Can Tell,* undated, and *Arms and the Man,* 1911, HRHRC; *Misalliance,* 1910, and *Pygmalion,* 1914, Hanley, HRHRC; *Man and Superman,* 1907, British Library, 50735.

35. *Shaw's Music,* vol. 3, p. 10; Shaw, *The Drama Observed,* vol. 2, p. 496.

36. Letters: to Janet Achurch, 20 March 1895, and Lawrence Langner, 1 February 1924, in Shaw, *Collected Letters,* vol. 1, p. 502; vol. 3, p. 862; to Martin Harvey, 26 November 1926, Houghton Library, Harvard College.

37. Rehearsal notes: *Pygmalion,* 1914, Hanley, HRHRC; *John Bull's Other Island,* 1907, British Library, 50736; *Pygmalion,* 1920, and *Arms and the Man,* 1911, British Library, 50644; *Misalliance,* 1910, Hanley, HRHRC; *Arms and the Man,* 1919, Burgunder.

38. Rehearsal notes: *Man and Superman,* 1907, British Library, 50735; *Heartbreak House,* British Library, 50647; letters to Gabriel Pascal, 26 and 28 July 1944, in *Shaw-Pascal,* p. 174.

39. *Shaw's Music,* vol. 3, p. 100–101; Shaw, *The Drama Observed,* vol. 2, p. 387.

40. "Notes to Act I [of *Cæsar and Cleopatra*]," Berg.

41. Letter to Charles Ricketts, 21 November 1910, in Shaw, *Collected Letters,* vol. 2, p. 952.

42. Letter to Lillah McCarthy, 25 January 1918, in McCarthy, *Myself and My Friends,* p. 192.

7. The Business of Theater

1. Shaw, *The Drama Observed,* vol. 1, p. 225.

2. Langner, *G.B.S. and the Lunatic,* p. 191.

3. Financial records are in Hanley, HRHRC, and the British Library, 50649 and 50731. Some of the accounts that Charlotte Shaw kept for her husband have been published in Janet Dunbar, *Mrs. G.B.S.* (London: Harrap, 1963), pp. 188, 223.

4. Letter to Trebitsch, 16 June 1904, Berg.

5. Letters to Trebitsch: 13 December 1904, Berg; 21 November 1907, 19 April 1921, in *Shaw-Trebitsch,* pp. 129, 223.

6. The following samples indicate the evolution of Shaw's prosperity and power. In 1894, when *Arms and the Man* played at the Avenue Theatre, London, he was to receive 10 percent of the gross nightly receipts when they exceeded £150, 7 1/2 percent when they exceeded £100 but did not exceed £150, and 5 percent when they did not exceed £100 (letter to Henry Arthur Jones, 14 April 1894, in Shaw, *Collected Letters,* vol. 1, p. 430). This did *not* mean 5 percent of the first £100, 7 1/2 percent of the next £50, and so forth. If the gross receipts were £100, his percentage was 5 percent, but if they were £100 and one shilling, he received 7 1/2 percent of the *entire* gross, if £150 and one shilling, 10 percent of the entire gross. By 1900, his fees went up. He was to receive 12 percent of the gross nightly receipts when they exceeded £150, 10 percent when they exceeded £100 but did not exceed £150, 7 1/2 percent when they exceeded £50 but did not exceed £100, and 5 percent when they did not exceed £50 (Draft of an Agreement between Shaw and Johnston Forbes-Robertson, 1900, Hanley, HRHRC). By 1916, his fees had gone up to 15 percent when the gross nightly receipts exceeded £300 (in the United States, when they exceeded $1,500), 10 percent when they exceeded £100 (or $500) but did not exceed £300 (or $1,500), 7 1/2 percent when they exceeded £50 (or $250) but did not exceed £100 (or $500), and 5 percent when they did not exceed £50 (or $250) (Draft of an Agreement between Shaw and the Theatre Guild, 1916, in Langner, *G.B.S. and the Lunatic,* p. 298; Memorandum of an Agreement between Shaw and Mrs. Virginia Compton, 1918, Yale University Library).

For one-act plays, Shaw's rule was a discount of half if there were another copyright play on the same bill, a discount of two-thirds if there were two other copyright plays on the bill. If there were no other copyright plays on the bill, he demanded full fees (letter to Mrs. H. H. Champion, 18 May 1926, Hanley, HRHRC).

7. Letter to R. E. Golding Bright, 22 October 1913, in *Advice to a Young Critic,* ed. E. J. West (New York: Crown, 1955), p. 193; Draft of an Agreement between Shaw and Richard Mansfield, 1894, Berg; Memorandum of an Agreement between Shaw and Robert Loraine, 1905, Hanley, HRHRC.

8. Langner, *G.B.S. and the Lunatic,* p. 298.

9. Ibid., p. 182.

10. Letter to Mrs. Patrick Campbell, 15 May 1915, in *Shaw-Campbell,* p. 196.

11. In 1904, for example, he made special arrangements with Vedrenne that the six matinées of *John Bull's Other Island* and the six of *Candida* would give him a

royalty of 10 percent only if the gross receipts exceeded £600 (as opposed to £100 or £150 elsewhere), 7 1/2 percent if they were over £300, and 5 percent if £300 and below (as opposed to over and under £50 elsewhere). Letter to J. E. Vedrenne, 26 October 1904, Hanley, HRHRC.

12. Letter to J. E. Vedrenne, 27 July 1907, in Shaw, *Collected Letters*, vol. 2, p. 703.

13. [Letter to the Federal Theatre, 22 May 1937, in Shaw, *Collected Letters*, vol. 4, p. 465; Shaw, *The Drama Observed*, vol. 4, p. 1483.]

14. Letter to R. E. Golding Bright, in *Advice to a Young Critic*, p. 156.

15. Memorandum of Agreement between Shaw and Roy Limbert, 1938, Berg; letter to Sir John Martin-Harvey, 26 October 1928, Houghton Library, Harvard College.

16. Letters to R. E. Golding Bright, 6 April 1904 and 3 March 1907, in *Advice to a Young Critic*, pp. 143, 179.

17. Shaw, *The Drama Observed*, vol. 4, pp. 1410–13; *Shaw on Theatre*, pp. 230–35. [Shaw gave professional terms to school theaters if they earmarked all of their profits for a fund used exclusively for performances of plays (Shaw, *The Drama Observed*, vol. 4, p. 1413).]

18. Letters: to H. H. Champion, 14 December 1911, and Maurice Browne, 17 March 1915, Hanley, HRHRC.

19. Letter to Trebitsch, 18 August 1906, in *Shaw-Trebitsch*, p. 109.

20. Letters: to R. E. Golding Bright, 8 March 1905, in *Advice to a Young Critic*, pp. 161–62; to Robert Loraine, no date given, in Loraine, *Head Wind*, p. 267; to Charles Ricketts, 7 October 1911, and Ricketts to Shaw, October 1911 (no day given), in Ricketts, *Self-Portrait*, pp. 167–68.

21. Letters: to Stephens, 21 May 1900, and to Rehan, 30 August 1904, in Shaw, *Collected Letters*, vol. 2, pp. 165, 449.

22. Letters: to Trebitsch, 29 January 1913, ibid., vol. 3, p. 146; to Faversham, 7 April 1916, Hanley, HRHRC.

23. Letters: to Barker, 20 August 1904, in *Shaw-Barker*, p. 25; to Lawrence Langner, no date given, in *G.B.S. and the Lunatic*, pp. 25–26.

24. Pencil draft of publicity release for the 1911 revival of *Arms and the Man*, British Library, 50644.

25. Postcard to Trebitsch, 14 February 1903, in *Shaw-Trebitsch*, p. 40.

26. Letters: to Barker, 27 September 1903, in *Shaw-Barker*, p. 20; to Langner, 30 September 1922, in Langner, *G.B.S. and the Lunatic*, p. 95.

27. Letter to Vedrenne, 26 November 1904, in Shaw, *Collected Letters*, vol. 2, pp. 468–69.

28. Shaw, *The Drama Observed*, vol. 3, pp. 836–37; vol. 4, pp. 1362, 1392–93.

29. Ibid., vol. 2, pp. 541–42.

II. The Director as Interpreter: Shaw's *Pygmalion*

1. Shaw, *The Drama Observed,* vol. 4, pp. 1381–86, 1516–23. The word is used on p. 1520.

2. HRHRC. Some of these and other rehearsal notes have been quoted in *Bernard Shaw, Director.*

3. (ii) British Library, 50644 and (iii) Hanley, HRHRC.

4. British Library, 50644. Herbert M. Prentice directed it, whereas Shaw directed the others.

5. British Library, 50639. Page references will be cited in the text after (v).

6. (vi) 11 April 1914, in Shaw, *Collected Letters,* vol. 3, pp. 224–25; (vii) c. 5 February 1920, in Shaw, *Theatrics,* pp. 153–55; and (viii) 15 May 1920, in Shaw, *Collected Letters,* vol. 3, pp. 675–76. Page references will follow small roman numerals.

7. Shaw, *The Drama Observed,* vol. 4, p. 1516.

8. Lewis Casson, "G.B.S.at Rehearsal," *Drama,* n.s. 20 (Spring 1951): 10.

9. Shaw, *The Drama Observed,* vol. 1, p. 186.

10. Letters to Trebitsch, 10 and 18 December 1902, in *Shaw-Trebitsch,* pp. 27, 28.

11. Letter to Lillah McCarthy, 8 February 1908, in Shaw, *Collected Letters,* vol. 2, p. 756.

12. Instructions to Producer, *Arms and the Man,* undated, in *Bernard Shaw's Arms and the Man: A Composite Production Book,* pp. 21, 29.

13. Letter to Lillah McCarthy, 23 January 1914, in Shaw, *Collected Letters,* vol. 3, pp. 217–18.

14. Shaw, *The Drama Observed,* vol. 4, pp. 1382, 1523.

15. Ibid., p. 1520.

16. Letter to Annie Russell, 27 November 1905, in Shaw, *Collected Letters,* vol. 2, p. 583.

17. Richard Huggett, *The Truth about Pygmalion* (London: Heinemann, 1969), pp. 78–80.

18. Letter to B. Iden Payne, 3 February 1911, in "Some Unpublished Letters of George Bernard Shaw," ed. Julian Park, *University of Buffalo Studies* 16 (September 1939): 126.

19. Letter to Barrymore, 22 February 1925, in Shaw, *Collected Letters,* vol. 3, p. 903.

20. Shaw, *The Drama Observed,* vol. 4, pp. 1367–68.

21. Huggett, p. 84. After the play opened, while Shaw was recuperating in the country, Tree performed this business. When Shaw saw it and disapproved, they supposedly had this exchange: "My ending makes money, you ought to be grateful." "Sir Herbert, your ending makes nonsense, you ought to be shot." Ibid., p. 162.

22. Huggett, p. 84.

III. The Theater in Bernard Shaw's Drama

1. Bernard Shaw, *Mrs Warren's Profession: A Facsimile of the Holograph Manuscript* (New York: Garland, 1981), p. 4.

2. For example, Eric Bentley, p. 160.

3. Henderson, *Shaw: Century,* pp. 593, 612; Ervine, *Bernard Shaw: His Life, Work and Friends* (New York: William Morrow, 1956), p. 431. In one respect, Henderson errs: if Shakespeare wrote an epilogue for *The Taming of the Shrew,* it has not come down to us.

4. *Shaw and the Nineteenth-Century Theater* (Princeton, N.J.: Princeton University Press, 1963), pp. 259, 333. Meisel errs (p. 259) when he says that Shaw puts onstage "five of the leading dramatic critics of the day" (he clearly does so with three of them). For further discussion of *The Taming of the Shrew, The Rehearsal,* and *The Critic,* see below.

5. Morgan, *The Shavian Playground* (London: Methuen, 1972), especially pp. 90–92; Gibbs, *The Mind and Art of Shaw* (New York: St. Martin's Press, 1983), especially pp. 93–94. I am indebted to both.

6. Dates after plays are years of completion.

7. *Ibsen: The Critical Heritage,* ed. Michael Egan (London: Routledge and Kegan Paul, 1972), pp. 270, 281–82.

8. Morgan, p. 51.

9. Berst, "*The Man of Destiny:* Shaw, Napoleon, and the Theater of Life," *SHAW: The Annual of Bernard Shaw Studies,* vol. 7, ed. Alfred Turco Jr. (University Park: Pennsylvania State University Press, 1907), p. 100.

10. Frederick P. W. McDowell makes two telling points: the Waiter "has some of Harlequin's magic [. . .] and produces by his gentle voice and affable demeanor the transforming effects associated with Harlequin's bat or wand"; and Philip's "bat is a magic wand that is in part emblematic of the harmonies being restored at the festive dance, as if by supernal forces." "Shaw's 'Higher Comedy' Par Excellence: *You Never Can Tell,*" *SHAW,* vol. 7, pp. 71–72.

11. The echo is of a passage between Glendower and Hotspur in *King Henry IV, Part 1,* III, i: "I can call spirits from the vasty deep." "Why, so can I, or so can any man; / But will they come when you do call for them?" They may not come for Glendower, but Bohun comes for Philip-harlequin.

12. Shaw, *Collected Letters,* vol. 1, pp. 734–35.

13. This section does not treat the Ra Prologue, written in 1912 and later published as "An Alternative to the Prologue." It is discussed below.

14. In Act IV, Cleopatra stages a ritual before a miniature sphinx. Although the natural light changes to sunset and a death cry follows an appeal to the voice of the Nile, suggestive of a play-within-a-play, the event is a rite and has no onstage audience.

15. See my introduction to Bernard Shaw, *Major Barbara: A Facsimile of the Holograph Manuscript* (New York: Garland Publishing, 1981), p. xiii, and the

manuscript. Shaw began to write Act I on 22 March 1905 and Act II on 7 April (pp. 2, 81), but he broke off, without noting the date, shortly after Barbara follows Snobby Price into the Salvation Army shelter and did not resume until 8 July, two days after he went to Ireland (pp. 97–98). After extensive revisions, he completed it on 15 October (p. 328), only twenty-two days before rehearsals began on 6 November, and he read it to the cast the preceding week (p. xiv).

16. He began it in May 1905 and completed it on 4 June. It was acted not at the Court but at the annual Theatrical Garden Party in Regents Park, London, in a benefit performance for the Actors' Orphanage, on 14 July, while he was in Ireland (3, 202–3).

17. In "The Avant-Garde Shaw," the final chapter that belies the subtitle of *The Unexpected Shaw: Biographical Approaches to G.B.S.and His Work* (New York: Frederick Ungar, 1982), Stanley Weintraub claims that with the sixteen cuckoo-clock chimes of this play, Shaw "anticipates Ionesco's *The Bald Soprano* (with its 'English clock' striking 'seventeen English strokes') by nearly half a century" (p. 227). In doing so, he follows Paul Silverstein, who in a splendid essay on Shaw's play, modestly says, "One might well be tempted to cite this passage as an example [. . .] of Shaw's anticipation of Absurdism" ("Barnes, Booths, and Shaw," *Shaw Review* 12 [September 1969]: 111) and cites the opening of *The Bald Soprano*. As a gag, Shaw's clock coincidentally forecasts Ionesco's, but the contexts are so different that any other linkage between the plays is tenuous. Eric Bentley hits the mark when, asked if this play anticipates the theater of the absurd, he replies, "I think it's just traditional zaniness." Alfred Turco, Jr., "Shaw 40 Years Later—Eric Bentley Speaks His Mind on Eleven Neglected Plays: *Getting Married, Overruled, On the Rocks,* and Others," *SHAW: The Annual of Bernard Shaw Studies,* vol. 7, p. 12.

18. "Tomfooling with Melodrama in *Passion, Poison, and Petrifaction,*" *SHAW: The Annual of Bernard Shaw Studies,* vol. 7, p. 139.

19. This is immediately succeeded by an echo of "If 'a do blench, I know my course" (*Hamlet* II,ii): "She but snooze in her sleep, I'll do't." If this seems far-fetched, note the allusion to Lady Macbeth's remark following the death of Duncan, "After life's fitful fever he sleeps well" (*Macbeth*, III,ii): Lady Magnesia says of her lover's and The Policeman's deaths, "After life's fitful fever they sleep well," and commands her maid, "Phyllis: sweep them up" (3, 219). Lord Fitztollemache's last line, "The rest is silence" (3, 220), is also Hamlet's last line.

20. The names Adolphus and Fitz, which Shaw uses in stage directions and speaker designations for Lord Fitztollemache, remind us that the interrupted *Major Barbara* was in the back of his mind when he wrote this farce. Adolphus is the given name of Cusins. As for Fitz, B. C. Rosset convincingly argues,

> Shaw's recurring use of names prefixed by "Fitz" indicates, in my opinion, his familiarity with its ancient usage. As defined in respectable sources—
>
> Fitz—a word in use from the 12th century in names of English families (esp. of French origin), meaning son; . . . used esp. for illegitimate

sons of kings and princes of the blood . . .

Fitz appears frequently enough in the fictive and dramatic works of GBS to attract attention [. . .].

One of Rosset's examples is Fitztollemache. *Shaw of Dublin: The Formative Years* (University Park: Pennsylvania State University Press, 1964), p. 147. In *Major Barbara,* every Andrew Undershaft has been illegitimate, which is a qualification for anyone to succeed to the inheritance. *Major Barbara* is also evoked by The Landlord, whose lower-class diction Shaw tries to render the way he tries to render Bill Walker's in *Major Barbara,* which he stopped shortly after Bill's entrance, for example: "Wots all this noise? Ah kin ennybody sleep through it" and "Ah could aw tell e wiz gowin te eat moy ceilin?" (3, 216–17).

21. "Tomfooling with Melodrama in *Passion, Poison, and Petrifaction,*" p. 139. "Shaw, who in the subtitle calls this farce 'a tragedy,'" says Weintraub, erroneously, "is thinking along the lines of the later Ionesco, who spoke of 'the tragedy of language'" (*The Unexpected Shaw,* p. 228). By "tragedy of language," Ionesco means the difficulty or inability of language to express or explain the verbally inexplicable, which is far from the world of Shaw, who confidently uses words to express and explain virtually everything under the sun. Silverstein, who also notes Ionesco's phrase, rightly marks it not as a similarity but as "a distinction" between the two dramatists (p. 114); but I disagree with him that such concepts as "death, love, honor, and jealousy" reflect "the noble, but superficial aspirations of society, while at supposedly the lower level," they reflect "the more realistic materialism of that same society" (p. 113). Rather, ideas of fate and death—for example, "It is a terrible night. Heaven help all poor mariners at sea!" (3, 206)—seem to me to evoke merely the diction of formulaic melodrama.

22. Lady Britomart may seem to foreshadow Snobby in the opening scene of Act I by performing the role of womanly woman, transparently aping submissiveness to get her son Stephen to give her the advice she wants, but she does not. The first page of the scene contains demands—"Dont begin to read," "Dont make excuses," "Dont fiddle with your tie"—and a dismissive exclamation, "Nonsense!" (3, 68)—none of which is submissive or what a womanly woman would say if she attempted influence. When Stephen says "No" when she asks if his advice is to put her pride in her pocket and ask Undershaft for money, she reacts: "(*sharply*) Stephen!" When, in response to her refusal to assume all responsibility for the decision, he "*obstinately*" says he "would die sooner than ask him for another penny," she "*resignedly*" states, "You mean that I must ask him. Very well, Stephen: it shall be as you wish" (3, 77). This differs from getting him to give her the advice she wants. Although she goes through a few verbal motions, she does not attempt to play a role.

23. Unlike the subtitle of the earlier play, this subtitle is not satiric.

24. By contrast, Shaw's self-references in *Misalliance* are implicit. "Democracy reads well," says Lord Summerhays; "but it doesnt act well, like some people's plays." Tarleton thinks "the superman may come. The superman's an idea. I be-

lieve in ideas. Read Whathisname" (4, 169). Unlike the explicit allusion in *The Doctor's Dilemma,* whose "playful shifting in and out of illusion enlivens" it, as Weintraub notes (p. 226), these implied self-references seem to be in-jokes. He may have been more fortunate than me in seeing productions of *Misalliance* with Shavians in the audience, for he believes that Shaw thinks "his audience knows very well indeed that he is the author of *Man and Superman*" (p. 227). I have attended performances in which the line fell flat among uncomprehending spectators and others in which some wondered why those who caught the joke laughed; I have also seen productions whose directors played it safe by deleting the lines.

25. This short play was denied canonical status by Shaw, who did not publish it in collected editions of his works. Following his lead, Dan H. Laurence relegates it to the appendix of *The Bodley Head Bernard Shaw* along with "abandoned fragments" and works Shaw considered to be "of too specialised or ephemeral a nature to be of interest to the general reader," "occasional pieces" which he dismissed "as trifles not fit to be published even among the 'Tomfooleries' or the 'Scraps and Shavings'" (7, 481). Michael Holroyd does not mention it in *Bernard Shaw,* 5 vols. (London: Chatto & Windus, 1988–92). Yet there is justification to include it in the canon. First, unlike the other works in the appendix, *The Inauguration Speech* was both performed (by Cyril and Mrs. Maude [Winifred Emery], for whose newly renovated London theater, The Playhouse, Shaw wrote it) and published in Shaw's lifetime (as *The Interlude at the Playhouse* in the *Daily Mail* and *Behind the Scenes with Cyril Maude,* as *Lest I Forget* in America [1928]). Second, Archibald Henderson, tutored by Shaw, cites *The Interlude at the Playhouse* in his three Shavian biographies—*George Bernard Shaw: His Life and Work* (New York: Stewart & Kidd, 1911), *Bernard Shaw: Playboy and Prophet* (New York: Appleton, 1932), and *Shaw: Century,* the last of which calls it "a little gem, quite perfect of its kind" (p. 567); and Raymond Mander and Joe Mitchenson list it in *Theatrical Companion to Shaw* (London: Rockliff, 1954). Third, the text in *The Bodley Head Bernard Shaw,* which derives from Shaw's handwritten manuscript, uses not the names of the actors for whom he wrote it, but Edwin and Mrs. Goldsmith (Angelina), which suggests that he may have originally intended the piece for performance after that of the Maudes, which was the case with *How He Lied to Her Husband,* written for Arnold Daly. Myron Matlaw calls *The Inauguration Speech* "an amusing and typically Shavian, dramatic creation," "well worth restoring into the general body of Shaw's drama," and a piece that "reads better, I think, than the posthumously-published *Why She Would Not* and some of the slight pieces that are included among the fifty-one plays in the last edition of *The Complete Plays of Bernard Shaw*" ("Bernard Shaw and The Interlude at the Playhouse," *Shaw Review:* 3 [September 1960]: 12). Following Matlaw, and for the other reasons given, I claim status for *The Inauguration Speech: An Interlude,* a comic delight eight decades after it was written, as a neglected play in the Shaw canon.

26. This does not mean the start of the evening. In its inaugural performance, the main piece was *Toddles,* by American dramatist Clyde Fitch, preceded by the

National Anthem, Austin Strong's one-act drama *The Drums of Oude,* and *The Inauguration Speech,* which was, as Maude and the *Daily Mail* titled it, an interlude at his Playhouse Theatre. After *Toddles* was a duologue, *Sixes and Sevens,* an address by Herbert Beerbohm Tree, and a thank-you speech by Maude, followed by an orchestral performance of "Auld Lang Syne," during which the audience filed out. According to the *Times, The Inauguration Speech* or *Interlude* was "the clou [chief attraction] of the evening" (quoted in Matlaw, p. 9). As the *Daily Mail* printed it the next day, with Shaw as author, and as reviewers cited Shaw (Matlaw, p. 11), his anonymity in the program insert was an open secret.

27. Slight misquotation of Samuel Johnson's prologue for David Garrick at the 1747 opening of his management of Drury Lane Theatre. A dozen years earlier than this play, Shaw used the same quotation as a theater critic and added, "But you cannot get out of an argument by simply telling a lie in a heroic couplet. The drama's laws the drama's patrons do n o t give, nor ever can give [. . .]." Then, he viewed the audience-actor relationship differently: "The public cannot do without the theater; and the actor and the dramatist are therefore in a position to insist on honorable terms." Shaw, *The Drama Observed,* vol. 2, p. 431.

28. Blanco also quotes nondramatic poetry. After the townswomen "*rush at him, vituperating, screaming passionately, tearing at him,*" calling him a coward and demanding he be lynched and burned, he ironically quotes Sir Walter Scott's *Marmion:* "'Oh woman, in our hours of ease, / Uncertain, coy, and hard to please'" (3, 768).

29. The one production of *The Merchant of Venice* that Shaw reviewed was Henry Irving's in 1880. Blanco's assessment of the actor who played Shylock mirrors Shaw's of Irving. Shaw's notice was not published during his lifetime. It is in *The Drama Observed,* vol. 1, pp. 3–11.

30. Shaw, *The Drama Observed,* vol. 3, pp. 1157–58.

31. Ibid., vol. 1, p. 209.

32. Peter Gahan, "Ruskin and Form in *Fanny's First Play,*" *SHAW: The Annual of Bernard Shaw Studies,* vol. 15, ed. Fred D. Crawford (University Park: Pennsylvania State University Press, 1995), p. 87.

33. Shaw bristled when critics compared him to Gilbert, whose comedy differs from his own. As he told William Archer on 23 April 1894, "Gilbert is simply a paradoxically humorous cynic. He accepts the conventional ideals implicitly, but observes that people do not really live up to them. This he regards as a failure on their part at which he mocks bitterly." Shaw does not accept these ideals. To him, a character "is ridiculous through the breakdown of his ideals, not odious from his falling short of them." Shaw, *Collected Letters,* vol. 1, p. 427.

34. My analysis of Shaw's reviewers and the real reviewers is indebted to Charles A. Carpenter, "Shaw's Cross-Section of Anti-Shavian Opinion," *Shaw Review,* 7 (September 1974): 78–86; and Leon Hugo, "Shaw and His Critics: Fanny's First Play," *Bernard Shaw: On Stage,* ed. L. W. Conolly and Ellen M. Pearson (Guelph: University of Guelph, 1991), pp. 61–80.

35. Quoted in Michael Holroyd, *Bernard Shaw,* vol. 2 (London: Chatto and Windus, 1989), p. 281.

36. Hugo, p. 79.

37. The irony is Shaw's, not the Count's, since the play has ample evidence that he is polite to his guests and none that he is hostile toward critics. Perhaps the Count draws on his memory of Shakespeare to find an apparently flattering quotation to charm or disarm the critics.

38. From the Proceedings of the Committee, quoted in Shaw, *The Drama Observed,* vol. 3, p. 1241 n.

39. *The Times,* 2 November 1904; *Shaw: The Critical Heritage,* ed. T. F. Evans (London: Routledge & Kegan Paul, 1976), pp. 125–26.

40. Hugo, p. 75.

41. Holroyd, p. 281; Hugo, p. 72.

42. Evans, p. 108; Hugo, p. 73.

43. Letter, 21 March 1910, in Shaw, *Collected Letters,* vol. 2, p. 912.

44. Arthur Nethercot hints at the significance of the surname when he suggests that it "should perhaps be pronounced 'O'Dowdy'" because of the Count's obsolete attire. *Men and Supermen: The Shavian Portrait Gallery* (New York: Benjamin Blom, 1966), p. 294.

45. Shaw, *The Drama Observed,* vol. 3, pp. 606, 608.

46. Gahan, p. 89.

47. Evans, p. 182.

48. Hugo, p. 78.

49. Although Fanny attends Cambridge University, she is not studying for a degree. Count O'Dowda's words are precise: "my daughter left me to complete her education at Cambridge" (4, 356). Women were admitted there when Girton College, its first college for women, was opened in 1869, but they received lectures separately from male students and could not take honors examinations until 1923. Not until 1948, more than a third of a century after this play and three years after World War II ended, did Cambridge grant degrees to women.

50. Katherine E. Kelly, "Shaw on Women Suffrage: A Minor Player on the Petticoat Platform," *SHAW: The Annual of Bernard Shaw Studies,* vol. 14: *1992: Shaw and the Last Hundred Years,* ed. Bernard F. Dukore (University Park: Pennsylvania State University Press, 1994), p. 77.

51. This analysis of Fanny's play and its relationship to the induction and epilogue draws on my *Bernard Shaw, Playwright,* pp. 173–77.

52. Shaw's ending differs from that of earlier English comedies with plays or rehearsals within plays. *The Taming of the Shrew* (c. 1593) has an Induction about the gulling of Christopher Sly, for whom this comedy is performed; but no epilogue with Sly has survived. In Ben Jonson's *The Magnetic Lady* (1629), Damplay (the meaning of whose name is obvious) and Probee (who gives supposedly penetrating analyses) are in an Induction and discuss the inner play after its first four acts; but after Act V Jonson replaces them with a Chorus who dismisses them and appeals

to the king for judgment of the play. In *The Rehearsal* (1671), by the Duke of Buckingham and others, the two spectators depart before the rehearsal of the play-within-the-play ends; the author, discovering this, leaves; and the actors go to dinner. Sheridan's *The Critic* (1779), in which critics and the author discuss his play, concludes abruptly when, after the inner play's naval battle, during which the author applauds every theatrical effect, he announces they will rehearse again tomorrow. Shaw was familiar with Shakespeare's comedy, which he reviewed, and Buckingham's and Sheridan's, to which he refers in his preface (1916) to *Overruled* (4, 840), but he was very likely not acquainted with Jonson's work, which remains neglected.

53. Shaw wrote the lesson and performance sequences for the 1938 movie version of *Pygmalion*. Ordinarily, I would not consider them in a study of his stage plays, but his "Note for Technicians" provides a loophole of which some theater companies, notably the Royal National Theatre in 1992, have taken advantage to justify their inclusion on stage: "A complete representation of this play as printed [. . .] is technically possible only on the cinema screen or on stages furnished with exceptionally elaborate machinery" (4, 657). Because the film episodes have been staged, I analyze them.

54. At the time, doctors knew that opium was addictive but prescribed it as a traditional, or "old-fashioned," remedy. In *Long Day's Journey into Night*, set in 1912, one year before Shaw began to write *The Music-Cure*, Eugene O'Neill used dramatic license to make the prescription of it by Mary Tyrone's physician evidence of her husband's cheapness in hiring a quack doctor.

55. Dan H. Laurence, *Bernard Shaw: A Bibliography*, vol. 2 (Oxford: Clarendon Press, 1983), pp. 650–54.

56. "Sir Almroth Wright's Case against Woman Suffrage," *Fabian Feminist*, ed. Rodelle Weintraub (University Park: Pennsylvania State University Press, 1977), p. 245.

57. Shaw, *The Drama Observed*, vol. 1, p. 137.

58. Yes, "dollars," not pounds (4, 954).

59. This is how it was done in the (Canada) Shaw Festival's 1986 production. Robert Benson, who played Burge-Lubin, recalls the difficulty of performing with the constraint of fixed timing imposed by interaction with a filmed and recorded actor. For providing this information, I thank Mr. Benson and Denis Johnston, Co-Director of the Academy of the Shaw Festival.

60. For Shaw's views on silent and talking films, see *Bernard Shaw on Cinema*, ed. Bernard F. Dukore (Carbondale: Southern Illinois University Press, 1997). As early as 1912, he was familiar with inventions that synchronized silent films and talking records, and he predicted that the theatrical world was on the verge of a revolution (p. 4). Since the revolution had not occurred when the Theatre Guild first produced the play in New York in 1922 or the Birmingham Repertory Company first produced it in England in 1923, how well—in fact, how—did they stage this vanguard theatrical effect? In the Guild production, the answer to the first

question is "apparently not strikingly enough to compensate for the play." Reviews in the *New York Times*, the *Evening Telegram*, and the *Evening Post* on 7 March 1922 do not mention the videophone (I am beholden to David Johnson for the *New York Times* review and to the Billy Rose Theater Collection of the New York Public Library at Lincoln Center for the others). The photograph of the Guild production in Raymond Mander and Joe Mitchenson, *Theatrical Companion to Shaw*, p. 194, looks like the wrong picture, because it contains two women seated at a table, whereas the play has one woman onstage, and because its costumes and setting suggest the 1920s, not the future. The photograph in Norman Nadel, *Pictorial History of the Theatre Guild* (New York: Crown, 1969), p. 17, shows a woman on what looks like the deck of a ship (for a copy of this, I thank Dan H. Laurence). Whether she is on film or standing behind a scrim (theatrical gauze which, when lighted from behind, becomes transparent) is unclear, but as the scale of her body and that of the man onstage seem the same, I suspect the latter, which is less expensive and conforms to the Guild's usually low budgets. On the evidence of this photo, the device is unimpressive. Supporting my suspicion is the illustration of this scene in a book by the production's designer, Lee Simonson, *Part of a Lifetime* (New York: Duell, Sloan & Pearce, 1943), Plate 24, which looks like a scrim, not a movie screen; and it shows the setting to consist of folded screens, which are inexpensive. Simonson does not discuss the production of *Back to Methuselah*. On the other hand, Maida Castellum's review in the *New York Call*, 7 March 1922 (Billy Rose Theater Collection), states, "Motion pictures in color, thrown on a screen, enable people to see each other on the telephone even though they are hundreds of miles apart." If she is accurate, then my inference goes into the garbage can. I should note that what the card catalogue of the Billy Rose Collection calls a prompt book is not a prompt book, but a copy of the first 1921 edition of the play, with Burge-Lubin's lines marked vertically, as actors sometimes mark dialogue to be memorized.

Of the Birmingham Rep's production, the *Birmingham Post*, 12 October 1923, carried a notice by "R.C.R." (probably R. Crompton Rhodes, according to Dan H. Laurence): "The new telephone, by which one could see the speaker as well as hear the voice, was not so startling as it should have been, as the mechanical device was not perfect" (quoted in H. M. Geduld, "An Edition of Bernard Shaw's *Back to Methuselah*" [Ph.D. dissertation, London: Birkbeck College, University of London, 1961], vol. 5, p. 77). An unsigned review in the *Evening Standard*, 12 October 1923, called the "theatrical" device "The Indiscreet Photophone" because it made "possible the broad joke of the switching on of the Minister of Health as she sits in a petticoat at her dressing-table." The joke is not the director's but Shaw's, and was in the first edition. A hint that the Birmingham Rep used a scrim is a pre-opening interview with director H. K. Ayliff ("Task of Producing *Back to Methuselah*," *Birmingham Mail*, 11 October 1923). One of the production's "'special difficulties,'" said Ayliff, was the "'photo-telephone screen business in "The Thing Happens,"'" since "'the shallowness of the stage render[ed] the screen more transparent when it should have been opaque than was desirable, as changes had to be made behind it.'" Had a motion picture been used, I suspect he would have mentioned keystoning as a problem when a film is rear-projected on a shallow upstage space. In any case, he added, his technical staff surmounted this difficulty "'by certain changes in the working and lighting.'" For the *Evening Standard* review and the Ayliff interview, I am grateful to Ben Payne, Literary Manager of the Birmingham Rep, and Mrs. Diane Arnold of the Birmingham Central Library.

61. *Bernard Shaw, Playwright*, pp. 110–17.

62. *Shaw's Music*, vol. 3, p. 444.

63. Shaw, *The Drama Observed*, vol. 4, p. 1292.

64. Stogumber also states that at Orleans an English arrow pierced her throat— "a death wound; yet she fought all day"—and that when she led the French to the English fortress wall, "our men were paralyzed, and could neither shoot nor strike whilst the French fell on them and drove them on to the bridge, which immediately burst into flames" and plunged them into the river (6, 129). He calls them not miracles but witchcraft; but, says Cauchon, both are "capable of a natural explanation. The woman's miracles would not impose on a rabbit: she does not claim them as miracles herself." Her victories only prove that she is smarter than the English commanders (6, 131). Shaw's dramatization of these events in his screenplay of *Saint Joan* supports Cauchon: the wound in her neck is a flesh wound whose bleeding "a bandage of tow" stops; when Lord Salisbury rewards the archer who shot Joan, the archers interrupt the battle for him to do so, thus giving Joan's forces a chance to bombard them; and the bridge bursting into flame results from her ordering a fire ship to be anchored under it and then firing a cannon at the ship. *The Collected Screenplays of Bernard Shaw*, ed. Bernard F. Dukore (Athens: University of Georgia Press, 1980), pp. 196–98.

65. Bentley, p. 120.

66. Of the last quotation, for example, Robert Brustein claims that "the autobiographical note is unmistakable" (*The Theatre of Revolt* [Boston: Little, Brown, 1964), p. 205); and Arthur Ganz says of Shaw's protest that "the despair here expressed was the character's and not his," that "the sorrow rings true and the protestation does not" (*George Bernard Shaw* [New York: Grove Press, 1983]), p. 207.

67. Peters "Shaw's Double Dethroned: *The Dark Lady of the Sonnets, Cymbeline Refinished*, and *Shakes versus Shav*," *SHAW: The Annual of Bernard Shaw Studies*, vol. 7, p. 301. My analysis is indebted to her study, which unlike mine is biographical and psychological.

Index

KING ALFRED'S COLLEGE
LIBRARY

Bernard F. Dukore is University Distinguished Professor of Theatre Arts and Humanities Emeritus, Virginia Polytechnic Institute and State University. He is the author or editor of more than thirty books and numerous essays, articles, and reviews about drama, theater, and film.